In Remembrance
and
Hope
The Ministry and Vision
of Howard G. Hageman

by
Gregg A. Mast

The Historical Series of the Reformed Church in America

No. 27

In Remembrance
and
Hope
The Ministry and Vision
of Howard G. Hageman

by
Gregg A. Mast

Wm. B. Eerdmans Publishing Co.
Grand Rapids, Michigan

© 1998 Wm. B. Eerdmans Publishing Co.
255 Jefferson Ave. S.E., Grand Rapids, Michigan 49503 /
P.O. Box 163, Cambridge CB3 9PU U.K.

Printed in the United States of America

01 00 99 98   5 4 3 2 1

ISBN 0-8028-4613-0

Body text set in Adobe New Caledonia
Chapter titles set in Adobe Garamond

The Historical Series of the Reformed Church in America

This series has been inaugurated by the General Synod of the Reformed Church in America, acting through its Commission on History, for the purpose of encouraging historical research and providing a medium wherein this knowledge may be shared with the academic community and with the members of the denomination in order that a knowledge of the past may contribute to right action in the present.

General Editor

The Rev. Donald J. Bruggink, Ph.D.
Western Theological Seminary

The Reverend Dr. Howard G. Hageman

A Tribute to Howard G. Hageman

This volume is published with the assistance of many friends of Howard G. Hageman. The following individuals and organizations have helped to underwrite the expense of its publication. It is presented with gratitude and affection in memory of Howard, our teacher, colleague, pastor, and friend.

Names appear as provided by the subscribers

David Alexander NBTS '80
Eleanor & Robert Alexander
George F. Ammerman
Mavis & Clynton Angus
Anonymous
Dave & Lynn Armstrong
John Assini
Carolyn Jones-Assini
Charles R. Ausherman
John Howard Austin
Donald R. Baird
Mrs. Pamela Leaper Bakker
George W. Barrowclough
The Rev. Robert W. Barrowclough
The Rev. Fred Baumgardner
William A. Beardslee
Peter W. Berry
Dick Beving NBTS '45
Mrs. Ludwig R. Binder
Robert J. Block
Derrick W. Bluschke
Randall B. Bosch
Marcia & Kenneth Bradsell
The Rev. David M. Brechter
Mrs. George H. Bricker
Mrs. Jean Brinser

Lynn Brown
Scott D. Brown
Donald J. Bruggink
Elaine & Elton Bruins
The Rev. James L. H. & The Rev. Kathleen Hart Brumm
The Rev. Nathan S. Busker
The Rev. Robert E. Butcher
Mrs. Douglas C. Buys
Ekdal J. Buys
William Cameron
Wilbur D. Canaday, Jr.
Paul D. Carey
The Rev. & Mrs. Alvin Cason
Jack & Deb Cherry
Mrs. Louis H. Chisman
Peter & Florence Christoph
The Church Herald
Sandee Clark
The Rev. Richard Coffill
Janet R. Conti
The Rev. & Mrs. David G. Corlett
Ms. Madaline N. Crowell
The Reverend Carol Cortelyou Cruikshank
George A. Damiano
The Rev. Thomas C. Danney

vii

The Rev. Kathryn L. Davelaar
Horton M. Davies
Linden & Mary De Bie
The Rev. Fran De Jong
John R. de Velder
Marion & Edith de Velder
Walter de Velder
The Rev. John F. DeVries
The Rev. Thomas D. DeVries
Roger De Young
The Rev. Barbara L. Dickens
Fred & Barbara Diekman
Chester J. Droog
Bob & Donna Drum
The Rev. Robert B. Dunbar
Miss Elizabeth W. Durham
Miss Elizabeth G. Durkee
John Dykstra
James P. Ebbers
The Rev. Micheal Edwards
The Rev. Robert Engel
Mark William Ennis
Pamela Pater-Ennis
Shirley M. Farrell
Paul C. Ferenczy
Barbara D. Fillette
James D. Folts
Russell & Grace Franck
The Rev. Douglas W. Fromm
Jeff Gargano
Russell & Maria Gasero
The Rev. & Mrs. Stephen
  Giordano
Harold J. Goldzung, Sr.
The Rev. Adrian C. Gray, Sr.
Joann Green
Herman Harmelink III
The Rev. John Hart
Adrienne Flipse Hausch
Amy Jo & Jim Hawley

Andrew A. Hendricks, M. D.
Mary R. Hendricks
Warren J. Henseler
Mr. & Mrs. Arnold M. Hess
Robert L. Hinshalwood
Dr. Marvin D. Hoff
The Rev. Craig & The Rev. Jan
  Hoffman
Edward T. Hoffman
Steven Hoffman
Judith Gravell Hornstra
Betty Hageman Houghtaling &
  Walter W. Houghtaling
David W. Houghtaling
Nancy Houghtaling Behun
Renée S. House
Elizabeth & Patricia Huba
Marian I. Hughes
Ms. Muriel M. Hunter
Chaplain William Mill Hunter
Earle W. Hutchison
Kent E. Huyck
John I. Itzen
Wilbur & Martha Ivins
Allan Janssen
Paul Janssen
The Rev. David W. & Susanne S.
  Jenks
Joyce L. Jennings
The Rt. Rev. William C. Johnson
Chaplain Robert A. Jones
Lynn T. Joosten
The Rev. Lewis E. Kain
Dr. Leonard V. Kalkwarf
Norman & Mary Kansfield
Thomas & Kathleen Kelly
Thomas Kendall
The Rev. Dr. Earl Wm. Kennedy
Ruth & Khodamorad Kermani
The Rev. Dr. Martin Kessler

Dr. Claudia A. Kirkpatrick
The Rev. Jeffrey A. Kisner, Ph. D.
The Rev. Dr. & Mrs. Carl M.
  Kleis
Cornelius G. Kors
Harold Korver
Mark A. Kraai
The Rev. Dr. Henry C. Kreutzer, Jr.
Fritz Kruithof
Ruth Lang
Samuel LaPenta
Tom Larkin
Ian & Edith Leet
Roger Leonard
Dr. Blaise Levai
Kurt R. Linde
Laura Lee Linder
Don Lindskoog
Ronald D. Lokhorst
The Rev. Ronald Lowry
Herman E. Luben
John & Helga Lucius
Mr. & Mrs. Daniel R. Madia
John Magee
The Rev. Warren G. Martens
  NBTS '55
Neal & Stella Mast
Vicki Ann Mast
The Rev. Donald A. McCabe
Mary K. McCann
Thomas McCann
The Rev. Martha L. McCracken
The Rev. Bruce Menning
The Mercersburg Society
The Rev. Nickolas M. Miles
Albert & Barbara Miller
Audrey R. Ming
Bob & Joan Mitchell
The Rev. & Mrs. Frederick Mold, Jr.
E. Andrew Mondore

Mr. & Mrs. Edward Mondore
Charles & Deborah Morris
Robert Dean Morrison
The Rev. Howard Moths
Fred & Barbara Mueller
Edwin & Luella Mulder
Theodore C. Muller
Frederick H. Musson
Carol Myers
James A. Neevel
John P. Newton
The Rev. Leroy Nixon, Ph. D.
North Reformed Church
The Rev. Paul F. Nulton
The Rev. Dr. Victor & the Hon.
  Betty Nuovo
Gert O'Hare
Eleanor B. Onderdonk
The Rev. Art & Ann Opmeer
John & Marilyn Paarlberg
Donald S. Pangburn
George W. & Natalie R. Parry
The Rev. Russell F. Pater
The Revs. Roy & Marie Paterik
Thora H. Paton
Diana Paulsen
Peter & Elizabeth Paulsen
Peter Paulson
The Rev. Dr. Rand & Sally
  Peabody
The Rev. Bruce E. Penn
Dave Peters
Wanda Austin-Peters
Richard A. Petrie
Elizabeth M. Pierce
Dan Plasman
Richard F. Plechner
A. J. Poppen
The Rev. Linda S. Powell
Samuel M. Priestley, Jr.

Pultneyville Reformed Church
The Rev. Karyn A. Ratcliffe
Harlan E. Ratmeyer
James B. Reid
Charles L. Rice
Fowler & Mable Riddick
The Rev. Ruth A. Fries Robbins
Chap. Lt. Col. Michael Romano
Garrett C. Roorda
Peter G. Rose
Mr. Kenneth E. Rowe
The Rev. Harold L. Rutherford, M. Div.
The Rev. Nancy E. Ryan
Dr. Leopold Schneider
The Rev. David & Janice Schreuder
Tom Schwanda
Adrian Leiby Scott
Carl Scovel
The Rev. Robert M. Shaw
Dr. & Mrs. John C. Shetler
Peter John Shortway
Robert S. Skinner
Calvin Eugene Spann
The Rev. Louis O. Springsteen
William & Sandra Staats
The Rev. Ronald C. Stockhoff
The Rev. Dr. Richard Munn Suffern
Larry & Jane Suntken
Edward & Linda Sweetman
Kenneth Tenckinck
Dr. Ed Tenhor
Norman & Myrtle Thomas
Mrs. Bard Thompson
Ian S. Todd
Donald Troost

Dr. Walter J. Ungerer
Merwin Van Doornik
Gerard Van Dyk
Arthur O. Van Eck
The Rev. Lynn Carol Van Ek
George H. Van Emburg
Rowland & Judy Van Es
Clarence Van Heukelom
Glenn N. Van Oort
Harold J. Vande Berg
Dr. Lyle Vander Broek
Dr. Allen Verhey
David & Janet Waanders
Mildred & Ted Wagner
Roy W. Wagoner
Jack Wahlberg
Richard Wallace
Paul & Debby Walther
Wilbur T. Washington
The Rev. Dorothy Knigge Waters
Paul D. Wesselink
Ross Westhuis
David E. White
John C. White
Robert & JoAnne White
The Rev. Arlene R. Wilhelm
Jane Wilkinson
The Rev. Mildred Williams
Rich Williams
The Rev. Glenroy B. Wolfsen
Woodcliff Community Reformed Church
Youngsville Community Reformed Church
John E. Zavacky
Nancy Anne Zeller
Edith E. Zindle

Contents

Acknowledgements

James Luther Adams once told the story of a young Jewish student, named Louis Finkelstein, who was being interviewed for admission to the Jewish Theological Seminary in New York. The president of the institution, Solomon Schecter, an imposing man whom many thought resembled Moses, asked why Finkelstein wanted to attend seminary. He responded that he wanted to learn more about the Torah. "That's not a good reason," responded Schecter, "you can do that at home." "Why should I come?" Finkelstein nervously asked. "You come here for one reason—to meet a great person. If you do not meet a great person while you are here, then your time with the faculty will be wasted."[1]

I arrived at New Brunswick Seminary in 1974 to study with Howard Hageman, and for the next decade continued doctoral studies at Drew University so I could maintain my association with this remarkable scholar and teacher, who had become my mentor. It was Howard's faith however, always pointing beyond himself to an evangelist from Nazareth, which inspired both my vocation and my life in the church. Howard would have been the first to confess that "greatness" belongs only to God. I offer this book in thanksgiving for the grace of God so abundantly seen in the remarkable gifts of Howard G. Hageman.

[1]John D. Spalding, "Remembering James Luther Adams," *Christian Century* (July 19-26, 1995): 714.

It is a pleasure to acknowledge those who have supported and aided this portrait of Howard's ministry and visions. The First Church in Albany graciously provided a summer sabbatical in which to do the research and writing. The First Reformed Church in Schenectady generously offered office space and quiet. The staff of the Gardner Sage Library of New Brunswick Seminary worked tirelessly to provide Howard's columns and articles published in the *Church Herald* from his first contribution, in 1946, to his last, in 1990. The New Netherland Project in Albany, New York, shared a computer diskette of a bibliography of most of Howard's publications saving countless hours of research and typing. Russell Gassero, the archivist of the Reformed Church in America, sought out unpublished minutes and manuscripts that added color and nuance to this story of Howard's work and witness.

My colleagues and friends, The Rev. Amy Jo Hawley, The Rev. Wilbur and Martha Ivins, and Steven Hoffman, read the manuscript and provided invaluable suggestions to bring clarity to the work. My wife, Vicki, and our children, Andrew, Katherine, and David, each offered their own help and considerable support as they watched with some bemusement as I finally learned to use a computer for this project. A concluding word of thanks to Carol Hageman, friend and collaborator on this labor of love. Carol not only has written the foreword to this book, but she also shared Howard's unpublished manuscripts and, more importantly, her memories of their almost fifty years together, as she reminded me often of the spirit that inspired his work.

Gregg A. Mast
Guilderland, New York

Foreword

I was pleased to be asked to lay before you a brief description of the events and lives God used to help mold the life and ministry of my husband, Howard Hageman.

Howard was born in Lynn, Massachusetts, in 1921, the son of an energetic, charismatic young Methodist minister not too removed from his graduate work at Boston University, and his wife Cora, an educator and a born teacher with a sensitivity to the needs of the poor and unloved. When Howard was two years old, the family moved to Albany, New York, a pleasant small city which would become home. He was fortunate to receive an excellent education at the Albany Academy for Boys, where he won honors in academics and oratory. During these early years he became accomplished at the keyboard, both piano and organ. Indeed, he gave his first concert at the great organ at Trinity Methodist Church while still in his early teens.

This rather sheltered and pleasant boyhood came to a shattering halt early one August morning in 1937, when Howard's father drowned in a fishing accident on Lake Champlain. His boyhood matured into manhood overnight.

The year following that tragic event, also his last at the academy, Howard gravitated to the First Church in Albany (Reformed). M. Stephen James was the pastor at the time. Dr. and Mrs. James had been longtime friends of the Hageman family, and "Uncle Jimmy" naturally took a special place in

Howard's life. It was Dr. James who introduced Howard to Reformed theology, a theology he truly appreciated and over time made his own.

The fall of 1938 saw Howard and his mother driving to Cambridge, Massachusetts, for his entrance into Harvard College...directly into the teeth of a record-breaking hurricane! There were no warning systems in those days. Despite an unavoidable delay and his late appearance, the rest of his college years were calm and productive.

The Classics Department at Harvard was relatively small, and at that time even the professorial "stars" did their own teaching. They took an interest in the special gifts of their students and guided them gently toward fulfilling avenues of study. This was a form of pedagogy Howard appreciated and would make his own in his teaching career.

Anxious to pursue his new theological foundation, Howard sought out a Presbyterian church in Boston, a rarity, and found the Church of the Covenant with G. Campbell Wadsworth in the pulpit. Campbell, a Canadian, was a recent product of Edinburgh University graduate school, a compelling theologian and preacher. He was drawn to this rather lost young man and promptly took him home to share lunch, and the hearts of the family! There started a friendship and theological dialogue that lasted until Howard had the honor of preaching Campbell's funeral sermon fifty years later. The Wadsworth family included an energetic four-year-old son and infant twin daughters at that time, yet both Campbell and Margaret felt that their home was an integral part of Campbell's pastoral ministry. Howard appreciated this ministry style and would make it his own in his parish career.

At the Church of the Covenant organ bench was Maurice C. Kirkpatrick, an accomplished musician and teacher who held himself to extremely high musical standards. Kirk and Effie took Howard into their circle, and he enjoyed both a friendship and an education in church music which he also would eventually pass on.

The advent of World War II brought many changes. The Wadsworths returned to Canada. When America entered the conflict, several of Howard's classmates enlisted. Full of patriotism but poorly prepared, they lost their lives in the first year. Seminary bound, Howard did not serve in the armed forces but was employed for a brief time as a civilian by the U. S. Navy in its decoding program.

Howard entered New Brunswick Theological Seminary in the fall of 1942. Dr. James had left the parish in Albany to assume a professorate at the seminary. I believe Dr. James was the only person Howard really knew in the Reformed Church in America at that time. New Brunswick was a very small, rather informal school then. However, it held a formidable place in the theological world, due in part to the extraordinary scholarship of its president, John W. Beardslee II.

During Howard's junior year he followed up on a study he had begun at Harvard about Mercersburg, a liturgical movement in the German Reformed church of the mid 1800s. He made a trip to Reading and Lancaster, Pennsylvania, to meet Scott Brenner and George Bricker, who introduced him to the movement. Dr. Bricker, connected with Lancaster Seminary, was particularly helpful in later years, finding printed materials to help in what became Howard's life-long study and commitment.

At the end of his junior year, Howard became the student assistant to David VanStrien at the Woodcliff Community Church (Reformed), where he would remain until his graduation. Dr. VanStrien was a wise and kindly man who introduced Howard to the joys and frustrations of parish ministry.

Upon his graduation in 1945, Howard surprised friends and family by putting aside his plans for immediate graduate work at Yale to accept a call to the North Reformed Church in Newark, New Jersey. His decision was unusual at a time when the move of white Protestant middle-class folk from the city to the suburbs was just gathering strength. Many churches were also pulling up stakes and following their congregations. In Newark, the void caused by the out-migration was fast filled with an in-migration of folk from the rural south and the coal mining towns of western Pennsylvania, all seeking employment in the diversified industry of the city. The church was facing an increasingly indifferent and sometimes hostile population. The situation at North Church was compounded by some internal strife. Because Howard felt passionately that it is precisely at the point of weakness and need that the church must dig in, plant a banner high and proclaim Christ's gospel boldly, he set aside his plans and cast his lot with a church which had made a decision to stay the course.

While Howard was student assistant at Woodcliff, he became romantically involved with a young woman in the congregation. Our wedding took place soon after his ordination. God is good and I am grateful we had forty-eight years together.

Renewing the North Church was a long hard road, taking literally years of afternoons and evenings in parish calling, imaginative new programs, solid biblical preaching, and the efforts of a truly dedicated small congregation undergirded by the knowledge that it was doing God's work. However, the day came when a congregation at peace with itself was strong enough to address the folks at the door in the name of Christ. In the process, Howard found in the parish his heart's work.

Shortly after starting his work at North Church, Howard enrolled for graduate study at Princeton Seminary. However, it was soon evident that the reward did not justify the time spent away from the parish. Therefore, he set out on the unorthodox road of self-education. The search for books, the struggle to buy them, the long nights spent at his desk, after hours, all attest to the degree of discipline he imposed on himself. Of course, learning for him was pure joy.

In time, Dr. John Mackay, then president of Princeton Seminary, asked Howard to deliver the prestigious Stone Lectures on the subject of Reformed worship. These lectures evolved into *Pulpit and Table,* published in 1962, a small volume which nevertheless secured Howard's place in the scholarly world both at home and abroad. It was very satisfying, of course, but more importantly to him, he was able to prove in his own life that at least in the church there ought to be no gulf between scholar and practitioner.

Howard served as pastor of North Church for twenty-eight years, and as sometimes visiting professor at New Brunswick in homiletics and liturgics. In 1973 he became president of New Brunswick Seminary, where he also continued to teach for the next twelve years. In these years he was pleased to work with Bard Thompson, dean of the graduate school at Drew University, and Horton Davies, the Henry W. Putnam Professor of the History of Christianity at Princeton University, formulating a Ph.D. program in liturgics to be offered at Drew. It was satisfying to see the program up and running, teaching in it, and experiencing the pleasure of seeing New Brunswick graduates complete the course. Then, in 1985, he moved into active retirement until his illness and death on the last Sunday of Advent, 1992.

If all the above makes you think "all work and no play," please dismiss the thought. Howard had a zest for life and loved people. The easy smile and glib remark were not among his gifts, but his friends enjoyed his sense of humor and gentle wit. He enjoyed sharing the gifts he had been given–be it knowledge, a book, his table, his beloved Lake Champlain, or later the Hudson River. He took great pleasure in planning events that would please;

like outings, dinner parties, trips, and unexpected gifts. In the words of an old friend, "Howard made things happen."

Despite his pleasure in his colonial Dutch ancestry, I believe one of Howard's greatest gifts came from his Irish maternal grandmother; the ability to laugh in the face of trouble and shed a tear in the face of prosperity; to take one's work very seriously, but not one's self. I once heard an author explain his compulsion to write this way, "It was for this purpose I was put on earth." I can think of no better way to describe the life and ministry of Howard Hageman.

To God alone be the Glory!

Carol W. Hageman
Guilderland, New York

Introduction

Howard Hageman loved to read the published diaries of historical figures. He found in their flesh and blood stories the raw material for many of his sermon illustrations and examples to prove points in his scholarly articles. He was convinced that if one looks closely enough at the world one will discover the fingerprints of God in every life and in every corner of the globe. Howard was a kind of detective on the trail of the divine in the common experiences of life.

At first glance it may seem a shame that he did not leave a diary of his remarkable life. But Howard did leave for us an amazing record of the events between 1961 and 1988. It was between these years that he wrote the "Focus on the World" column in the *Church Herald*. For more than half of the twenty-seven years the column was published weekly and consequently, Howard wrote almost 1,000 columns and addressed more than 1,600 topics.

For the historian, this record is a gold mine of material, because Howard Hageman served as a virtual religious news service for the denomination. His focus on the world included a commentary on the social changes and crises in our own country during a turbulent era. A review of the articles reveals that he shared news from churches in more than forty nations. India and Italy, Chile and Canada, Taiwan and Cuba, all found a way into his column and therefore into the consciousness of the Reformed Church in America. The ecumenical world of dialogue and disagreement was a favorite topic, especially in the 1960s. The relationship between church and state was often described in the very real issues from our evening newspapers. Roman Catholics and our Jewish neighbors regularly appeared in his writings, as did an occasional article about the Islamic countries.

Howard loved to read and write about the Netherlands, and the Reformed Church in America was often reminded of its roots and the continuing developments in both the Dutch nation and church. The greatest number of columns was committed to issues of church union (in the 1960s), the struggle for justice and reconciliation in Ireland and South Africa (in the 1970s), and the continuing concern for liturgical renewal. Howard saved some of his most courageous articles for the deeply troubling issue of race relations in the United States. Although he did not expect people always to agree with him, and I suspect there were those who seldom did, there was very little question where Hageman stood on the issues he addressed. Nevertheless, he never identified himself with any partisan agenda, so readers were left to guess his political leanings.

It is the intent of this book to identify the issues and concerns that found their way into the very core of the ministry and vision of Howard Hageman. It is to that end that the book has been organized around the threefold foci of our worship, our work, and our witness. After an initial chapter to introduce the reader to Hageman and his personal and spiritual roots, we will turn to the issues of word and sacrament, praise and prayer. The second section, entitled "Our Work," focuses on the common ministry of all believers and the ordained service of elder, deacon, and minister. The last section addresses the witness of the church in the world with special emphases on the country of South Africa and the challenging call to urban ministry.

In each of these chapters it is hoped that the reader will not only catch a glimpse of the remarkable ministry of Howard Hageman, but most important, will begin to appreciate his profound vision for the Reformed church. It will become clear that Howard had a deep and abiding commitment to the Reformed faith that formed his life and actions.

Howard wrote a great deal of material which has not found its way into this text. He had an insatiable hunger to learn more about hymnody and music, Dutch colonial history and liturgical renewal, homiletics and church history, the Mercersburg movement, and the arts. With such a renaissance man, it is important to limit our inquiry so we can begin to understand the impact he had on the life and common ministry of the Reformed Church in America.

For Howard, the Christian faith is both personal and cosmic. It embraces the life of the spirit and the life of the most mundane concern. He was fond of reminding people that it was John Calvin who worked to create a new sewer system in Geneva in response to a terrible plague. The call of the church is one that follows Jesus into all parts of life to claim the world for God. Howard often quoted these memorable words of Albert Schweitzer. They are a fitting introduction to this text, for they are a reminder that this book is not so much a monument to the past as it is a vision of the future.

> As one unknown and nameless He comes to us, just as on the shore of the lake He approached those men who knew not who He was. His words are the same: "Follow thou Me!" and He puts us to the tasks which He has to carry out in our age. He will reveal Himself through all that they are privileged to experience in His fellowship of peace and activity, of struggle and suffering, till they come to know, as an inexpressible secret, Who He is.[1]

[1]Albert Schweitzer, *Out of My Life and Thought* (New York: Henry Holt and Company, Inc., 1933): 48-49.

I
Ministry and Vision:
The Secret of Our Destiny

Howard often told the story of driving through the New Jersey countryside sometime in the 1940s and discovering on the bulletin board of a village church the words: "The secret of our destiny lies in the recovery of our heritage." Although he could never discover the author of the quotation, it will become clear as we study the ministry and visions of Howard Hageman that the inscription on a bulletin board became for him a creed and hymn of faith. Before turning to Howard's remarkable career however, it is important for us to catch a glimpse of the personal and spiritual roots which gave him life.

The Hageman family roots ran deep into the soil of the Netherlands. Although Howard was fond of quoting Matthew 25:35 regarding his relationship to the Reformed church, "I was a stranger and you welcomed me," his family began its ministry in the seventeenth century when it resided in the small Dutch village of Vorchten in the province of Gelderland. In the year 1624, one of his direct ancestors was called to serve as the village dominie. Quite amazingly, the story in the Netherlands did not end with the death of the first dominie; the Hageman family provided the parish with ministers for 113 years, with one seventeen-year hiatus, between 1660 and 1677. The first dominie's son came to America in 1652 to serve as a schoolteacher in the new world and a founder of Flatbush, Long Island. In this country the Hageman clan contributed eight of its sons to the ministry of the Reformed Church in America.

Howard's father was born in Bucyrus, Ohio, the son of a farmer. He attended a rural school as a child and taught for five years before entering Ohio Wesleyan University. After winning a scholarship, Hageman Sr. entered Boston University School of Theology. He served pastoral charges in Ohio and Massachusetts before accepting the call to Trinity Methodist Church in Albany, New York, in 1923. The Hageman family provided young Howard with an environment that nurtured his interest in music, architecture, and academic disciplines. It also provided him with a deep love of the church and an abiding interest in its worship and life.

Early on a Monday morning, long before the light had dawned, Howard Sr. rose to drive eight miles to collect his fishing companion, James Martin. Both men were dressed in heavy fishing garb and were prepared to spend the day on Lake Champlain. As Hageman stood to drop anchor about a half mile from shore, the boat capsized and the men were thrown into the water. Martin was rescued by two campers who heard his shouts for help, but Hageman drowned. A newspaper that covered the tragic story described how the sixteen-year-old son of the minister had telephoned the news of his death to the Albany church. Howard's commitment to the heritage of the church and his personal and spiritual priorities were tragically and quietly inspired by the event which took place just before dawn on an August morning on Lake Champlain.

A year after his father's death, Howard graduated from the Albany Academy and entered Harvard at the age of seventeen. His love of history and his natural gifts as a linguist prompted him to become a classics major and, in 1942, he was honored to provide the graduation address in Latin. During his time at Harvard, Howard was to make a discovery that would change his life and ministry. Buried in the library stacks was the record of a creative church movement of the mid 19th century called Mercersburg. He devoured the record of its conception and birth and the controversy which surrounded its growth. As he read, he found that he was discovering the roots of his family's worship in Pennsylvania. Years later he explained:

> "Well, I had relatives in Pennsylvania who were members of the German Reformed Church who had been influenced by Mercersberg, so as a kid I used to visit uncles, aunts, grandparents

and so forth and without thinking much about it, became familiar with a liturgical form of service. Then I got involved in the First Reformed Church in Albany. M. Stephen James was there and, of course, his mind went in that same direction... And somewhere along the line, while I was still in Harvard, I ran across the name of Nevin."[1]

Howard's choice of New Brunswick Seminary was not only influenced by the presence of his father's seminary classmate and friend, Dr. M. Stephen James, who had arrived there in 1942 to serve as professor of preaching, but also by the misconception that the Dutch Reformed church was deeply influenced by and appreciative of the Mercersburg movement.

While at Harvard, Howard began to prepare for his service in the Reformed church by teaching himself Dutch. He bought a Dutch Bible at the Massachusetts Bible Society and began to read passages he knew by heart. He readily confessed that his reading ability of Dutch was far superior to his speaking skill. Nevertheless, his success at learning French in school and at teaching himself German and Afrikaans as well became an important bridge to information and theology for the Reformed church in decades to come. It was Dr. Milton Hoffman, a professor at New Brunswick and an early visitor to the Netherlands following the Second World War, who returned to the United States and observed, "Never forget that from now on America is the old world and Europe the new." Howard's skill and commitment to languages allowed the worlds to find a mediator and friend. His vision for a new world encouraged him to share often the insights of Europe with North America.

As Howard prepared to graduate from New Brunswick in 1945, he applied to do graduate work at Yale but instead embarked on a career in parish ministry. What turned this brilliant student toward parish ministry? In his presidential inaugural address at New Brunswick some twenty-eight years later, he recalled a conversation with Dr. Frederic Berg, who had left the faculty at the seminary to assume a pastorate in Flatbush. Dr. Berg remarked that during his years of teaching he never found a student who could ask him a question that puzzled him. That discovery, he observed, compelled him to go back to the parish where every week people would ask

[1] John D. Spalding, "Remembering James Luther Adams," *Christian Century* (July 19-26, 1995): 714.

him questions he could not answer. When Howard graduated, he received not only the Senior Class award for excellence, but also the Lodewick Prize for Preaching. With the encouragement of his family friend and mentor, Dr. James, Howard accepted a call to the North Reformed Church in Newark, New Jersey.

On the twenty-eighth anniversary of his call to North Church, in 1973, Hageman returned to his theological alma mater as president, during a very trying time in its history. He concluded his tenure as president in 1985 when he and Carol retired to a small Hudson River village, New Baltimore, New York, just south of Albany.

In the fall of 1984, Howard announced his plans to retire from New Brunswick Seminary. Dr. Paul Fries, interviewing him for an issue of the *New Brunswick Newsletter*, prompted him to identify the people who had most influenced his life and ministry. It should come as no surprise that Howard first mentioned the name of John Williamson Nevin, the theologian of the Mercersburg Movement in the German Reformed church. It was Nevin's focus on the theology of John Calvin that brought Hageman to a realization that the Reformed tradition was not only deeply sacramental but also theologically committed to a high view of the body of Christ and the ministry of all believers. While at Harvard, Howard was also intrigued by the writings of John Henry Newman, one of the first people he had read who wrestled with issues of both faith and reason. His father, before his death, had told him to watch a young theologian named Karl Barth. Upon Barth's death, Hageman wrote in his "Focus on the World" column, "I for one am deeply grateful that this theological giant belonged firmly in the Reformed tradition, that the theology of the Word of God was his home territory."[2]

During his time at New Brunswick, Howard discovered George Washington Bethune, whose mosaic portrait hangs prominently in the seminary's Gardner Sage Library. He was deeply impressed with his elegance as a preacher, his passion for books, and his commitment to the ecumenical church long before it was fashionable. Hageman cited the Dutch theologian and liturgical scholar Vander Leeuw as someone who challenged him to learn Dutch because he was inspired by the direction of his writing. To his gallery of theological heroes, Howard added a Reformed

---

[2]Howard G. Hageman, "Homage to Karl Barth," *Church Herald* (February 7, 1969): 11.

pastor by the name of Kohlbrugge who confronted the privatizing of the gospel with a clear and objective view of the work of Christ and the gospel.

From 1961 through 1988 Howard wrote a column in the *Church Herald* entitled, "Focus on the World." During that twenty-seven-year period, he also remembered with a column or comment some significant people in his life. He once noted that Dr. John Beardslee, Jr., who was president of New Brunswick when Howard was a student, was one of the most influential teachers in his life and training. He remembered his colleague and friend, Erik Routley, one of the great hymnologists of our time. Howard had recruited Erik to serve as editor of our hymnal, *Rejoice in the Lord*, and deeply grieved his untimely passing. Hageman loved poetry and often quoted a verse from memory in his many writings and sermons. He paid special attention to the work of G.K. Chesterton, whom he had discovered in college. Indeed, he once remarked that he knew of no place outside the four gospels that more winsomely shared the Easter story than the chapter dedicated to the life of Christ in *The Everlasting Man*. In the last paragraph of chapter three, Chesterton writes:

> On the third day the friends of Christ coming at daybreak to the place found the grave empty and the stone rolled away. In varying ways they realized the wonder; but even they hardly realized that the world had died in the night. What they were looking at was the first day of a new creation, with a new heaven and a new earth; and in a semblance of the gardener God walked again in the garden, in the cool not of the evening but the dawn.[3]

Hageman also lauded the work of other poets whom he often quoted in his writings. T.S. Eliot and W.H. Auden were both Christians, considered by Howard and many others as two of the greatest poets in the English language. He derided the fact that Christian folk often ignored Eliot. He once exclaimed with some exasperation: "Lazy Christians find it far more palatable to amuse themselves with the threadbare images and worn out clichés of traditional religious doggerel than to try to think their way through Mr. Eliot's difficult and new statements."[4]

---

[3]G. K. Chesterton, *The Everlasting Man* (Garden City, Long Island: Image Books, 1955): 212.

[4]Howard G. Hageman, "The Two Cultures," *Church Herald* (February 5, 1965): 21.

Henry Thoreau, in a quotation Howard loved to cite, observed after someone announced that Harvard College taught all of the branches of human knowledge, "That's right; all of the branches and none of the roots." Hageman left Harvard in 1942 with the writings and visions of Mercersburg in his mind and soul to attend New Brunswick Theological Seminary. It was there that he nurtured the roots that would sustain his life and ministry.

Early in the 1940s, Howard was moved by his Boston pastor, G. C. Wadsworth, to explore the Scottish theologians Henry Wotherspoon, Thomas Leishman, and James Cooper, in whose writings he found references to Mercersburg. The discovery inspired him to initiate a life-long search of its literature and history. He devoured the description of the controversy that surrounded its introduction into the German Reformed church by the *Mercersburg Review*. He read again and again the writings of John Williamson Nevin, Phillip Schaff, and Henry Harbaugh. Hageman once exclaimed, "When I graduated from Harvard in 1942, I was as well informed on Mercersburg theology as any college senior in the United States!"[5]

As he began his seminary studies, Howard was not aware that although a significant portion of the German Reformed church embraced the Mercersburg renewal, an equally large portion of the Dutch Reformed felt very uncomfortable with its conclusions. His knowledge of the liturgical work Dr. James had done in the worship of the First Church in Albany had led him to believe that the liturgical tradition represented there would be found at New Brunswick and in the denomination as a whole. During his first year as a student at the seminary, he quickly learned otherwise, and so he sought and received an invitation to attend the annual convocation on Mercersburg at Lancaster Seminary. It was then that he considered joining the Evangelical and Reformed church. Many years later Hageman tellingly wrote: "Perhaps the only reason I did not do so was some distant vision of my having a liturgical and sacramental mission in the Reformed Church in America....In any event, I was ordained as a complete convert to Mercersburg and I hope my role to implement my convictions in my own church is sufficiently a matter of record."[6] What he found in Mercersburg was a theology that was churchly, sacramental, and liturgical. These were

---

[5]"A Personal Word," undated, Hageman Collection, Gardner Sage Library, New Brunswick Theological Seminary, New Brunswick, New Jersey.
[6]Ibid.

characteristics of ecclesiastical renewal which would guide him throughout his ministerial career.

The Mercersburg movement revived Calvin's doctrines of church and sacraments, which had been almost totally replaced from the sixteenth century with Zwinglian theological perspectives. In the early 1840s, John Nevin was called by the German Reformed church to serve its young seminary in Mercersburg, Pennsylvania. He was soon joined by a classically trained German church historian by the name of Phillip Schaff. The two of them moved to confront the prevailing atmosphere of "new measures" which had invaded the Calvinist denomination. They affirmed the call for faith to be deeply experiential while urging the church to assume its appropriate role as a community of education and nurture. Nevin pointed to Calvin's understanding of our mystical union with Christ as the foundation of church life and ministry and the sacrament of the Lord's Supper.

George Bricker, one of Howard's mentors in Mercersburg, has written:

> When Nevin began his work at Mercersburg he became alarmed at the drift of the German Reformed Church and American Protestantism away from biblical faith, the spirit of the early church, and the insights of the Reformation. In his estimation the German Reformed Church partook of the general malaise of American Protestantism. It was unchurchly, unhistorical, and unsacramental. It was based on a faulty Christology.[7]

When Nevin was called to write a defense of the new liturgy, which he and those sympathetic to Mercersburg theology had prepared at the request of the General Synod of the German Reformed church, he described it as a document that was Christocentric, firmly rooted in the faith of the Apostles' Creed, and one that was objective and historical. Nevin described the cardinal principle of the movement as "the fact of the Incarnation."

> The incarnation should be viewed not as a doctrine or speculation but as a real transaction of God in the world. It is regarded as necessarily the essence of Christianity, the sum and substance of the whole Christian redemption. Christ saves the world, not

[7]Charles Yrigoyen, Jr., and George Bricker, eds., *Catholic and Reformed Selected Theological Writings of John Williamson Nevin* (Pittsburgh: The Pickwick Press, 1978): 5.

ultimately by what he teaches or by what he does, but by what he is in the constitution of his own person. His person in its relations to the world carries in it the power of victory over sin, death, and hell, the force thus of a real atonement or reconciliation between God and man, the triumph of a glorious resurrection from the dead, and all the consequences for faith which are attributed to this the grand old symbol called the Apostles' Creed.[8]

The Mercersburg theology led Howard to make some important commitments early in his career from which he would never waver. Therefore, we read in his early writings in the 1940s the same themes that permeated his interest to the end of his life. For example, in the mid 1980s Howard was an active participant in the North American Academy of Liturgy's working group on the historical study of the liturgy. Among his papers was a proposal to study the impact Mercersburg had on the parish life of local congregations in the German church. At the same time, he was instrumental in establishing the Mercersburg Society, which continues to study the visions of the movement for the modern church. Hageman served as its president until his death in 1992. Describing the first convocation of the society, he wrote:

> The large majority of those present were working pastors (and some laypeople) who are uneasy about the integrity of the Reformed tradition in today's America. Repelled by the sterility of a fossilized Calvinism, appalled by the success of a mindless Evangelicalism, and discouraged by the emptiness of classic liberalism, they are looking for a fresh understanding of the Reformed tradition. Mercersburg, with its emphasis on incarnation, church, sacraments, and ministry as essential elements of that tradition, seems to offer at least an interesting possibility.[9]

Hageman was not blind to the problems of the movement. While it attempted to be a vindication of Calvinistic doctrine, Mercersburg was strangely silent about the importance of preaching for the church and the world. Hageman also observed that it was possible to follow the teaching of Mercersburg as an end in itself and for it to become almost cultic for those who lived in the last century as well as this one. But for Hageman and for

[8]Ibid., 408-409.
[9]Howard G. Hageman, "Back to Mercersburg," *Reformed Journal* (August, 1985): 5.

others within the Reformed tradition, Mercersburg became a bridge to the church catholic and to a church constantly reforming itself according to the Word of God.

As we turn toward a deeper appreciation of the ministry and vision of Howard Hageman, it is appropriate for us to pause to catch an overview of his theology and the themes that came to him from his mentors, his commitment to Mercersburg and his abiding dependence on the constantly reforming Word of God. These major themes became a consistent melody in the almost 1,000 articles and columns that he wrote and published.

In January of 1981, Howard was invited by Central College to serve as the presenter of the Staley Lecture Program. His five days on campus included eight opportunities for him to address his topic, "Reformed Theology in Practice." The titles of these lectures are instructive concerning the theological themes of his academic study and pastoral ministry. The first lecture was entitled "Grace Reigns," and clearly it articulated the primary role of God's grace and sovereignty in the life of the church and the world. His second chapel lecture focused on the title, "Who Chose Whom?" and defended a biblical, historical, and Calvinistic understanding of the divine foundation of our salvation. It is clear from his third lecture entitled "No Church-No Christian," that Hageman wanted his audience at Central to affirm the central role of the church in our life as the body of Christ. Howard was fond of quoting Calvin, who once wrote that it was impossible to claim God as our father without also claiming the church as our mother. The "Cosmic Christ," the fourth lecture, reminded his audience that the reign of Christ is not only personal but also universal in its embrace. Throughout his life, Hageman mourned the loss of Ascension Day as a symbol of the church's lack of understanding of such a Christ. The concluding address was entitled, "From the Service to Service," and it clearly called the church to remember that our liturgy does not end, but begins, at the doors of the church. In all of the lectures, Hageman had the opportunity to address the issue of integrity in the worship life of the Reformed church and to remind his audience of the vertical and horizontal dimensions of our liturgy.

In 1947, in one of the first columns Howard published in the *Church Herald*, he addressed the character of the church catholic. During an age that was often suspicious of, if not hostile to, the universal dimension of the body of Christ, he concluded the article with these words:

We need to realize that the Reformed church we attend is not just the Reformed church in our town and nothing more. It's the Reformed church in our town, part of the Reformed Church in America, part of the churches of Christ in America, part of the Reformed and Presbyterian churches of the world, part of the World Council of Churches, a part of the body of Christ, at work in the world He came to redeem.[10]

Howard was acutely aware that when he began to write his regular column in the *Church Herald* in the early 1960s there were many who were confidently predicting the demise of the organized church and the ordained ministry as well. Hageman's position regarding the church, however, did not change. He remained committed to a community that was constantly reforming itself according to the Word of God. This dynamic quality provided a creed and cultus that are always looking to share an eternal Word in an ever changing world. In the midst of all of the chaos and confusion of the mid 1960s, especially concerning church union, Howard wrote:

I glory in the confessional stance of the Reformed church, in its vow to obey only the Word of God, in its Biblical and its theological seriousness. I am proud of its liturgical inheritance which avoids the errors of both formalism and license. I delight in the evangelical freedom of its style of church order. I envy no other church anything at any of these points. In the Reformed Church in America these are mine and I am glad to have it so.[11]

It was this deep commitment to the Reformed church that prompted Howard regularly to call the denomination to become true to its heritage. In 1952, he observed that we seem to be the least selfconscious group of people in the world.

We have our saints, our martyrs, our prophets, our poets — but we have allowed them to lie forgotten in the dust....The plain fact of the matter is that a people without history is a people without a

---

[10]Howard G. Hageman, "World Churches Present A United Front," *Church Herald* (January 10, 1947): 14.
[11]Howard G. Hageman, "From My Corner," *Church Herald* (March 17, 1967): 11.

future. If the Reformed Church in America has lost its sense of direction, it could be because it first lost its sense of origin. People who do not know where they are going! And that, too often, describes us."[12]

When invited by the *Church Herald* in 1961 to identify the greatest issue facing the denomination, Hageman reiterated his position that "the first task that we have to face is the rediscovery of who we are." During his first visit to Geneva in 1950, he stood in front of the great Reformation Monument and vowed that he would try to rescue from obscurity the heroes of the Reformed Reformation whom God had used to bring light from the shadows.

In an untitled and unpublished document, Hageman explored the forces of Christianity under the classifications, Catholic, Evangelical, and Reformed. He identified the Reformed tradition as grounded in the sovereignty of God. For Reformed folk, he wrote, there is no other authority than the Word of God. A rigorous adherence to such a standard means that our confession, *Ecclesia reformata semper reformanda*, which Howard translated "a reformed church is itself always being reformed," calls the church to be always self critical or more accurately to be constantly re-formed by the Word of God. Another unique feature of the Reformed tradition is the creative third use of the law as expounded in Calvin and clearly illustrated in the Heidelberg Catechism. This use of the law calls us to a life of obedience and an ethical stance that is fully engaged with the world. Hageman concluded the piece by suggesting that the time had come for all three traditions, Catholic, Evangelical, and Reformed, to embrace the best in each other as we seek to serve a world where we are a colony of heaven and an outpost of grace.

Howard G. Hageman was a faithful pastor, a brilliant scholar and teacher, an engaging preacher, a prophetic presence, a lover of the church and its worship, and most importantly, a servant of the Word of God. His legacy to us is a gift for which many of us are deeply grateful. Because the secret of our destiny lies hidden in the recovery of our heritage, it is appropriate for us to study the ministry and vision of Howard Hageman regarding our worship, our work and our witness.

---

[12]Howard G. Hageman, "When the Reformed Church was Young," *Church Herald* (November 14, 1952): 15.

II
The Pulpit:
In the Beginning was the Word

As dusk was turning to darkness on the fourth Sunday of Advent, December 20, 1992, Howard Hageman died. His funeral was held at the North Reformed Church in Newark, New Jersey, where he had served for twenty-eight years as pastor. Some days later, a memorial service was celebrated at the old First Church in Albany, where as a young man he was introduced to the Dutch Reformed tradition. The lectionary reading for that Sunday was the familiar passage from the first chapter of the Gospel of John, that includes the words: "In the beginning was the Word and the Word was with God, and the Word was God."

The Word and words were Howard's life. He read voraciously, he preached and taught with passion and eloquence, and he wrote extensively in a broad range of theological, historical, and liturgical areas. Howard loved words! Most important, Howard committed his life to discovering the Word among the words of the world. In 1977, Hageman estimated he had preached in more than 250 congregations in the Reformed Church in America. By the time of his death, he had graced the pulpits of almost one third of the churches. Yet, in spite of his widely acclaimed role as the favorite choice to preach anniversary and special celebration services, Howard did not write a great deal about preaching.

In 1952 Hageman was invited to preach at the General Synod meeting and he chose his text from 1 Thessalonians: "When ye received the Word of God which ye heard of us, ye received it not as the word of men, but, as it is in truth, the Word of God...." It is from the body of this sermon that we learn a great deal about Howard's theology of the Word that inspired his preaching:

> If we are to be more than talking shops, lecture halls, schools of doctrine, if we are to be fellowships of living power, then one of our desperate needs is to recover a right sense of what it means to preach and to hear the Word. I cannot but think that one of the most pernicious things that has happened to us in this regard is the exclusive way in which we have come to identify the Word of God with the Bible. Let there be no mistaking it; the Bible is the Word of God, but neither in a primary nor in an exclusive sense. How can we forget that primarily the Word of God is He that became flesh and dwelt among us, full of grace and truth, who still lives at the right hand of His Father? Any attempt to replace His primary position by a book stands condemned as idolatry.[1]

This clear and emphatic defense of a Christocentric view of preaching led Hageman finally to confess the sacramental dimension of the pulpit. Indeed if Howard could have unilaterally declared preaching the third sacrament, he would have done it. Sermons are more than lectures about the Bible, or even opportunities to do biblical exegesis in a public setting, but the place and the time when the Christ comes again to live among us and within us. Preaching is the act of identifying the presence of the Word in our midst and listening closely to where he calls us to go, what he calls us to do, and, most important, who he calls us to be. Howard had not always held such a high view of preaching. He once confessed that in the early years of his career the pulpit was primarily understood by preachers as a place and time for the education of the congregation. Hageman wrote: "This writer has destroyed his first sermons because they were really biblical and theological lectures, fairly well done 'head trips' but little else."[2] Hageman went on to recall with some horror the first sermon he preached on Trinity Sunday in the early 1940s when he attempted to explain all the Athanasian mysteries in fifteen minutes!

[1]Howard G. Hageman, "Preaching the Word," *Church Herald* (September 19, 1952): 5.
[2]Howard G. Hageman, "Preaching is Alive and Well," *Theology Today* 37 (January, 1981): 493-497.

His critical eye did not only turn toward his own work, but also toward a church that he feared had often lost the resolve to preach life's changing messages of resurrection. Hageman was fond of quoting Ralph Waldo Emerson's description of the Reverend Barzillal Frost, the minister of the church Emerson attended in Concord. In Emerson's diary entry for March 18, 1838, a stormy, snowy day, these words appear:

> At church all day, but almost tempted to say I would go no more. Men go where they want to go, else had no soul gone this afternoon. The snowstorm was real; the preacher merely spectral. Vast contrast to look at him and then out of the window. He had no word intimating that he had ever laughed or wept, was married or enamored, had been cheated, or voted for or chagrined. If he had ever lived or acted, we were none the wiser for it.[3]

What the entry emphasizes is the lack of flesh and blood in the young preacher's sermon. For Howard, preaching was the opportunity to share the real presence of Christ. He shuddered when he heard preaching which would talk about God as an object of our study rather than the subject of our love and devotion. Preaching is not talking about faith, but creating faith. It is not talking about the resurrection, but raising the dead. The pulpit is finally a place where one person speaks of the pain and joy of an entire congregation and the word of hope and challenge God has already spoken in the life of a carpenter.

In a lecture Hageman apparently delivered at New Brunswick in 1984 entitled "The Spirituality of John Calvin," he shared what he believed to be the understanding of preaching in the writings of the great reformer. It is interesting that Calvin never identified a separate place for the lesson in his liturgies, because the reading and the preaching of the Word were the same act. To highlight some important aspects of Calvin's theology of preaching, Hageman used a brief portion of the lecture to analyze the following prayer, which Calvin used before the Word.

> As we look into the face of the Son, Jesus Christ, our Lord, whom (God) has appointed Mediator between himself and us, let us

---

[3]"On Being A Real Parson," May 18, 1978, Hageman Collection, Gardner Sage Library, New Brunswick Theological Seminary, New Brunswick, New Jersey.

beseech him in whom is all fullness of wisdom and light to
vouchsafe to guide us by his Holy Spirit into the true understanding
of his holy doctrine, making it productive in us of all the fruits of
righteousness.[4]

Hageman suggests we see in this prayer the real presence of Christ who
comes to us in the preached Word through the power of the Holy Spirit. In
response to being in the presence of the living Christ, our understanding of
him is enlarged so that we may produce fruits of righteousness. It is
immediately clear to the reader that these insights can be equally applied to
the celebration of the sacrament of the Lord's Supper. Hageman's suggestion
is that the church needs to embrace the sacramental quality of preaching
which is eloquently illustrated in this brief commentary on Calvin's prayer.

I suppose it is possible for the reader to assume that Hageman had a
minimalist view of scripture, considering his high regard for the identification
of the Word with the person of Christ. Nothing could be further from the
truth! For Hageman, a sermon without its biblical moorings often was
carried into the unchartered waters of the preacher's imagination and
private theology. He described this as the great failure of the liberal church.
He also criticized the conservative church as simply reciting biblical material
as proof for theological propositions.

"We need to remind ourselves," he wrote, "that Calvin was not afraid of
the equation, *Predicatio Verbi Dei est Verbum Dei* (the preaching of the
Word of God is the Word of God)."[5] Such a high view of preaching meant
that Hageman assumed the task of preaching with the utmost seriousness.
The preacher's first responsibility, according to Hageman, is to read all the
lections for the week and to listen and look for that word or text that catches
his or her attention. Once the text is selected then the preacher is called to
do the homework of a homilitician. Commentaries and lives must be read
and savored. The interaction between the text and the congregation is
crucial. If a preacher does not know his people, then the great risk is that the
preacher, who is not quite a real person, will speak to a congregation filled
with not quite real people about not quite real things.

---

[4]Bard Thompson, *Liturgies of the Western Church* (Cleveland: The World Publishing
   Company, 1982: 209.
[5]Howard G. Hageman, "The Need and Promise of Reformed Preaching," *Church
   Herald* (October 17, 1975): 6.

In 1969, Hageman dedicated part of his column to a parish paper produced by a Reformed congregation in Rotterdam. The Dutch newsletter included an inspiring piece written by a lay person in response to the question: "What do I expect from our ministers in the pulpit?" After focusing on the corporate dimension of preaching, the author concluded with these words:

> Then the sermon will be the point at which the vertical line (which comes from God) touches the horizontal line (which comes from us). A real flash of lighting! Sunday church-going then becomes an event, something which always remains open and free. But seen this way, the congregation is just as much responsible for the sermon as the dominie....[6]

The weekly interaction between the preacher and congregation is the time to let the text "simmer" on the back burner of the preacher's mind and soul. In Hageman's own preparation, he moved from exegetical study to writing the entire sermon in a single sentence by Wednesday morning. This discipline saved him countless hours of wandering the theological landscape when he finally put his hand to writing. Hageman then spent the rest of the week collecting his thoughts and insights on small cards and pieces of paper that he would empty onto his desk at the time of his Saturday composition. "Because you have been living with the text all week, talking to it, arguing with it, looking for it, most of the materials which you need are going to be there," he writes.[7]

It was his personal discipline to write every sermon he preached. Realizing that there are many preachers who bristle at such a routine, Hageman observed that for him "good craftsmanship demands the discipline of writing." As he organized each sermon, he attempted ruthlessly to excise everything that did not address the central idea. This homiletical mode produced a structure that was clear and clean in its lines. Although a congregation may not in the end agree with what a preacher has shared, it is crucial that they know what he or she has said, Hageman observed. Finally

---

[6]Howard G. Hageman, "A Layman Looks At Preaching," *Church Herald* (February 28, 1969): 9.

[7]Howard G. Hageman, "Preaching is Alive and Well," *Theology Today* 37 (January, 1981): 493-497.

the choice of language is crucial to the enterprise because a congregation must see what it hears.

Having followed Hageman through a normal week of sermon preparation, we need to catch a glimpse of him in the pulpit. He was considered by many to be one of the finest preachers of the latter half of the twentieth century. Howard was as dramatic in the pulpit as he was quietly self-deprecating out of it. He gestured with hands which literally directed the symphony of words. I often thought of a great thunderstorm rumbling across a lake as an image of his finely honed voice. Each sentence would begin gently and build as it reached its crescendo. In and through it all, the congregation had an abiding sense that this preacher believed what he saying. Sermons, for Howard, had to come from an intersection between the Word and the world. The situation had to exegete the Word as the Word interpreted the world. It was Isaac Da Costa, a Dutch leader in the religious movements that finally prompted Albertus van Raalte to come to Michigan and Hendrik Scholte to Iowa, who wrote: "When you prepare a sermon, put your newspaper next to your Bible." As we move to consider the work of the sermon after its delivery, Howard was fond of quoting B. A. Gerrish, a modern Reformation scholar, who once observed:

> (Luther) preached the Word, slept, and drank beer; and while he did nothing more, the Word did it all. With Calvin things were quite different. As he lay on his deathbed, he fell to reminiscing about the course of his life and remarked: "When I first arrived in this church, there was almost nothing. They were preaching and that is all. There was no reformation.[8]

For Hageman the act of preaching and worship can be seen poetically in the walk of two disciples along the Emmaus road. Into the midst of their crucified lives a stranger appears and shares with them all that the scriptures had to say to their buried hopes. As importantly, the stranger becomes known to them in breaking bread, which prompts these weary travelers to run back down the same Emmaus road to share new life. There is no place in the story for the disciples to sit back and rest secure in their private knowledge of the resurrection. The work of Easter is the work of helping

[8]Brian Gerrish, *The Old Protestantism and the New* (Chicago: University of Chicago Press, 1982): 109.

change the world into the new creation. The pulpit and the preacher are at the cutting edge of that divine task.

Hageman often lauded the Roman church for its recovery of an appreciation of preaching in its life. As we will discover in the next section, he also called the Protestant tradition to move toward a parallel recovery of the sacraments in our ecclesiastical life. Howard was convinced that first the Reformed church needed to understand and appreciate the sacramental nature of preaching. He asked: "How can we talk about the real presence of Christ in the breaking of bread if we have not first been made aware of the real presence of Christ in the preaching of the Word?"[9]

J.D. Benoit, a French liturgical scholar, put the challenge in this way:

> This, it seems to me, is the great lack in our preaching; it does not nourish souls. It does not take them by the hand, so to speak, and bring them to God, but always leaves them in the same situation, that of the morning after confirmation....It does not address itself to their spiritual development. It is the pastor who must distribute the bread which makes souls live and grow spiritually.[10]

It is to that challenge that Howard wrote and preached. It was to that challenge that Howard called the church to wrestle with God in a time when people all too often live a life of quiet desperation. Hageman loved to quote Francis Thompson, who wrote not only the well-known poem, "The Hound of Heaven," but also a smaller poem that he entitled "The Kingdom of God," with the subtitle, "In No Strange Land." A few lines call us to the task of the pulpit and the pew:

> O world invisible, we view thee,
> O world intangible, we touch thee,
> O world unknowable, we know thee,
> Inapprehensible, we clutch thee....
>
> The angels keep their ancient places;
> Turn but a stone, and start a wing!

[9]Howard G. Hageman, "Sacramental Seriousness," *Reformed Journal* 35 No.3 (March, 1985): 4.

[10]J. D. Benoit, "Les Deficits de la Predication" (an address delivered at the synod of the Reformed Church of Alsace-Lorraine, September, 1952): 4-5.

'Tis ye, 'Tis your estranged faces
That miss the many splendored thing....

Yea in the night, my soul, my daughter,
Cry — clinging heaven by the hems:
And lo, Christ walking on the water
Not of Gennesaret, but Thames![11]

[11]Howard G. Hageman, "In No Strange Land," *Princeton Seminary Bulletin* 68
    (Autumn, 1975): 51.

III
The Table:
In Remembrance,
in Communion,
and in Hope

The year 1959 was a remarkable time in the comparatively young life of Howard G. Hageman. He not only served as one of the youngest presidents of General Synod at the age of thirty-nine, but he also was invited by Dr. James Mckay, then the president of Princeton Theological Seminary, to present the prestigious Stone Lectures in 1960. Such an invitation was a unique honor for any scholar, but for a person who had neither a terminal graduate degree nor extensive teaching credentials, it was a rare accolade. Howard's surprising decision to serve the parish instead of going on to graduate school was publicly confirmed within the scholarly community by Mckay's invitation. The substance of his lectures became the text for *Pulpit and Table,* published by John Knox Press, a few years later. The premise of the lectures and the book was that although John Calvin was clearly the theological leader of the Reformed tradition, Ulrich Zwingli had become our liturgical master. Although Hageman would have preferred a different historical outcome, his honest appraisal of our worship life allowed him to trace the events that had contributed to the ascendancy of Zwingli and Zurich over Calvin and Geneva. What contributed to our liturgical dependence on Zwingli and the apparent impotence of Calvin's ideas and practice?

The response to that question, and more importantly the investigation into the reappearance of Calvin's liturgical agenda, makes the book a fascinating one for historians and church members. A clue to the mystery of the reassessment of Calvin's ideas is found in a chain of events which occurred in the nineteenth century. It should come as no surprise that Mercersburg is in the midst of the drama. Nevin, Schaaf, and Harbaugh appear as important players in the recovery of the Calvinistic understanding of the liturgy, the sacraments, and a deep appreciation for the historical growth of the church.

The concluding chapter of *Pulpit and Table* is entitled "Toward A Reformed Liturgic." The dynamic quality of Reformed worship is apparent in the title as Hageman does not attempt to propose a liturgy that will work in all times and places. Rather, he suggests the principles which are consistent with scripture and can guide the development of our liturgical work. This final section in the Hageman book will be the focus of considerable attention in our next chapter when we turn from the sacrament to the broader topic of our corporate life of prayer.

It is important for us to take notice of the title of Hageman's book, *Pulpit and Table*. The liturgical life of the Reformed Church in America was one that revolved exclusively around the sermon well into the twentieth century. However, Calvin had argued strenuously in the sixteenth century that the New Testament pattern of worship required both the pulpit and the table each time the church gathered. Because the Roman mass and medieval custom allowed congregants to commune only once a year, Zwingli's proposal for quarterly communion seemed more than adequate to the authorities. What they failed to appreciate was that the separation of the table from the normal Sunday morning service tore asunder 1,500 years of church tradition and, more importantly, the New Testament pattern of Word and sacrament. Zwingli placed his Communion service in the afternoon as a separate celebration further emphasizing the rift between these complementary ways of receiving God's Word. It was Calvin's conviction that each service of the church should include the Word, experienced in both the preaching of the minister and the reception of the sacrament. It is this liturgical insight that the Mercersburg theologians had rediscovered and promoted and of which Hageman had become convinced early in his career.

When Paul Fries interviewed Hageman in 1984, he began their session by asking which of Howard's views had not changed over the years. Howard responded:

I think when I graduated from seminary almost 40 years ago, I had some fairly definite ideas about the sacramental life of the church. I remain convinced that we need to give them a greater role in the life of the church. That's the one thing I started with and ended with. Other things have come in and out, and I presume if I read what I wrote about sacraments 40 years ago, it would look a little different from what I would write today, but concern for the sacraments remains.[1]

This emphasis on the sacraments, especially the Lord's Supper, led Hageman to commit almost half of his forty-year ministerial career to the revision of the liturgy of the Reformed Church in America. Before we turn to that story however, it is important that we identify one theological debate that Hageman anticipated by almost twenty years in his writing about the sacraments. In 1962, just a year after he had begun his regular column in the *Church Herald*, he discovered a religious news story that highlighted a debate in the Lutheran churches in this country and in Europe. The discussion focused on the relationship between baptism, confirmation, and participation in the Eucharist. Although the Reformed tradition does not embrace the term "confirmation," we had firmly tied the right to participate at the table with confession of faith. At the end of this first article on the subject, Hageman raises another question which the churches of all traditions have yet to confront: "If participation in the Lord's Supper depends upon baptism, then how can churches refuse the Sacrament to members of other churches if, as is indeed the case, they recognize their baptism?"[2]

The issue of children at the table comes into full view in a column in 1969 entitled *Kindercommunie*. After reviewing the developments in the Dutch Lutheran church, Hageman predicts that not only must the Reformed church begin to talk about the relationship between the sacraments and confession, but that it would become a topic of lively debate in the ecumenical community as well. Although Howard was not willing to state a position in 1969, by the following year, he was more than eager to push the Reformed tradition to reconsider the whole issue. He writes:

[1]Paul R. Fries, "An Interview with Dr. Hageman," *New Brunswick Theological Seminary Newsletter* vol.13, no.9 (November, 1984): 6.
[2]Howard G. Hageman, "When is a Member Not a Member?" *Church Herald* (October 19, 1962): 8.

The Reformed answer to the problem has historically been that instruction in the Christian faith ought to be a prerequisite of admission to the Lord's Table. While no one certainly wishes to question the importance of instruction in the Christian faith (for which there is ample justification in both the New Testament and Christian tradition), one can question by what authority this is connected inseparably with communion in the body and blood of Christ.[3]

This brief detour allows us not only to see Hageman's ability to anticipate, through his regular correspondence with European churches, issues that could become important in the Reformed church, but it also shows his clear appeal to biblical authority when attempting to settle the concerns that finally did come before us.

In 1950, Hageman was invited to serve on a committee of four people given the responsibility of recommending a revision of the Reformed Church liturgy. The General Synod had dismissed a committee with the same responsibility in 1947 as it anticipated a possible merger with the United Presbyterian Church. When that union did not occur and the Reformed Church in America received correspondence from the Reformed Church in the Netherlands regarding their increased interest in liturgical issues, the General Synod of 1950 was inspired to appoint Howard's mentor, M. Stephen James, as chair of a committee consisting of Richard Oudersluys, Gerritt Vander Lugt, and Hageman. The committee's first report to the following year's synod noted that there had not been a revision of the liturgy since 1906, and that the church in the Netherlands was moving forward with serious liturgical studies so that it could reform its worship. The committee proposed that the Reformed church should do the same and received the synod's blessing not only to revise the liturgy but also to nurture a revival of understanding in our common worship life. The responsibility of describing their proposals from 1950 through 1968 is far too ambitious a task for this book. What does concern us is that Hageman committed his time and energy to the vision and saw it as one of his most significant contributions to the life of the Reformed church.

[3]Howard G. Hageman, "What Makes a Church Member?" *Church Herald* (September 11, 1970): 21.

Before we look at the specific contributions Hageman made to the revision process and the theology that undergirded his work, it would be helpful to allow Howard to speak for himself regarding the importance of the Lord's Supper. In a deeply moving article published by the *Church Herald* in 1952, entitled "Discerning the Body of the Lord," he addresses those who come to the table and calls us to expect the presence of Christ to meet us there:

> You can come to Holy Communion and discern the Lord's memory, understanding how when we break the bread and lift the cup we are calling to mind and even dramatizing the long ago and far away events of Calvary. And that's true, but it's not enough. You can come to Holy Communion and discern the Lord's influence, reflecting on the wonder of the fact that one Jewish carpenter should have had such force of personality that almost 2,000 years later in a completely different quarter of the globe, men and women should still be obeying His command to do this. And that's true too, but it is still not enough. You can come to Holy Communion and discern the Lord's spirit, finding the things for which He stood, the character which He bore. And that also will be true, but still not enough.
>
> You must come to Holy Communion and there discern the Lord's body, find His Personal presence, His living comradeship, His sovereign love. Here in that sacred hour you must find Him not as a spirit, a memory, an influence, but as a friend, as personal and real as the man sitting next to you.[4]

The genuine piety of this piece reminds us that Hageman's spirituality was deeply formed by the sacrament. His work on the history and theology of the Lord's Supper flowed out of an abiding sense that God meets the church at the table in the person of the Christ. It is crucial in Reformed theology, and thus for Hageman, that the sacrament be understood as an action rather than an object. It is in the act of eating and drinking that Christ feeds us with his presence through the power of the Holy Spirit. Hageman wrote extensively on the history and theology of the Eucharist in the Reformed tradition, and

[4]Howard G. Hageman, "Discerning the Body of the Lord," *Church Herald* (September 12, 1952): 11.

in all of his work, he consistently holds up the theology of John Calvin as the foundation to our appreciation of the sacrament.

In an article entitled "The Spirituality of John Calvin," Hageman borrows from B.A. Gerrish in identifying six characteristics of Calvin's understanding of the Eucharist that continue to guide our theology and experience. He begins with the premise that the Eucharist is a gift rather than a good work. The gift is that Jesus Christ himself comes to us not only in the sacraments but also in the sacramentality of preaching and through the ever present work of the Holy Spirit. For Calvin, the gift came through the sign, which made it far more than the empty vehicle suggested by Zwingli. The gift is given by the power of the Holy Spirit, and thus Calvin regularly writes about the spiritual real presence of Christ in the sacrament. The gift is given to all who commune, but it is received only by those who have faith. Finally the gift evokes gratitude in the church and inspires us to live an ethical and obedient life.[5]

At the very heart of this understanding of the Lord's Supper is the sense that the Word of God comes to us *audibly* in the preaching of the pulpit and *visibly* in the meal of the table. The Reformed tradition has lived with the Zwinglian theology of the sacrament for so long that we have failed, observes Hageman, to recognize the implicit Manicheanism, which makes the audible more spiritual than the visible. A far healthier theology embraces the entire world of the senses as the place where God comes to meet us. Such a tradition has a great deal to offer the ecumenical community as it struggles to find consensus at the table.

In a two-part lecture delivered at Western Theological Seminary in 1979, Hageman suggested four areas that we have to offer to the ecumenical conversation regarding the Lord's Supper. He first identifies the presence of Christ in the dynamic actions of eating and drinking at the table. Although Calvin had clearly moved beyond the medieval categories which clung to the Lutheran and Roman eucharistic theologies, he remained bedeviled with the "geography" of the person of Christ. To Calvin's credit, he finally declared his deep appreciation for the mystery of the sacramental presence that should keep the church humble as it communes. The second contribution, which is intimately connected to the first, is the role of the Holy Spirit in this

[5]"The Spirituality of John Calvin," February 24, 1984, Hageman Collection, Gardner Sage Library, New Brunswick Theological Seminary, New Brunswick, New Jersey.

sacramental moment and action. The sacrament is not effected by the repetition of words or formulas or made real through our faith but depends on the work of the Spirit in the meal. A continuing issue in ecumenical discussions is the role of sacrifice in the sacramental action. Hageman cites a passage from Calvin's *Institutes* that may provide some important new perspectives for the entire church to consider. Calvin writes:

> The cup and also the bread must be sanctified in accordance with this practice in order that the wine may be a figure of the blood of our Lord Jesus Christ and bread of his body in order to show that we have truly fed upon him and being, as it were, grafted into him may have a common life and that by that his death and passion that he has undergone may belong to us and that sacrifice by which we are reconciled to God may be attributed and imputed to us now as if we had offered it ourselves in person.[6]

Finally, the eschatological dimensions of the supper call the church to remember that we commune in hope and expectation of the banquet which will be shared in the kingdom yet to come. This trait reminds us that the meal is not only a foretaste but also a prophetic call to work in this world so God's reign becomes more real "on earth as it is in heaven." The Reformed tradition at its best is constantly weaving our life of ethical obedience out of the gratitude for the grace received at both the table and pulpit.

It is now time for us to return to the story of the revision of the liturgy of the Reformed church. The initial work of the committee was placed before the classes for approval in 1954 and, much to the surprise and consternation of the authors, it was not adopted. In 1956, Hageman and James were given the task of revising the Communion service that would turn out to be Howard's most significant work on the committee and for the church. Having learned their lesson regarding the cautious mood of the denomination and proposed changes to its worship, the committee returned in 1958 with a proposal that the church should take five years to use the provisional liturgy before being asked to vote on it. By the following year, 15,500 copies had been sold as the Reformed Church in America warmed to the idea that its liturgical life was on the move.

---

6. John Calvin, *Institutes of the Christian Religion* (Philadelphia: Westminster Press, 1960): IV 18:11.

One would have expected that with such enthusiasm and a five-year plan for study and use, the church would have been eager to offer its suggestions regarding revision and finally embrace the liturgy. The minutes of the General Synod reveal that classes were slow to respond, however, and by the early 1960s, the committee thought it wise to recommend an extension of the trial period. The Committee on Revision used the time to stay abreast of the liturgical developments in other Reformed churches and within the ecumenical community. For instance, in their minutes of November 1960, we learn that the committee listened to an audio tape of a Communion service sent to them by the Reformed Church in the Netherlands. In the following year Howard shared with them a translation of the liturgical work of the French Reformed church. Indeed, some years later, Hageman revealed that it was the French liturgy and the worship of the Church of South India that had influenced his composition of the Eucharistic prayer in our own revision.[7]

After sixteen years of dialogue, the General Synod of 1966 adopted the revised liturgy and the labor of love was concluded. If one reads the reports of the committee to the synods over those years, one is struck with the clear vision that the group wanted not only to issue a new liturgy but also to revive interest and commitment in the denomination for our worship life. At times the committee grew frustrated with the apparent lack of appreciation for their work and the direction they hoped for the church. Therefore, the committee worked to sponsor educational forums and classical workshops so that Reformed church ministers and leaders could have opportunities to reflect on their worship and become active partners in the liturgical revival.

In the late 1960s, following the adoption of the liturgy, the committee decided to publish a small booklet for the church as it attempted to integrate the new forms into its worship. Hageman was invited to write the chapter on the Lord's Supper. He identified the three principles that had guided the original committee in its work. First, the Communion service needed to be faithful to the New Testament understanding of the meaning of the supper. Second, the service needed to be consistent with the theology of the supper set forth in the Belgic Confession and Heidelberg Catechism. Third, there

---

[7]"The Lord's Supper I & II" (lectures delivered at Western Theological Seminary) undated, Hageman Collection, Gardner Sage Library, New Brunswick Theological Seminary, New Brunswick, New Jersey.

needed to be "sensitivity to liturgical language that will be meaningful to Christians of the mid-twentieth century while still conveying the essentials of our historic faith."[8]

The task of bringing the liturgy, specifically the Communion service, into the heart of the life of the local congregation was an important vision for Hageman. When asked to reflect on his almost fifty years of ministry, Howard would regularly cite the wide acceptance of the 1967 Communion liturgy in the Reformed church and greater frequency of congregational celebrations of the sacrament as signs that his work had not been in vain. The committee, which was established in 1950, produced a liturgy that brought the sacrament back into the normal Sunday service, if not always in practice, at least in theology. Hageman loved to observe that the battle for the sacramental soul of the Reformed church was one fought between the Zwinglian notion of the sacrament, which had dominated our life for almost half a millennium, and the Calvinistic understanding, which prompts us to celebrate the real presence of the Christ instead of his real absence. It is from the 1967 liturgy that we have received some of the most recognizable words in all of our common worship life. In five brief paragraphs Hageman caught the dynamic quality of the sacrament for the worshiping congregation. They are words which describe the life and experience of a sacramental and liturgical church. We conclude this section by quoting the "Meaning of the Sacrament" as it is found in our liturgy:

> Beloved in the Lord Jesus Christ, the holy Supper which we are about to celebrate is a feast of remembrance, of communion, and of hope.
>
> We come in remembrance that our Lord Jesus Christ was sent of the Father into the world to assume our flesh and blood and to fulfill for us all obedience to the divine law, even to the bitter and shameful death of the cross. By his death, resurrection, and ascension he established a new and eternal covenant of grace and reconciliation that we might be accepted of God and never be forsaken by him.
>
> We come to have communion with this same Christ who has promised to be with us always, even to the end of the world. In the

[8]Garrett C. Roorda, editor, *A Companion to the Liturgy* (New York: The Half Moon Press, 1971): 36.

breaking of the bread he makes himself known to us as the true heavenly Bread that strengthens us unto life eternal. In the cup of blessing he comes to us as the Vine in whom we must abide if we are to bear fruit.

We come in hope, believing that this bread and this cup are a pledge and foretaste of the feast of love of which we shall partake when his kingdom has fully come, when with unveiled face we shall behold him, made like unto him in his glory.

Since by his death, resurrection, and ascension Christ has obtained for us the life-giving Spirit who unites us all in one body, so are we to receive this Supper in true love, mindful of the communion of saints.[9]

[9]Eric Routley, editor, *Rejoice in the Lord* (Grand Rapids, Michigan: William B. Eerdmans Publishing Company, 1985): 567.

IV
Prayer:
Toward a Reformed Liturgic

During his half century of public ministry, Howard Hageman published almost 1,000 columns and articles. A quarter of them focused on the worship life of the church. There is little doubt that Hageman cherished the worship of the Reformed tradition and sought to promote knowledge of its history and commitment to its constant reformation. This chapter will primarily draw from the principles Hageman enunciated in the last chapter of *Pulpit and Table*, entitled "Toward a Reformed Liturgic." Before we turn to his visions however, we will look at the resistance he encountered in his own congregation—the same kind of resistance to change that many pastors face.

In 1969, following denominational approval of the new liturgy, it appears that Hageman committed a consistory meeting at the North Church in Newark to a discussion of some possible changes to their morning worship. The minutes of the meeting reveal that of the six proposals one was rejected, a second vote was evenly split, two of the ideas were referred to other groups within the church for discussion, and two others were approved with a split vote. There is no magic in the call to reform the worship life of a local congregation. Hageman knew as well as any minister that the vision of the Reformed church is constantly calling us to renew ourselves in ways consistent with the Word of God.

Hageman was quite emphatic when discussing liturgical renewal that there is no liturgy that epitomizes Reformed theology for all times and places. Instead, he proposed a series of principles or characteristics which should mark Reformed worship. It would be inappropriate to consider these traits as unique either to Howard Hageman or, for that matter, to the Reformed tradition. They are Christian in character and could be applied to Christian worship in all traditions.

1. Worship is primarily doxological. The vertical dimension of worship needs to undergird its horizontal character. In this regard, it is important that the worshiping community be aware that it has gathered to offer itself and its praise to God as it receives the gift of grace in return. In 1974 Hageman was invited to review the new *Worshipbook* of the Presbyterian church. While he found a great deal to celebrate in the work, he was concerned that it had failed adequately to address this first principle. Hageman wrote: "Successful as it may be at provoking us to a new awareness of our horizontal obligations as Christians, it fails notably to provoke us to a similar awareness of our transcendental relationships. The language, with a few lapses, is efficiently expressive, but fails to be equally evocative."[1]

2. Especially in the Reformed tradition, we need to recognize the false duality we have created between the spiritual and material worlds and to embrace a sacramental view of worship. Such a view encourages us to worship God with all of our senses and the gifts of the created order because God comes to us through the material at hand. This emphasis calls for a renewal in the area of the arts, which have served the church so well through the centuries.

3. As we have already noted in the previous chapters, both word and sacrament belong together as complementary ways for the Word of God to come to us in worship. Their separation has been a tragic part of our liturgical history and has led to a denigration of the created world as the channel of God's grace.

4. The joy of worship has often been lacking in the Reformed tradition. We have confused our call to do things decently and in order with a sober and often static view of worship. Hageman regularly emphasizes the fact that every Sunday is a mini Easter in which we are to celebrate our new life in Christ.

[1] Howard G. Hageman, "Old and New in the Worshipbook," *Theology Today* 31 (October, 1974): 207.

5. The shape of Reformed worship is one that follows the pattern of the Christian life outlined in scripture and the Heidelberg Catechism: guilt, grace, and gratitude. Each time we overemphasize or underplay one of these dimensions of the Christian experience, we fail to express the fullness of the gospel. For example, the temptation to forget guilt in a world that is constantly looking for painless salvation cheapens grace. On the other hand, when we underemphasize gratitude, we become a self-satisfied spiritual people who have turned the gospel into a private affair between themselves and God.

6. Reformed worship is corporate worship. Although we confess with our mouths the creed of the Reformation, "the priesthood of all believers," our experience is often characterized by a liturgy dominated by the pastor and at times by the choir. Hageman emphasizes the fact that the Reformation called for the priesthood of all believers, rather than every believer or each believer. This distinction reminds the church of its corporate identity as it worships as one people. This principle can be heard in the words of the committee given responsibility for liturgical revision in 1871. It used as one of its primary guidelines that it would work for greater congregational participation, conscious "that the Gospel minister is not by virtue of his office a priest, but that the people themselves are a royal priesthood, with all the power and privilege of prayer."

7. It has been clear from the time of the Reformation that prayer in the Reformed liturgical tradition can be either "free" or from a book, observes Hageman. When not done well, the former can be sloppy and sentimental and the latter cold and impersonal. Worship leaders need to strive for a tone that is both relevant and dignified, personal without being private, expressive as well as evocative, and contemporary while embracing the eternal.

8. The worship of the church should be the worship of the wilderness rather than that of a permanent temple. In other words, our worship needs to reflect an eschatological dimension that reminds us that we are a pilgrim people offering our praise to a God who is ever before us. This principle finally means that all of our liturgies are provisional in character. As people on the way, our opportunity to worship is, in the words of Hageman, a "rendezvous with eternity."

9. At its very heart, worship is dialogical. The church has often understood this trait as an exclusively horizontal conversation between the minister and the congregation rather than a vertical conversation between the worshiping

community and God. The dialogue is one marked by both authenticity and grace. We are called to be honest and humble as we approach, hear, and respond to God's Word. One of Hageman's favorite terms for the church was "meeting house." He heard in the phrase an echo of the call for God to meet humanity and for us to meet each other. The vertical and horizontal dimensions of worship are both acknowledged and affirmed when the church is a meeting house.

10. The twentieth century has reminded us of the ecumenical character of our worship. When we confess that we believe in one holy catholic church, we confess that the liturgical gifts of the church belong to all of us. Obviously, we need not all worship in the same way, but we can appreciate the traditions that are consistent with the Word and indigenous to other communions. This trait of the modern church has allowed us to "borrow" from other parts of our common tradition and creates worship which better expresses our oneness in Christ.

11. The Reformed tradition does not claim that one or more liturgies are required in all times and places. We are called to obedience to the Word of God, which allows us, at our best moments, to be creative and fresh. Through the years there have been those who have interpreted this principle to mean that we are limited in our worship to only those words and actions expressly commanded in scripture. The Reformed tradition however, believes that our call is to obey the Word, which guides us into ways of worship that are consistent with, rather than mandated by, scripture.

12. The liturgy, which means the work of the people, begins in our sanctuaries and continues in the communities in which we live. It is not coincidental that the same word "service" is used to describe what we do in our sanctuaries and in the world. Hageman observes:

> The Christian liturgy was the total response of the body of Christ expressed in worship, obedience, and service. Our fatal blunder has been our effort to make a distinction here. Obedience and service that are not rooted in worship are as unthinkable in New Testament terms as worship that does not issue in obedience and service. Whenever we attempt to isolate these elements, we falsify the basic concept. There is but one Christian liturgy, focalized in Word and Sacrament, continued in mission and service.[2]

[2]Howard G. Hageman, *Pulpit and Table* (Richmond: John Knox Press, 1962): 130.

13. David once exclaimed that "I will not offer burnt offerings to the Lord my God which cost me nothing" (2 Sam. 24:24). The church is called to offer the best it has to God in its worship. While acknowledging the potential collision between the need for broad congregational participation and the need for excellence, we should not ignore the words of David. The quality of our offering is in direct proportion to our sacrifice. Hymns and sermons, readings and prayers, which are spontaneous can reveal a lack of seriousness about the vocation of worship.

To these principles for worship renewal in the Reformed tradition, Howard published in 1984 an article entitled "Changing Understandings of Reformed Corporate Worship." It is a defining document for Hageman in that it attempts to trace the understanding of worship in the Reformed tradition from the time of the Reformation into the twentieth century. The premise of the article is that the Reformed tradition has passed through four understandings of worship since the Reformation, leaving an indelible mark on our liturgical self understanding and experience.

For John Calvin, the foundational theme for worship was one of glory. A worshiping congregation is called to give glory to God as it offers its life in God's service. The adoration of God was emphasized by Calvin, according to Hageman, in juxtaposition to the Roman emphasis on "procuring grace and forgiveness through the sacrifice of Christ," on the one hand, and the Anabaptist emphasis "in which worship was seen primarily as an exercise to stimulate and assure the believer."[3] For Calvin, giving glory to God included not only what we do Sunday morning but also a life of obedience and ethical service. Thus, the Calvinist *Gloria in Excelsis* is, liturgically and theologically, the Ten Commandments.

While Calvin was in the pulpit he was never able to forget that he was called to be a teacher as well as a preacher. Consequently, there is a sizable didactic element in the Calvinistic worship tradition. The doxological dimension of Calvin's liturgical theology, however, kept this instructional quality in check. Hageman claimed that in New England Puritanism and American Presbyterianism, worship became seen primarily as the time and place in which instruction was provided to the congregation. It was clearly in this second historical stage that the Reformed church gained a reputation

---

[3]Howard G. Hageman, "Changing Understandings of Reformed Corporate Worship," *Reformed Liturgy and Music* 18 (Fall, 1984): 155.

for being an intellectual and cerebral community of faith. This understanding of worship was questioned frequently in the eighteenth century as the Congregational, Presbyterian, and Reformed churches were divided into "old side" and "new side" regarding the purpose of worship.

Following the American Revolution, this division blossomed into a new understanding of worship. The early nineteenth century witnessed the arrival of the converting role of worship within the Reformed community. This meant that for some, perhaps many, congregations, the sermon was moved to the end of the service to make an altar call intimately connected to the preaching of the Word. This development calls into question whether worship remains a corporate activity of the church or simply a setting in which a group of individuals gathers to have their personal souls challenged and converted. Hageman writes at this juncture of the story:

> During its history the Reformed understanding of corporate worship has involved three phases, to give glory to God, to instruct the faithful, and to convert the sinful. What makes the story of Reformed worship delightfully confusing is the way in which one understanding was blended with another so that today all three can be found co-mingled in our common practice.[4]

We come now to the characteristic that marks the late nineteenth and twentieth century. Through the work of Mercersburg and other movements like it, the Reformed tradition began to perceive the ecumenical dimension of its liturgy. Although we do not have time in this work to follow the influence Mercersburg theological and liturgical insights had on other English-speaking Reformed churches, Mercersburg marked the beginning of liturgical renewal not only in the German Reformed church but also in the Scottish church and through it in the American Presbyterian and the Reformed Church in America. With Mercersburg, the historic riches of both the eastern and western parts of the church catholic became available to the Reformed tradition again. By way of Mercersburg, the Reformed churches reentered the traditional biblical understanding of worship that held Word and sacrament as complementary in their roles as channels of God's grace.

4Ibid., 157.

It became apparent to Hageman that it is not our responsibility or even an option to choose one tradition over another. Each development added an important dimension to our liturgical experience. Hageman suggests the dynamic weaving of these historical insights into a pattern of worship that is truly Reformed.

There is no question that our basic point of view must be the doxological one, though certainly with the ecumenical dimension. That is not only our Reformed heritage, but it is the heritage of catholic Christendom as well. We also would do well to remember in this ecumenical age that full doxology demands the celebration of the Eucharist as an integral part of the liturgy.

But certainly no Reformed or Presbyterian person can ever turn his back on his didactic heritage. Indeed, it could be argued that the American church suffers today because it has so largely ceased to be a teaching church. Our production of mature Christians is disappointing because our evangelical inheritance has so often replaced teaching with appeals to conversion. That block of material in the service involving the reading and preaching of the Word ought to be zealously guarded and winsomely used.

Even though the excesses of evangelicalism have done us great liturgical damage, we cannot ignore what it was trying to say to a form of worship which had become coldly intellectual and conceptually sterile. Though conversion may not be our aim in the worshipping congregation, renewal, and recommitment certainly are. It is there that our corporate worship must sound a clear evangelical note.[5]

The renewal of our worship has generally been aided by the increased interest in, and commitment to, the liturgical year. Hageman complained in a column in 1962 that the church year was for most folk a strange mixture of national and denominational occasions dressed up with whatever ecclesiastical extras the local dominie thinks are nice. To be sure, words like "Lent" and "Advent" were unknown to most of the Reformed church until the 1960s and 1970s, although their revival began in Reformed circles with the liturgical renewals of the nineteenth century. While Hageman was

[5]Ibid., 158.

convinced that the church year was not only an appropriate annual remembrance of the life and ministry of Christ and a response to a very deep human need for continuity in matters of faith, he regularly expressed misgivings about the way the church year was kept by the Reformed church.

For example, Advent is the preparation for the coming of Christ. Hageman often commented that most observances of Advent are used to prepare for the coming of Christ to Bethlehem, rather than an opportunity to ready ourselves to meet Christ in glory when he comes as our Judge. This latter emphasis puts a sharp edge on a season that for many has become comfortable with images of mangers and shepherds. The call not to lose Christ in Christmas always prompted a return question from Hageman: which Christ? The Christ of the manger appears harmless and domesticated, while the Christ of the great white throne is one who calls us to sacrificial obedience in a world where power still murders the innocent and refugees still flee across borders to save the lives of their children. Hageman observed that the temptation to focus on the child in a manger finally leads us toward a "department store" Advent instead of an ecclesiastical one. It was Krister Stendahl who once lamented that Americans were in danger of losing their necessary eschatological itch. Howard's musing regarding Advent is a wake-up call to a church that all too often is keeping an incomplete season.

The church of the Middle Ages devoted the four Sundays of Advent to a consideration of the four last things: death, judgment, hell, and heaven. Hageman wrote in one of his final columns in 1988, "The One who came in lowliness to Bethlehem is now the One who comes in Judgment against all the selfish cruelty of our human societies. He also comes in mercy for the poor and the needy whom in our selfishness we have neglected. Of course we should celebrate the beginning of our redemption at Christmas, but not at the expense of forgetting about the end of it, the promise that all things will be under Christ's control."[6]

The Lenten season also drew from Howard some words of caution regarding the way the church was keeping the liturgical time. As early as 1962, he observed that while there was a great deal of talk of "the green hill far away" there seemed little concern with the cross of the contemporary world. He also noted that the call to confession of sin was one that often

---

[6]Howard G. Hageman, "Advent 1988," *Church Herald* (December 2, 1988): 30.

focused on the personal if not private misdeeds of Christians while ignoring the failures and pride that are equally true of the community of faith.[7]

The final crusade for Hageman, and it was a crusade, was an attempt to resurrect the liturgical celebration of Ascension Day. Perhaps the large mosaic of the ascending Christ that fills the apse of the North Church in Newark inspired Howard's commitment to the day. In the column closest to Ascension Day in 1962, Hageman wrote: " Especially in times like these a Risen Christ is not enough. He tends to become the possession of personal piety, assuring us of our own immortality. We need a cosmic Christ, a Christ who is already King of the world which he has redeemed, even though all things are not yet put under Him. We need a sovereign Christ who is the Master of history. And this is what Ascension Day proclaims. Indeed I should not hesitate to argue that the Christian interpretation of history, which we so desperately need, is rooted in the Ascension."[8]

The renewal of worship in the Reformed Church in America was the call Hageman heard when he came to the denomination out of New Brunswick Theological Seminary. It was a call he heard first during a childhood spent in the Methodist church of his parents, the Episcopal church of his grandmother and the old First Church in Albany where his mentor Stephen James introduced him to the Reformed tradition. It was a call heard in his discovery of the Mercersburg divines and nurtured in his years of study of the movement. Finally it was a call extended to him by a denomination that sought for its worship to be a precious gift to God. Hageman heeded the call.

---

[7]Howard G. Hageman, "On Hanging Purple Curtains," *Church Herald* (March 23, 1962): 8.

[8]Howard G. Hageman, "A Forgotten Feast," *Church Herald* (May 18, 1962): 8.

V
Praise:
Songs in the Night

Just a couple of years before his death, Howard wrote a brief article published by the *Reformed Journal* under the title, "Songs in the Night." The piece began with a moving exclamation: "There must be a simple psychological explanation for my experience, but I wonder why it is that in my 70th year I find myself waking up in the middle of the night singing parts of songs that I know I have not heard for more than 60 years."[1] Hageman's deep love of music and hymns began as a child when he learned to play both the piano and the organ. His skill developed when his father, who played the violin, would hand him a piece of music that Howard was expected to sight read as they played together. While he was still a young man, the Madison Avenue Church, which was the Dutch Reformed congregation located just a few blocks from where the Hageman family lived, burned to the ground. Howard and his father took a winter walk to view the tragic night fire, after which the young Hageman, not yet sixteen, penned a hymn in response to the memorable event.

In the mysterious providence of God, the hymn found its way into the archives of the old First Church in Albany, where it was discovered just a year before the church's 350th anniversary in 1992. The Madison Avenue Church, which was the original Second Reformed Church in Albany, had

---

[1]Howard G Hageman, "Songs in the Night," *Reformed Journal* (November, 1990): 8.

39

reunited with the North Church in 1938, to create the present First Church. On Reformation Sunday, as part of its anniversary celebration, the congregation sang Hageman's hymn in what was to be Howard's final Sunday present in worship before his death a few months later.

The hymn speaks eloquently of a deep faith and profound appreciation for the church, still being held by divine grace, in the midst of its earthly struggles.

> O Lord, most high, most holy,
> We gather here today
> To render thanks and praises
> To hymn Thee and to pray.
> For Thy Church Universal
> Our heartfelt thanks we pour,
> Oh, teach us in Thy mercy
> To love Thee more and more.
>
> Though forces consume Thy temples,
> Thy Church still forward goes,
> Though storms harsh beat against her,
> Thy saving power she knows.
> Though roaring flames may ever
> Around her towers rage,
> Still stands Thy Cross unshaken,
> Still lives Thy sacred page.
>
> Though temples where the fathers
> Have worshiped year on year
> Are buried, and all relics
> forever disappear,
> Yet stands Thy Word eternal,
> Thy power to save we know,
> Thy Church cannot be wounded,
> Still onward shall it go.

It is evident that Hageman had a profound love of both the church and music at a very young age. He never faltered in this affection as he spent a lifetime urging the church to reclaim the best of its heritage, the singing of the psalms, and to be open to the creative work of the Spirit in the contributions of new composers and musicians. Hageman was convinced that, next to the Bible, the hymnbook of any congregation was the most influential volume in the church. Consequently, he was regularly perplexed at what he judged to be faulty theology being sung by congregations which claimed orthodoxy in every other way. In 1950, just five years out of seminary, Hageman wrote in an article published in the *Church Herald*, "If someone will start a society for the recovery of the music of the Reformed Church in America in the Reformed Church, I will become a life member!"[2] Although such a society was never formed, Hageman did spend a lifetime singing his creed. It was a creed that confessed that the secret of our destiny lies in the recovery of our heritage in the area of hymns and church music as well as the other parts of life together.

Both Zwingli and Calvin had strong opinions regarding music and its relationship to worship. In 1960 Hageman was invited to address a church music conference being held at Hope College and the title of his presentation was, "Can Music Be Reformed?" The role of music in the medieval church was one that excluded the congregation, as professional choirs sang the difficult pieces composed for the mass. Although Zwingli was an accomplished musician, he banned all music from his services because he was convinced that music was essentially seductive and would lure the minds and hearts of the congregation away from the Word of God. For Zwingli the Word needed to be spoken, not sung, in order for it to be truly heard. Calvin softened this approach and from the beginning of his liturgical career included the singing of psalms in the worship he led. Hageman observed however, that Calvin was not happy with the congregation singing in parts and had his choirmaster thrown in jail for overriding his opposition to the choir singing a descant or counter melody to the morning psalm. For Calvin, worship needed to be corporate in its constitution, or it failed to be worship.

The proper role for music in worship, according to Hageman's reading of Calvin, was to provide a suitable opportunity for the congregation to "respond to the Word of God, whether in terms of thanksgiving, penitence, affirmation, or dedication."[3] The music of the church should be offered by

[2]Howard G. Hageman, "The Reformed Battlecry," *Church Herald* (January 13, 1950): 13.

the congregation as a gift to God. The primary role of choirs is to lead a congregation in its offering of praise. The text of the hymns included in the liturgies that Calvin created included not only the psalms, but also the New Testament canticles such as the *Magnificat, Nunc Dimittis* and *Benedictus*. One exception to the rule that the text of a hymn needed to be of biblical origin was the singing of the Apostle's Creed.

Although we no longer hold to the principle that the text of hymns must be exclusively from scripture, Hageman suggested some guidelines to determine what is appropriate and acceptable in worship. Hymns need to be consistent with our understanding of the gospel, even when the text may not be a quotation of scripture. In other words, our hymns should always be biblical. They also need to be honest in their melodic line and honest to the experience of the church. Erik Routley often said that hymns needed to be modest in that they should not call attention to themselves but be servants of the Word. Hageman would not allow the church to ignore what he believed to be the dominant theme of worship in the Reformation, which was that the congregation was called to give glory to God in its worship. At the heart of worship is a sense that we have come together to offer our gifts of adoration to God. This of course presents a thorny issue in that many hymns are written for the benefit of horizontal relationships or the inner life of a person or congregation. Hageman argued that there is great temptation toward an egocentrism in our worship when such hymns dominate our liturgical life.

In this regard, he once cited the interesting popularity of the hymn, "How Great Thou Art." While most gospel hymns are musical testimonies, songs that we address to each other for encouragement and inspiration,[4] this hymn made famous by Cliff Barrows and the Billy Graham Crusades, is one that clearly addresses great praise to God. Hageman suggested that the hymn's popularity revealed an important corrective to the horizontal focus of many gospel hymns and thus met a deep and abiding thirst for the transcendent. Hymns must not tempt or seduce the worshiping community to forget the core of worship, which is that we have been called together not for our own enlightenment or even inspiration, but to give glory to our Creator and Redeemer.

[3]Howard G. Hageman, "Can Church Music Be Reformed?" *Reformed Review* 14 (December, 1960): 19-28.
[4]Howard G. Hageman, "How Great Thou Art," *Church Herald* (July 10, 1981): 30.

In a *festschrift* for Howard Hageman, Norman Kansfield has contributed a chapter entitled, "The Pastoral Hymnologist: The Contribution of Howard G. Hageman to the Hymnology of the Reformed Church in America." Part of the chapter analyzes the almost forty columns Howard wrote in the *Church Herald*. Kansfield has grouped the columns into seven categories: (1) Some columns sought to make the RCA aware of its hymnological history. (2) Some attempted to help us understand what other Christian bodies were doing about hymns or hymnbooks. (3) Some explored the ways that congregations use hymns and church music. (4) Several asked why some hymns last while others pass out of usefulness. (5) Others attempted to suggest what makes a hymn "good." (6) A few focused on the issues involved in textual alteration. (7) After 1978, a number of columns dealt with the processes and progress of *Rejoice in the Lord*.[5]

This chapter does not have the space nor the inclination to study all of these categories, but it is clear that for Hageman, doxology is at the center of our worship and thus must be at the heart of good hymnology. But what makes a good hymn? Howard once observed that for too long some of us have allowed the musicians of the seventeenth and eighteenth century to define good music and acceptable hymnody. There are others who have decided that if a hymn or song is contemporary, it must be good. While listening to a lecture one day on the radio concerning opera, Howard remembered that the lecturer observed "In opera the text must always be subordinate to the musical line." Hageman responded:

> As soon as he had finished his sentences, I said to myself, "With hymns it is just the reverse; the music must always be subordinate to the text." Then I began to reflect: Isn't this really the problem we have with much of our hymnsinging? The purpose of the music is to enhance and make memorable the text, not to provide a catchy melody which we can whistle on the way home. For how many church members today has opera replaced hymnody? The words they sing are ignored; so long as the tune is one which they like, they

[5]Norman J. Kansfield, "The Pastoral Hymnologist: The Contribution of Howard G. Hageman to the Hymnology of the Reformed Church in America" (May 15, 1992) Hageman Collection, Gardner Sage Library, New Brunswick Theological Seminary, New Brunswick, New Jersey.

could just as well be singing from the yellow pages of the phone book![6]

Hageman turned to Bernard Lord Manning of Cambridge, a competent church historian and lay theologian, who had published a small volume on the hymns of Wesley and Watts in 1942, to provide another perspective regarding the issue of "good hymnody." It is in the introduction to this volume that Manning writes:

> What makes a good hymn? ...First, (good) hymns combine personal experience with a presentation of historic events and doctrines. Full of the intensest and most individual passion as they are, why contain more than that: the writers look back from their own experience to those experiences of the incarnate Son of God on which their faith was built. This gives them a steadiness, a firmness, a security against mere emotionalism and sentimentality which more recent writers, trying to lay bare their souls, have found it difficult to avoid.[7]

Howard was also deeply concerned that choral music had become opportunities for performance rather than an organic part of the Sunday morning worship. One can hear echoes of the Reformation struggle as Hageman critiques the minister for being far more dominant than any medieval priest and the choir more central than in any medieval mass. Hageman once wrote:

> A choir's first obligation is to master the hymns that are to be sung in a service so that it can give leadership and support to the singing of the congregation. I suspect that sometimes this could best be accomplished by its forsaking the choir loft and scattering itself around in the congregation.[8]

This commitment to a choir's call to lead a congregation meant that anthems and solos became for Hageman a great source of concern. He once

---

[6]Howard G. Hageman, "Opera in Church," *Church Herald* (November 15, 1985): 30.
[7]Bernard Lord Manning, *The Hymns of Wesley and Watts* (London: The Epworth Press, 1942): 138.
[8]Howard G. Hageman, "A Word About Church Music," *Church Herald* (April 4, 1969): 11.

told the story in a column of a choir director who had made as part of his annual report this observation:

> [We] have been selecting anthems which feature solo parts and in this way each choir member gets an opportunity to "show off" his or her ability as a soloist. This new approach to our Sunday services has met with unanimous approval.[9]

This not only received quite a negative reaction from Hageman but also prompted him to relate a delightful story concerning Handel. After the first performance of *The Messiah* in Dublin, the Earl of Kinnoull, who had been present in the audience, exclaimed, "Mr. Handel, I wish to thank you for the magnificent entertainment you have given us tonight."

"My Lord," responded Handel, "I did not wish to entertain you. I wished to make you better men and women."[10] The role of choirs in public worship is to make our gift to God not the entertainment of each other but the adoration of God and the edification of the church.

It was in 1978, the 350th anniversary of the Reformed Church in America, when Hageman suggested that the denomination consider giving itself a birthday present. Not since 1869 had we had a hymnbook which we could call our own. In the intervening years, the church had either embraced the work of others or worked cooperatively with other denominations in producing hymnbooks. Howard was fully aware that the expense of such an endeavor was an intimidating challenge that had caused many churches to pause, or to mortgage their future to accomplish the dream. Hageman, in spite of the obstacles, hoped the idea would be embraced by the denomination and would yield benefits being a treasury of hymns. He wrote in his column: "For one thing, such an effort might have a unifying effect on some of the divisions which so many deplore. For another, such an effort might surprise us into realizing that our tastes are not really as different as we had supposed."[11]

The General Synod of 1978 heard Howard's suggestion and cautiously directed a small subcommittee "to study the various possibilities for future hymnals for the Reformed Church in America." In the report to the General

[9]Howard G. Hageman, "Church Music Revisited," *Church Herald* (June 13, 1969): 9.
[10]Ibid.
[11]Howard G. Hageman, "A Birthday Present," *Church Herald* (April 7, 1978): 30.

Synod of the following year, the subcommittee opted not to recommend or endorse a hymnbook but suggested that the church think seriously about producing its own. Since Hageman had been appointed to the committee, it comes as no surprise to hear echoes of his concerns in the description of a Reformed hymnal of excellence:

> a. a hymnal that recognizes our Calvinist heritage of psalmody as a central element in the praise of God;
>
> b. a hymnal that uses Biblical and theological integrity as a primary criterion in its selections;
>
> c. a hymnal which, while accepting the best in contemporary hymn writing, strives to avoid the ephemeral and the trendy.[12]

The synod responded positively to the report but still was not prepared to embrace the project without some clear parameters. A hymnbook committee was formed with the mandate to develop a plan for such a book and to return to the next General Synod for further instructions. It appears evident from the report in 1980, which included a budget for the project of a little less than $50,000, an amazingly small sum for such a large task, that at least one major concern had to do with how we were to pay for our "birthday present." Dr. Erik Routley, a professor at Westminster Choir College and considered by many one of the greatest hymnologists in the English language, had also promised to serve as editor at a very nominal expense to the denomination. With such good news before it, the synod adopted the proposal to move forward with the project.

In perhaps one of the most creative decisions of its tenure, the committee decided to arrange the new hymnbook by following the scriptures: the first section dealing with creation and Genesis and the last with eschatology and Revelation. New hymns were tested by many congregations that volunteered for the task and more than 200 hymns were retained from the 1955 edition of *The Hymnbook*. Howard recalls how the committee of seven, which he was invited to chair, sang every hymn with Routley at the piano to gain a sense of its "singability."

The report to the General Synod of 1983 begins with a painful announcement:

---

[12]*Minutes of the General Synod* (June, 1979): 164.

The Hymnbook Committee suffered a severe blow last October in the sudden and unexpected death of our editor, Dr. Erik Routley. The committee had met with Dr. Routley for several days in late September. At that meeting, the final selection of the contents of *Rejoice in the Lord* (which is the title chosen for the new book) was made. All that remained to be done was the editorial preparation of the manuscript for the publisher.[13]

The loss was a very difficult one for Hageman, who counted Routley as a close colleague and a personal friend. In his column in November of 1982, just a few weeks after Dr. Routley's death, Hageman recounts the deep debt the denomination owed to this minister and hymnologist from the United Reformed Church in England. Routley often referred to their hymnbook as "a lyric commentary on the biblical faith." Both Routley and Hageman were proud of the number of metrical psalms returned to Reformed church repertoire. The committee had also worked hard to include hymns written by Reformed church authors and composers, and to include the great composers from a wide range of Christian traditions.

The editorial work of the hymnbook was assumed by Ann McKenzie, a friend of Routley and competent musician in her own right. Because of a fiscal decision to have the book printed in Korea, the introduction of *Rejoice in the Lord* did not occur until 1985. In reviewing the committee's work, Hageman identified the greatest practical problem as "the vexing question of inclusive language." He goes on to explain the issue in this way:

> A great deal of offensive material was easily dealt with, e.g., that *men* may know easily became that *all* may know. The Committee honestly believes that it has just about completely changed all of this kind of thing in *Rejoice in the Lord* and we were surprised to discover how much of it there was, especially in the hymnody of the nineteenth century. At other points the Committee took a somewhat conservative stance. It was early decided that we would not go beyond Biblical data. *Father* is *Father*, *Son* is *Son*, *Lord* is *Lord* etc.... The knottiest problem was posed by the simple fact that the English language has no genderless pronoun, a fact which means that all references to the Deity are *he*. In prose writing it is easily

13*Minutes of the General Synod* (June, 1983): 148.

possible to use the he/she alternative, but the metrical requirements of poetry make that impossible. Until a genderless pronoun is added to the language (because of its neuter quality *it* will hardly do) we felt that we had no choice but to follow tradition and use *he* when referring to God.[14]

As Howard looked back over his life he reflected that the two contributions he was most proud to have offered to the church of his adoption was his role in the development of the 1967 liturgy of the Lord's Supper and the production of our own hymnbook, *Rejoice in the Lord*. He would have been the first to observe however, that the Reformed church is a community of faith that always must be reforming itself according to the Word of God. Therefore, there is no liturgy or hymn that is not provisional in character, because we are always a people on the way. For Hageman, it was enough to add his voice to a faithful chorus of those who have sought to sing an eternal hymn of praise in a foreign land.

[14]Howard G. Hageman, "The Story of *Rejoice in the Lord*," *New Brunswick Theological Seminary Newsletter* Vol. 14, No. 12 (Spring, 1986); 9.

VI
Our Common Ministry:
A High and Holy Calling

"When is a church a church?" The question was asked by Hageman only half in jest in a March column in 1978, the 350th anniversary of the founding of the Reformed Church in America. The denomination has always dated its beginning here to the arrival of the first ordained minister on these shores. Church historians have pointed to the presence of Dominie Jonas Michaelius and the celebration of the Lord's Supper above a mill with a consistory of three as the first official act of our denomination. Behind Hageman's question is a challenge to the underlying assumptions that embrace the 1628 date. The liturgy and catechism were certainly being read in America before the pilgrims landed at Plymouth Rock. By 1614 the settlement at Fort Orange, an early name for Albany, New York, undoubtedly included faithful members of the Dutch Reformed church. By 1624, some years before the arrival of the first minister, two "visitors of the sick," Jan Huyck and Sebastian Krol, were sent to Fort Orange and New Amsterdam to care for the sick and to conduct simple services of worship. They were allowed to read the prepared sermons of ordained ministers, baptize, offer written prayers, and conduct marriages. To be sure, the two men were far from educated, but they were courageous and faithful at the beginning of our history on these shores. The birth of the Reformed Church in America was midwifed by lay people, making ours a lay movement from the earliest days.

49

Consider the number of congregations served by lay readers in the first centuries of our existence. For instance, in 1720, there were twelve congregations in what is now the State of New Jersey with only one ordained minister. As one would expect, the dominie traveled between the churches and visited each as often as he could. In his absence, the *krakenbezoeker,* the visitor of the sick and lay leader of a congregation, held the church together and ministered faithfully to his flock.[1]

The common work of ministry to which the church is called was identified by the Reformation as the priesthood of all believers. Hageman was convinced that we too often have ignored the substance of this great biblical insight and have returned to a clergy-dominated church. In an article written as early as 1955, Howard held up a mirror to the face of the Reformed church and explained what he saw:

> Imperceptibly, slowly, but surely, in our way we have come to depend upon our ministers almost as much as the Church in the Middle Ages did upon its priests. To be sure, the pattern is a completely different one but the essential fact remains about the same. Who is expected to read the Bible to us and explain what it means? The minister. Who is expected to say our prayers for us, whether in public or in private? The minister. Who is the center of attraction about whom the entire worship of our churches revolves? The minister. Who is expected to attract people into our fellowship and enlarge our congregation? The minister.[2]

It is an important pillar of the reformation movement of the sixteenth century that every believer is called to ministry. This vocation to ministry is one that is shared by the butcher, the baker, the housewife, and the minister. The partition between the sacred and the secular world was a wall that came tumbling down in the battle for the soul of the church. And so, as Hageman looked at the founding date of our ministry on these shores, he was led to ask an obvious question: "When is a church a church?" The query reminds us that the priesthood of all believers arrived long before the first minister and, frankly, before the first visitors of the sick as well.

---

[1]Howard G. Hageman, "Back to the Beginning," *Church Herald* (May 15, 1981): 30.
[2]Howard G. Hageman, "Every Man's Ministry," *Church Herald* (May 13, 1955): 12.

While doing some teaching at New Brunswick Seminary in the mid 1960s, Hageman remembered an interesting conversation with one of his students. The role of the laity was an important topic in the life of the church in those days, and Hageman cautioned the class that elevating the role of laity was being touted by some as a way to minimize or even eliminate the ministry of the Word. Hageman writes: "But one of the students pointed out that the real thrust of the New Testament is to *clericalize* the church. The New Testament does not seek to reduce the minister to a layman; it seeks to elevate the layman to a minister."[3] It was this commitment to the important role of the laity in the church that prompted Hageman to encourage what he called the necessary education of all of our "ministers." Toward the end of his presidential address to the General Synod in 1960, Hageman exclaimed:

> When I consider the missionary conviction and training of the member of the communist cell and then compare it with that of the member of the Reformed Church, I want to run away and hide. Think what a concerned cell of persons in each of our congregations could mean! In our Reformed Church we have 220,000 potential missionaries — with perhaps 2,200 in active service! Even if the number were only to be tripled, we should be tripling the strength of our witness for the kingdom of God and His righteousness.[4]

The whole membership of the church enjoys the high and holy calling of being integral ministers in the movement of Christ. It is within such a context that we see the offices to which certain people are called. When reading Hageman's columns, articles, and lectures concerning the offices of the church, it is apparent that an office is finally not a congregational appointment but "the gift of the ascended Christ to his church."[5] Such language is intentional and thus appropriately intimidating. In truth there is but one ministry, that is the ministry of Christ to which all of us are called. Within the ministry there are offices, described in the New Testament, to help the church in its work. In different times and places, these offices, which we have come to know as elder, deacon, and minister of the Word,

[3]Howard G. Hageman, "Every Man a Minister," *Church Herald* (March 6, 1964): 9.
[4]Howard G. Hageman, "Report on the State of Religion, R.C.A.," *Church Herald* (June 3, 1960): 13.
[5]Howard G. Hageman, "The Gift of Office," *Church Herald* (September 30, 1977): 16.

may have different names. They remain, however, reflections of the one ministry, interdependent and necessary, in the work of the gospel.

In the next chapter we will focus especially on the minister of Word and sacrament, and so we now turn our attention to the lay offices of elder and deacon. Although for almost 500 years we have enjoyed the understanding that lay folk can be *ordained*, the Reformed church is regularly oblivious to this remarkable action, just as the ecumenical community is often surprised and delighted with our biblical insight. The reformers, especially John Calvin, wanted the church to reflect again the organization and worship of the New Testament church. To that end, the reformers sought to restore what they believed were the threefold offices of minister, elder, and deacon. If the deacon had a missionary role that prompted the office to turn outward toward the world, the elder had a pastoral role that meant that the office faced inward toward the community of the faith.

Both the offices of elder and deacon in Reformed church polity require the local congregation to ordain and install with prayer and the "laying on of hands," which is an ancient custom denoting a divine call confirmed by the church. Elders have followed the biblical roles that call for them to be concerned with the pastoral care of the congregation, the proclamation of the gospel in a needy and sometimes hostile world, the maintenance of a community of faith that exemplifies the ethical and obedient life to which Christ has called us, and with the deacons and ministers to sit together to serve the mission of Christ in the world. If Hageman could have emphasized one of these roles in the modern world, he would have had the church become far more serious about the preaching role of elders. The presbyter in the New Testament church proclaimed the gospel in a local congregation.

The vision of the role of the elder is one that is inward focused and primarily pastoral in nature. In a lecture given to a group of elders in 1960 at Warwick Conference Center, Hageman suggested that the church often fails to nurture the gifts of those it confirms in the offices through education and prayer.[6] The very popular lay schools, which were sponsored by New Brunswick Seminary during Hageman's presidency, attempted to address this vacuum through placing the theological professors of the church in the church to help form and educate lay leaders. The emphasis of recent

---

[6]*Workshop for the Consistory* (April 23, 1960), Hageman Collection, Gardner Sage Library, New Brunswick Theological Seminary, New Brunswick, New Jersey.

synodical actions regarding lay spiritual formation and education raises the same issue before us. It remains the tragic custom in most settings, however, to confirm the call of a person to a lay office of the church without providing any instruction or assistance in the performance of his or her ministry.

Hageman often cited the survival of the office of deacon, something that did not occur in the Presbyterian church, as a glory of the Reformed Church in America's tradition. Calvin had built into Reformed polity an office which responded to human need. Deacons were first described by Paul in the book of Acts. Although it was an office that was never fully developed by Calvin, it was one the early settlers to America brought with them, thanks to the Synod of Dordt. In many congregations deacons have become junior elders or simply the property committee or ushers. The liturgy of the Reformed church is clear that the role of the diaconate is one that responds to the needs of the world in very concrete ways. In the early years, it was the Deacon's Fund that fed the hungry, housed the homeless, cared for widows and orphans, and responded to the needs for charity within any community. Over time this role was supplanted by the state, and the church quietly cared for its own.

It is fascinating to note that the Roman church has taken the role of deacon quite seriously in the twentieth century and has established courses of training for a permanent diaconate. In a 1973 column Hageman noted that the Archdiocese of Boston had just established a program for deacons that included the standard academic subjects: Bible, theology, sacraments and church history. The program was designed to last two years and produce a new class of servants within the church.[7] In the last few years, the Reformed church has initiated a national program of fellowship and education for the diaconate. Implicit in the program is an understanding of the role of the deacon that embraces the response of both charity and justice to a world of need. The vision of the diaconate is one that faces outward, embracing the needs of whole people in search of a whole gospel. It is a vision that confesses that the whole creation yearns for God's redeeming presence. Hageman knew that the foundation for such a vision is biblical and thus reformed.

[7]Howard G. Hageman, "Permanent Deacons," *Church Herald* (September 21, 1973): 19.

In 1985, the year he retired as president of New Brunswick Seminary, Howard must have been invited to imagine how the seminary would look in the year 2000. His response included these words:

> I look forward to much more happening on Holy Hill in terms of theological education not only for prospective ministers, but for concerned lay persons. As a secular world demands more and more that we be able to give an account of the faith that is in us, the Seminary will have a larger role to play in helping people to sharpen and deepen their understanding of the Christian faith and apply it to the world in which they are living. It is not too much to imagine that the classroom of the future will contain both candidates for the ministry and concerned members of the church.[8]

It is such a vision that takes seriously the question when is a church a church? Until the church takes itself seriously we have no right to expect that an increasingly cynical but searching world will do the same. The priesthood of all believers emphasizes the call and the responsibility of every member of the body of Christ. It does so not by minimizing any office or role but by reminding us that the ministry of Christ is one that everyone assumes at his or her baptism and does not lay down until we find our way into God's glorious presence.

In 1953 Howard Hageman was invited to write a book for new members of the Reformed Church in America. It was intended to be an orientation to our identity and what we are called to do. *Lily Among the Thorns*, a volume that stayed on the desks of pastors and educators for more than thirty years, was reprinted five times and revised in 1975. Chapter after chapter tells the story of our denomination and the visions that kept us true to the Word of God. It was Howard's hope that the reader would have a better sense of what it means to worship, work and witness as a part of the Reformed church. He also hoped that each person would assume his or her important task as a member of our ministry and mission. The final paragraph of the 1983 version of *Lily Among the Thorns* reminds us that the search for a reforming community of faith is one that all of us need to pursue.

---

[8]*Into the Third Century* (January 18, 1985), Hageman Collection, Gardner Sage Library, New Brunswick Theological Seminary, New Brunswick, New Jersey.

It is a cardinal doctrine of the Reformed Church that each one of us must make the search for himself. The Catechism, Confession, and Liturgy are all there to help us. The living Church of which we are a part can certainly give us guidance. But finally, we cannot be told why we are Reformed. The minister or the church that could tell us does not exist. Only when we stand in the same spot where the Reformers once stood and experience the same power they experienced shall we finally know. Only when we come to a sense of our complete helplessness, and of the all pervading grace of God in Christ Jesus, only when in gratitude for that discovery we dedicate all our living to His glory — only then can we know what it means to be Reformed.[9]

---

[9]Howard G. Hageman, *Lily Among the Thorns* (New York: The Reformed Church Press, 1983): 150-151.

VII
Minister of Word
and Sacrament:
V.D.M.

"In preaching, the minister ought to become thoroughly frightened. What are you doing, you human being, with God's Word on your lips? How did you get this role as mediator between heaven and earth?"[1] These words of Karl Barth, quoted by Hageman in an article entitled, "The Office of the Minister in the Reformed Church," haunt all those who believe that they have heard the call to become a minister. As described in the last chapter, Hageman was convinced that the ministry, first the ministry of the entire priesthood of all believers, then of the offices of elder, deacon, and minister of Word and sacrament, do not exist by "virtue of any arrangement or convenience"; but it "was created by our Lord and is His gift to His Church, renewed by Him in each successive generation."[2] These words, written in 1949, express a high and yet very personal view of ministry, which Hageman consistently espoused throughout his career, and which is echoed in one of the last articles he published in the *Church Herald* in 1990, entitled, "Answering the Call":

> But at whatever age, the person must have heard the voice of the Lord saying, "Whom shall I send and who will go for us?" and have replied, however haltingly, "Here am I; send me." I realize how

[1]Howard G. Hageman, "The Office of the Minister in the Reformed Church," *Church Herald* (February 4, 1949): 13.
[2]Ibid., 12.

hopelessly old-fashioned I may sound in this day of professionalism, but unless some such experience is at the root of a person's desire to enter the ministry, I believe that the whole process is doomed to failure.[3]

This chapter focuses on the call and education of the minister of the Word and sacrament. The call to become a minister is not a single act or event, but a process that is confirmed again and again by the church. The validation of the call is crucial in this process and can cause considerable tension within the candidate and the church, because there are in a sense two calls that need to work in tandem. The inner call of the individual and the outer call of the church is required for a valid ministry to move forward. In some circumstances an individual's call is not validated by the church, and in other circumstances the church too strongly moves someone toward ministry who has not experienced a divine encouragement to serve. When either of these scenarios play out, the supposed call to ministry ends in disaster.

Hageman was fascinated by the question of the source of new ministers for the church. As one can imagine, there are times of both "want and plenty" in any profession, and the ministry is no exception. Where do ministers come from? A survey conducted by the United Presbyterian church discovered that out of 1,666 candidates for ministry in the early 1960s, twenty percent of them came from just one percent of the denomination's congregations.[4] There is clearly an atmosphere established in some congregations that encourages people to consider the ministry as a career. Over the last few decades, we have also discovered that those candidates who have little or no exposure to a specific congregation as their spiritual home often enter ministry with some major liabilities. Both a theology and an experience of the church are crucial in the formation of a minister of Word and sacrament.

In an address at the graduation ceremony at New Brunswick Seminary in 1976, Hageman explored the role of ministry through a brief study of the titles we often use to describe our ministers. Howard suggested that perhaps we ought to return to the old custom of placing behind a minister's name the three letters V. D. M., which in Latin mean *Verbi Dei Minister*, Minister of

---

[3]Howard G. Hageman, "Answering the Call," *Church Herald* (January, 1990): 28.
[4]Howard G. Hageman, "Where Ministers Come From," *Church Herald* (April 27, 1962): 8, 22.

the Word of God. The title reverend or pastor often calls attention to the holiness of the person rather than the more appropriate focus that ministers are servants of the *Word of God*. The ministry of Word and sacrament is one that relies on the one who calls us rather than on some special quality a minister brings to the office. It is the Word that provides definition and direction to our service. It is the Word who uses our lives to incarnate the gospel in the midst of the church in these days. It is the Word that is the foundation to the priesthood of all believers, making all of our ministry one ministry.

Training for ministry has evolved through the years until we now have theological institutions dedicated exclusively to the task. In the earliest years in America, those who trained for ministry in the Reformed church returned to the Netherlands for their theological education. By the middle of the eighteenth century, however, part of the church felt this arrangement to be both costly and less than sensitive to our indigenous needs, and so "kitchen seminaries," as they were derisively called by their critics, were established. Hageman describes them for us:

> Certain ministerial leaders took young men as apprentices, taught them some Christian fundamentals while letting them observe the ministry in practice, and finally certified them to the brethren when they deemed their students ready for licensure and ordination.[5]

Hageman had a very personal interest in the whole area of education as his family traced its lineage back to one of the first schoolmasters in the town of Midwout on Long Island. Howard Hageman followed in the distinguished line of educators and pastors when he entered the ministry in 1945 and returned to his theological alma mater, New Brunswick Seminary, in 1973, as its tenth president.

Hageman has told the story of New Brunswick, the oldest seminary in the country, in his book *Two Centuries Plus*, published on its 200th anniversary, in 1984.[6] The congregations that sought independence from the mother country, especially over issues of language and culture, inevitably won the

---

[5]Howard G. Hageman, "Kitchen Seminaries," *Church Herald* (February 19, 1982): 30.
[6]This volume is part of the Historical Series of the Reformed Church in America and
   is published by Wm. B. Eerdmans Publishing Co., Grand Rapids, Michigan.

battle. John Henry Livingston, the first professor of theology and the "father" of the Reformed Church in America, established classes for interested students initially in New York and finally in New Brunswick in the early nineteenth century.

Before arriving as its president, Hageman was no stranger to New Brunswick, having served as lecturer in liturgics and homiletics on a regular basis throughout the 1950s and 1960s. He wrote many columns about theological education in the sixties. He was particularly impressed with the response of the Roman church in this country, and some European churches, toward second-career candidates for the ministry and education for laity. In a particularly direct and hard-hitting column in December of 1963 entitled, "Rethinking Our Seminaries," Hageman offered some probing questions that challenged our seminaries to reconsider their mission. "If the purpose of a seminary education is to prepare people for ministry in the contemporary world," Hageman asked:

> If this is your purpose, why are there not more men on your faculties who have ministered significantly in the contemporary world?... why does such a relatively high percentage of seminary graduates flee from the parish ministry or at best endure it only until something else can be found?... what can be done to strengthen the prophetic power and evangelical urgency with which our seminary graduates speak?...what is being done to implement the fact that the minister is, according to our liturgy, both pastor and *teacher*?[7]

Just a few years after writing this column, Hageman remained critical of seminary education as he continued to cite experiments in other traditions that he felt were more flexible and responsive to the needs of the world. He quoted the editor of the Maryknoll Fathers monthly magazine who exclaimed: "The purpose of a seminary is not to form theologians and scholars, but pastors and workers."[8] Facing the literal fires of the urban struggle in the mid 1960s, Hageman would neither be quiet nor patient with a seminary education that he believed was dramatically out of step with the overwhelming

[7]Howard G. Hageman, "Rethinking Seminaries," *Church Herald* (December 27, 1963): 9.
[8]Howard G. Hageman, "A New Seminary," *Church Herald* (January 15, 1965): 9.

needs of the church. In a column in 1965, Howard described the positive experience of a man, who, as a second-vocation candidate for the ministry, had been accepted into a flexible program at Eden Theological Seminary. With the tact of a man aflame with a mission, Hageman affirms the work of Eden and the United Church of Christ, but then he turns his attention toward his own denomination:

> And we? Well, I can tell you. If any such person comes to us, we politely inform him to take four years of college, three years of seminary, and if after that period, he is still alive, to come and see us again. And if you tell me that we have no real need for such a person, let me tell you, politely, that you are making loud noises through your LBJ hat! [9]

Hageman's focus was not only on second-career candidates, but he was acutely aware of the urban need for minority pastors as well. By the time Hageman was called to become president of New Brunswick Theological Seminary, he had developed a vision for theological education that embraced second-vocation candidates, urban needs, and lay spiritual formation, which only awaited the right time and resources to make it come alive. Hageman's arrival in the fall of 1973 was in the midst of a difficult time for the seminary. The multi-site program, which was designed to move students through two years of experience at both New Brunswick and Western seminaries, was being challenged by the practical economics of transporting households and procuring employment for student spouses. Hageman's inaugural address, entitled, "A Funny Thing Happened on the Way to New Brunswick," highlighted his commitment to congregational ministry and provided a blueprint for a remarkable future. A small portion of the address sounded the same tone as his 1965 article:

> To take a member of a minority group who has a real calling for ministry but may never have finished high school and at best has had an inadequate education in a ghetto school and ask him to complete four years of college and three years of seminary is about as sensible as asking him to preach a sermon in the Mandarin language! Yet the future of the church in many areas where we have

[9]Howard G. Hageman, "Are We Using Our Potential Ministry?" *Church Herald* (October 1, 1965): 9.

a heavy investment depends largely on our ability to develop such a ministry.[10]

Toward the end of his address, he offered a dream that would embrace both the needs of the church and the needs of those who have heard the call of God to prepare for ministry as part of the priesthood of all believers or in one of the offices of the church. In a prophetic moment, undoubtedly born out of the pain of urban ministry and a passion for theological education, Hageman exclaimed:

> Personally I long to see the day when some classes at New Brunswick, probably held in the evening, involve seminary students, members of minority groups, ministers and lay people together in their composition. I think the mix would be rewarding for all of us.[11]

The dream was not to wait long, as the report to the General Synod of 1975 described how New Brunswick was investigating "the possibility of working with New York Seminary to expedite the training of black ministers."[12] The Reverend Benjamin Alicea was appointed in 1978 as instructor in church history at New Brunswick and associate director of the Urban Theological Center Program. He remembers the way it all began in the final chapter of *Two Centuries Plus.*

> The genesis of the urban program can be traced to an informal and unexpected conversation in Hertzog Hall following a Lenten service....During the coffee hour after worship, the Rev. Dr. George W. (Bill) Webber, president of New York Theological Seminary (NYTS) in New York City, asked Dr. Hageman if New Brunswick Seminary was interested in providing instruction for a number of adults in New York City who felt a call to the Christian ministry and needed the master of divinity degree for ordination, but who, for a number of reasons, were unable to attend an accredited seminary on the customary full-time basis. NYTS was

[10]*A Funny Thing Happened on the Way to New Brunswick* (1973) Hageman Collection, Gardner Sage Library, New Brunswick Theological Seminary, New Brunswick, New Jersey.
[11]Ibid.
[12]*Minutes of the General Synod* (June, 1975): 31.

not accredited to offer the master of divinity degree and was seeking to establish a partnership with a local seminary which would grant the degree.[13]

The program was initiated in the fall of 1975 and served both New Brunswick and the urban area with an exciting new paradigm for theological education. The classes, offered both in New York and on the New Brunswick campus, could finally lead to a Master of Divinity degree in four rather than three years. Because many of the students were pastors in churches which valued, but did not require, the theological degree, or were full-time workers in other careers, the classes were normally held in the evening and during summer intensives. In 1982, New York Seminary decided to re-instate their Master of Divinity program, and New Brunswick was faced with the challenge of going on alone. Negotiations with St. John's University and the old First Reformed Church, both in Queens, finally produced an exciting urban alternative for the program.

How did the urban program change the character and profile of New Brunswick Seminary? Alicea provides us with a picture of change that is quite stunning.

> The dramatic change in the population of students at the seminary can best be illustrated by comparing the student bodies of 1973 and 1983. In 1973, there were 43 students enrolled, all white males, averaging 24 years of age. Ninety-eight percent were master of divinity students, and 84 percent were Reformed Church candidates, with 88 percent residing on Holy Hill. The contrast in 1983 is remarkable. There were 110 students enrolled, 64 percent male and 61 percent white, averaging 37 years of age. The percentage of master of divinity students declined from 98 percent to 81.8 percent, with 35.4 percent of the entire enrollment preparing for Reformed Church ministry (46.8 percent on the New Brunswick campus.) Only 27 percent of the students were now residing on campus.[14]

Howard's vision of a theological education that was relevant and accessible to the urban church, a vision conceived and nurtured in the soil of twenty-

13 *Two Centuries Plus: The Story of the New Brunswick Seminary* (Grand Rapids, Michigan: W. B. Eerdmans Publishing Co., 1984): 194.
14Ibid., 193.

eight years of ministry in an urban center, has changed the face and future of New Brunswick. Hageman's twelve-year tenure as president of New Brunswick is ably described by Alicea in his last chapter of *Two Centuries Plus*. The seminary enrollment was dramatically increased, especially through the efforts of the urban program. The campus was improved and the old Gardner Sage Library, the jewel of the seminary, underwent a major renovation. The faculty was slowly expanded to better reflect the multicultural and multidenominational student body. New Brunswick reached out to initiate joint programs in theological education and professional development with Rutgers University, Princeton Theological Seminary, the Graduate School of Drew University, and the Trinity Counseling Center. A cooperative international program was begun with Leiden University in the Netherlands, and the seminary worked with Reformed churches and agencies in training black South African pastors and students.

We would be remiss if we concluded this chapter without a word concerning the $2 million Call to Commitment program which raised the funds for the library renovation. New Brunswick has a long history of struggling to find adequate financial resources to underwrite the most important task of theological education, and the Hageman tenure was no exception in this regard. However, during Howard's years at New Brunswick, the support of not only the eastern congregations, but also the entire denomination, was inspiring. The successful completion of the Call to Commitment preserved the library for generations to come and promised to develop innovative outreach projects like the New York program. The vision was embraced by the church in part because of Hageman's faithful and long ministry in the Reformed Church in America, but, more importantly, because it resonated with a deep and abiding need for new ministers to serve the Word of God in a new age.

This chapter has focused on the call and education of the minister of Word and sacrament. The process culminates in the liturgical action of ordination conducted in our denomination by the classis. Hageman once wrote that the ordination service did not make a minister any more than a wedding service made a marriage.[15] But the service does make visible the calls of both candidate and church in confirming a ministry.

---

[15]Howard G. Hageman, "Answering the Call," *Church Herald* (January, 1990): 29.

In 1978 Hageman was invited to deliver the address at the New Brunswick graduation ceremonies, and he entitled his talk, "On Being a Real Parson." Buried deep in the heart of the manuscript is a very moving description of what it means to be a minister. As he speaks, I suspect that Hageman is describing not only his own call to ministry, but also the kind of minister he would seek to care for his own soul and for the life of the community in which he lived.

> Let's get the situation straight. In any parish, in any congregation, there is but one Person and that Person is Jesus Christ the Lord. But we are his representatives and as his representatives we are called upon to display what we tell, to demonstrate what we proclaim. It is only that finally that makes us parsons when we are incarnating the Person whose gospel we announce.
>
> Now the moment I say that I want to back off immediately from several conclusions which have from time to time been drawn from it. Personally, I want no part of the parson as the professionally holy man whose life style so sharply differentiates from his fellow Christians that he comes to resemble a kind of third kind of sex. Personally, I want no part of the parson who believes that his calling is to live outside this world with no contact with its passion and its woe. That kind of parson is no good to me because he does not represent the Jesus Christ of the gospels. What I want is the parson who, in the midst of the struggles, the frustrations, the ambiguities of actual human existence, is able to show what the power of Christ can do.
>
> I want someone who is fully aware of the power of temptation and the struggles which it involves, acquainted with grief and the problems which it poses, conscious of the subtle pressures of community conformity, knowledgeable about the powerful pull of material greed, worried about paying his debts and meeting his bills, but in the midst of all these things, able to display the power of Christ to order and rearrange priorities. I want a parson who knows what it is to be disappointed, to be angry, to be unkind, to be sorry, but who also knows and shows how the Spirit of Christ is able to help us grow up in all things unto Him.[16]

[16]*On Being A Real Parson* (May 18, 1978) Hageman Collection, Gardner Sage Library, New Brunswick Theological Seminary, New Brunswick, New Jersey.

VIII
South Africa:
A Dangerous Division

This section of the book will focus on the call of the church to bear witness in the world to its faith and hope in Jesus Christ as Lord of all creation. We might begin this last section with Hageman's pastoral ministry in one of the most challenging urban centers in the United States. We could focus first on the pain and the passion that Howard learned from serving twenty-eight years as minister of the North Reformed Church in Newark, New Jersey. Instead, we have chosen to leave that dramatic story until the end and begin with Hageman's articulate positions regarding South Africa and racism in our own country as illustrative of his deep commitment to a world-embracing gospel found in Jesus the Christ. We do this because it is also arguable that Hageman's pastoral ministry was one that was primarily formed and directed by his experiences in both the nation and the world. What he saw and heard and felt in South Africa in the mid 1950s seared its way into his very soul. South Africa. The name of the country at the tip of Africa recalls for us images of riots and apartheid, great natural beauty and rich mineral resources and, more lately, the peaceful, smiling face of Nelson Mandela.

A telephone call came from the State Department in 1955 inviting Howard and Carol Hageman to spend three months in South Africa attempting to understand the mind and spirit of the Dutch Reformed churches in South Africa. These Afrikaans-speaking churches in South Africa wielded considerable power in the Afrikaans government. The choice of Hageman was probably influenced by Dr. Joseph Sizoo, who had been the last minister of the St. Nicholas Collegiate Church in New York City, president of New Brunswick Seminary, and, by 1955, a prominent minister in Washington, D.C.

The trip was sponsored under the joint auspices of the Federal Council of the Nederduitsch Gereformeerde Kerken of South Africa and the U.S. Exchange of Persons Program. The itinerary called for Hageman to address seminaries and churches in Pretoria, Potchefstrom, Bloemfontein, Cape Town, Grahamstown, Stellenbosch, and Wellington. In addition, the Hagemans were scheduled to visit "native mission stations" and to live with church folk who were already in 1956 feeling very uneasy about the system of apartheid. The visit was an extraordinary opportunity for Howard to gain a sense of the problems and challenges facing the South African churches and society, as well as to see first hand the raw power and pain of the apartheid system. More than twenty years later, Howard quoted in one of his columns an Afrikaans dominie: "I know that the situation looks hopeless, but then I say to myself that for a Christian no situation can ever be hopeless."[1] These words deeply influenced Hageman's lifelong quest to find and support some hopeful signs in a very troubled country.

We do not catch a glimpse of Hageman's public response to the 1956 trip until the General Synod of 1960, when he served as president. In a letter sent to two Dutch Reformed churches in South Africa and signed by Hageman and James Hoffman, the stated clerk of the Reformed Church in America at the time, there are some themes that will remain consistent in all of Hageman's writings about South Africa. First, the letter calls for both the American and South African churches to unite in a common confession of "failure and guilt before our Lord Jesus Christ in whom the walls of partition have been broken down."[2] From the outset, the synodical letter wants to set a tone that readily acknowledges the failure in the United States to face the issues of race with the reconciling power of the gospel. Second, the letter does not presume to judge the church in South Africa for its obvious support of the apartheid system. Nevertheless, it states:

> But we summon you, brethren, to re-examine the Scriptures and
> to listen again to what the Spirit is saying to our churches from

[1] Howard G. Hageman, "A Word About South Africa," *Church Herald* (November 25, 1977): 30.
[2] *Minutes of the General Synod* (June, 1960): 290.

them. We hope that such an examination will lead you to say again that in Jesus Christ there can be no walls of partition....But we believe that the time has come for you to say with no uncertain voice that in Jesus Christ there is neither Afrikaaner, Colored, or Bantu—as we must in our situation say the same thing to our people with certainty and conviction.[3]

In 1961, Hageman began his regular column in the *Church Herald,* and he also began a litany of almost forty articles that would keep South Africa in front of the Reformed church for the next three decades. He followed the events in the African country through the public media, which he often criticized for being biased and blind to the complexities of the situation. He also received publications from South Africa, both in English and Afrikaans, which he learned to read, so that their views could come to him without first being filtered through the media.

In his first article, dated May 12, 1961, he related the story of a furious debate in the synod meeting of the Hervormde Kerk, which had finally resulted in a motion that would prohibit ministers and elders from expressing themselves on the "race question" outside the confines of the synodical session. Two theological professors, contemptuous of the action, were given a week to recant their opposition or resign from their posts. The president of the synod attacked the professors and charged them with weakening the witness of the church at a time when it was "fighting for self preservation." Hageman's response was to exclaim that in one of our sister churches "orthodoxy is now no longer doctrinal but political." In addition, he pointed out that the call to self preservation is not a New Testament principle which instead directs us to seek to lose our lives rather than save them. He concludes his response with these words:

Our brethren in South Africa have a difficult road to travel. They need our prayers. But when the witness of the church and the very nature of the church are perverted in this way, they also need a reminder that Churches of the Word must honor the Word above their own self-preservation.[4]

---

[3]Ibid., 291.
[4]Howard G. Hageman, "... And then the Judgment," *Church Herald* (May 12, 1961): 8.

One can detect three basic themes in Hageman's columns and articles regarding South Africa. He is constantly seeking the prophetic role of the church to be strengthened as he highlights those individuals and organizations that work to hold the society and church accountable to the expectations of the Word of God. In a time when the media was held in high esteem and clearly trusted, Hageman is openly critical of the media as it often ignored signs of hope, especially within the Reformed community of faith. Finally, Hageman connects the failure of the church to be faithful in South Africa to a similar problem in the American church regarding issues of race.

We turn first to those South African Christians Hageman held up to the American church so we would appreciate the prophetic responsibility of the gospel. In 1962, he lauded the work of a group of Reformed theologians that had published a book entitled, *Delayed Action*. Hageman explains that even in the Dutch Reformed church there are "sincere and concerned Christians who need our prayers rather than our censure to strengthen their witness."[5] In the same year, Hageman highlighted the founding of the new periodical *Pro Veritate*, which provided a forum for church people, including folk in the Dutch Reformed church, to express their opposition to apartheid. Early in 1963, Hageman reported the courageous decision of his friend, Dominie Beyers Naude, not only the pastor of a large congregation outside Johannesburg but also the moderator of the Southern Transvaal Synod, to leave his posts. Naude, in his farewell sermon to his congregation, explained his dramatic response to the tragic circumstances in the church and country he loved:

> It is a choice between obedience to faith and obedience to church authorities....Whose kingdom comes first with us, that of God or of the nation? Which is more important, that we stand together or stand with God?... [Unless as a church we] understand better what is meant by obedience to God, ...not only will we lose or frustrate our best intellectual and spiritual forces among ministers, but we will also lose the confidence of thousands of our members who seek Biblical light on these controversial problems of church and state, of race and color.[6]

[5]Howard G. Hageman, "When is a Dutch Reformed not Dutch Reformed?" *Church Herald* (November 17, 1961): 10.
[6]Howard G. Hageman, "For Conscience's Sake," *Church Herald* (November 1, 1963): 11.

Just a few years later, in 1966, Hageman held up the courageous work of the Christian Institute, the organization that Naude went to administer after his departure from his congregation. A leading Afrikaans newspaper had published the names of thirty Dutch Reformed pastors who had supported the work of the institute and suggested that they be drummed out of the church. In addition the newspaper intimated that the organization was a Communist front. Although the circumstances were not the same, Howard asked if all this did not have the feel of Nazi Germany. It was in Germany in 1934 that the confessing church stood in opposition to the national church and the government at a place called Barmen. Students of the struggle in South Africa will understand that Hageman anticipated the questions of leading Reformed theologians by almost two decades by closing the article with the challenge: "Will there be another Barmen in South Africa in 1966?"[7] These few examples of Dutch Reformed resistance to the apartheid system should not allow us to forget that it was the official position of the Reformed churches which provided the theological backbone to the governmental policy. Nor are they meant to divert our attention from the many courageous Christians of other traditions who literally laid their lives on the line in solidarity with those who were suffering. The point that Hageman was trying to make was that there were those within the Reformed camp who saw evil and opposed it. They were the prophets who needed our support and prayers.

The failure of the media to report all of the events in the South African tragedy was a source of great irritation to Hageman. Already in 1962 he entitled a column "A Conspiracy of Silence" and asked why the press had failed to report the opposition of certain Dutch Reformed ministers to a recently passed piece of apartheid legislation. Hageman was convinced that the media had a simplistic view of the powerful Afrikaans church that did not allow for the courageous opposition of some of its leaders. Howard concluded his column with some searching questions:

> Why this conspiracy of silence? Why this attempt to paint the South African Dutch Church in lurid colors? ...I think we owe our Dutch Reformed cousins in South Africa a fair hearing. I also think the time has come when we protest to the American press that they are not being given one![8]

[7]Howard G. Hageman, "Another Barmen," *Church Herald* (March 4, 1966): 9.
[8]Howard G. Hageman, "A Conspiracy of Silence," *Church Herald* (September 7, 1962): 10.

A few years later Hageman was equally insistent that the press was only reporting half the story. In a column in which he described the actions of a Reformed synod's critical pronouncements regarding governmental policy, he noted that the press had totally ignored the actions. Howard then exclaimed:

> I have no desire to whitewash South Africa or the Dutch Reformed Church. But I do not want to see them black washed either. If the church there is regaining its prophetic voice, let's welcome it and pray for it.[9]

Finally, in an article published in 1985 and entitled "Slanting the News," Hageman again took issue with a press that he felt had prejudged all members of the Dutch Reformed church as unrepentently racist. He also noted that the presence of the Black and Colored Reformed churches, which outnumber their white mother, seemed unknown among the media. Hageman could not help but take another swing at the press.

> It strikes me as subtle racism on the part of the news media to omit any reference to these ethnic churches as they further the assumption that all Dutch Reformed people in South Africa are white and segregationist....There are many Reformed Christians in that unhappy country with whom we can and do work. They need our prayers, but it is difficult to remember them if the news media try to pretend that they aren't there.[10]

Howard was adamantly opposed to apartheid and expressed his feelings and what he was convinced was the judgment of scripture on the demonic system. He also felt that the Reformed Church in South Africa needed the Reformed Church in America to support the prophetic voices of those who had placed everything on the line to fight the system of oppression. To ignore them or to lump them into the larger and far more powerful majority that supported the government was to fail at our task. Thus, the criticism of the press became a relatively small but still important theme in his writings.

The General Synod of the Reformed Church in America voted in 1967 to open correspondence with the Dutch Reformed Church in South Africa

---

[9]Howard G. Hageman, "Some South African Notes," *Church Herald* (January 7, 1966): 22.
[10]Howard G. Hageman, "Slanting the News," *Church Herald* (May 3, 1985): 31.

and did so with a strongly worded letter opposing the obvious support that the African church had provided the apartheid system. Although Howard found the tone of our letter a bit overheated, in an article he published in the *Church Herald* entitled, "A Plea for Understanding," he used the occasion to suggest his own set of questions to the South African church. He began with the query, "Why does the Dutch Reformed Church in South Africa apparently feel that its duty is to uphold governmental policy rather than judge it in the light of God's Word?"[11] He followed this question up by asking why the church was increasingly rejecting the prophetic ministry of people who felt called upon to oppose governmental policies. He then focused on the popular South African defense of the apartheid system: that it was linguistically rather than racially designed. If such were truly the case, then the "Colored" population, which spoke Afrikaans, would have been fully integrated into "white" society. Their continued segregation from the European community unmasked the truth that apartheid was blatantly racist. Finally, while affirming the clear call for fairness and justice in the South African response to our initial letter, Hageman wanted to know who was to judge such important qualities in South African society. His point, of course, was that the implementation of any policy without the involvement of the governed is the foundation for revolutions. One can detect the strong dependence Hageman placed on the authority of the Word and the subtle but forceful arguments that he had used in opposing the apartheid system.

The role of the United States government, and other governments as well, did not escape Hageman's attention. In 1962, he identified the crucial role economics played in keeping the apartheid system afloat. In a particularly hard-hitting and insightful article, Howard wrote:

> In the last ten years, said the report (a South African government publication), American capital invested in South African industry has trebled. The profit on this investment averages 27% annually! (And I thought I was doing well at the local savings bank!)
>
> Let's face facts. The present government in South Africa could not last five minutes nor could its racial policies survive till tomorrow if it were faced with a withdrawal of American and (even more) British economic support. While our government and that of Great

[11]Howard G. Hageman, "A Plea for Understanding," *Church Herald* (May 23, 1969): 21.

Britain shed tears over the sad fate of the African native, any bird brain knows that they are crocodile tears. Our two countries could alter the situation any time they wanted to. The purse is still mightier than the resolution when all is said and done.[12]

To those who saw a Communist conspiracy behind every bush, Hageman was openly contemptuous. While acknowledging that the Communists had an international design, he felt that all too often we judged anyone who questioned the *status quo* as a Communist rather than looking to judge the proposed change by the Word of God, which remains our true and everlasting measure.

In 1974, Hageman returned to South Africa for his second and last visit. He reported to the readers of the *Church Herald* what he had discovered after an absence of eighteen years. The continent of Africa had undergone the greatest changes with the movement from colonial control to nationally elected and administered countries. The economy of South Africa had grown tremendously through the presence of millions of urban blacks, which made transparent the great myth of the apartheid system; that the black population would some day go back to their tribal homelands. While the central tenets of apartheid remained immovable, the so-called petty apartheid, segregated public facilities and amenities, was slowly disappearing. Property and voting rights for all South Africans were still a long way from the negotiating table however. Hageman concludes the article with this sober observation:

The one thing that seemed to have changed least in eighteen years is the Dutch Reformed churches. For the most part they remain solidly behind the traditional government policy, reluctant to see it change.[13]

While Hageman was in South Africa he was introduced to the Rev. Elia Tema, who was the pastor of the black Dutch Reformed church in the Orlando section of Soweto. Tema arrived on the New Brunswick campus in the fall of 1974 and received a masters in theology in May of 1976. Pastor Tema then returned to South Africa just in time to be in Soweto for the

[12]Howard G. Hageman, "Our Common Guilt," *Church Herald* (September 21, 1962): 8.

[13]Howard G. Hageman, "South Africa Revisited," *Church Herald* (May 30, 1975): 11.

dramatic protest of black school children regarding education in the black townships. The date, June 16, 1976, is burned into the consciousness of South Africa because it marks the beginning of the final assault on the apartheid regime. Although it would take another fifteen years before the protest would issue in the release and election of Nelson Mandela as president of a free South Africa, there was a sense that if the children would not live with the old system of oppression any longer, it was doomed to die.

Tema's attendance at New Brunswick marked the initiation of a program that encouraged black and colored ministers to come to the United States to further their theological education. Generous gifts and support from local congregations allowed a chance meeting of two ministers, Hageman and Tema, to grow into a modest but still significant program of support between the Reformed Church in America and theological institutions that served Reformed people of color in South Africa.

In response to the Soweto uprising, Hageman penned a column entitled "The Curse of Babel." The match that ignited the protest in Soweto was the government requirement that instruction be in the Afrikaans language rather than English or the native language of the class. What made this law so ironic was the tremendous pain caused by a similar British law for the Afrikaaners following the Anglo-Boer war. Hageman, reflecting on that fact, wrote these words:

> How ironic, therefore, that it should be the same Afrikaaner who by insisting that black children must learn to speak his language precipitated the frightful riots in Johannesburg and Pretoria recently. I realize that the language question was only the end of a very long fuse, but it was the question that set off the explosion. The black South African was expressing his resentment at the very same policy imposed on him by the descendants of Afrikaaners who bitterly resented that policy years ago when the British sought to impose it on them. Language is identity and it still remains true that "the language of the conqueror on the lips of the conquered is the language of slaves."[14]

In 1988, the last year in which Hageman wrote his "Focus on the World" column, he made an interesting observation linking the struggle in South

[14]Howard G. Hageman, "The Curse of Babel," *Church Herald* (July 23, 1976): 30.

Africa and the violence in Ireland. Howard had followed the problems in Ireland with the same kind of intentionality as his focus on South Africa. Perhaps his interest in Ireland was kindled by a maternal grandmother who was of Irish extraction. Whatever the case, Hageman was quite clear that the Protestant church needed to assume considerable responsibility for the trouble in both lands. In Ireland, it is Ian Paisley, a minister of the Free Presbyterian church, who has come to symbolize an entrenched and prejudiced attitude. Of course in South Africa, the Dutch Reformed church stood firmly obstructing the path of change and peace for the entire country. While acknowledging the complicated nature of both situations and the fact that there are many folk who disagree with these two symbols of resistance to justice, it was the white Protestant church, in particular, the Reformed tradition, which caused untold suffering to occur. Hageman insisted that we need to confess our sins in this regard and try to begin to understand what there is in our theology which stands so firmly with the *status quo,* or worse, in the way of justice.

We conclude this chapter with a few observations regarding the relationship of the church to the world. There are many within the church who would argue that the church must by definition stay away from politics. Some of these same people argue that we need to choose between an evangelical faith and a socially conscious one. Hageman called such a division of the gospel tragic. In the midst of the fiery trials of the 1960s, Hageman wrote a column entitled, "A Dangerous Division," which ended with this very personal confession:

> One of the great reasons why I am Reformed is the way in which John Calvin united the two magnificently. Great as was his evangelical passion, it never prevented his involving the church in the world on scores of fronts. Daring as was his social involvement, it never became a substitute for the evangelical heart of his Gospel. That's the tradition in which we belong. And I for one want to stay there.[15]

[15]Howard G. Hageman, "A Dangerous Division," *Church Herald* (June 11, 1965): 9.

IX
The City:
To Fall in Love Again

Howard Hageman was born in the industrial city of Lynn, Massachusetts; grew up in the capital city of Albany, New York; served for twenty-eight years as minister of the North Reformed Church in Newark, New Jersey; and for a dozen years was the president of the theological seminary in New Brunswick, New Jersey. In a very real sense, Howard was a citizen of the city. He once observed that he lived happily in each city because the Christian community provided him with care and support for his witness in the world. In their retirement, Howard and Carol Hageman moved close to Albany, where Howard died just a few blocks from where he had grown up.

It was the Rev. Dr. James Armstrong, a Methodist minister from Indianapolis, who was often quoted by Hageman as saying, "If the church is to win the city, it must fall in love with the city."[1] The story of the Reformed church is one that begins in the cities of both Europe and North America, but it is also one that reveals a lack of understanding of the city and sometimes a fear of it and its inhabitants. Hageman was convinced that the history of the Reformed church and the resources that we inherited from our past could serve us well in city ministry if we could fall in love again with the place of our birth.

In Hageman's presidential address to the General Synod in 1960, he bemoaned the fact that the only apparent conviction the church displayed

[1]Howard G. Hageman, "The City Again," *Church Herald* (March 30, 1962): 10.

75

concerning the city was one that prompted it to *leave* it. While a new City Committee had just been established to countermand this pervasive movement out of our metropolitan areas, Hageman remained only cautiously optimistic. He pointedly declared to the synod:

> At this synod when our theme is drawn from the words of our Lord "Ye Are My Witnesses" we would do well to remember the next phrase "Beginning at Jerusalem." Let us hope that we have arrested the shameful betrayal of Christ in the city."[2]

What happened to our ministry in the city? Hageman regularly wrote articles that highlighted our long and distinguished record of ministry in the major cities in the Northeast and our betrayal of this rich past. For example, in 1850, there were probably as many as twenty Reformed churches located on Manhattan Island. Today there are only a half dozen left, with most of the imposing buildings and ministries only a memory. In an article written in 1983, Howard suggested that he may have found a clue to our dramatic decline. In describing the great success of one of the churches in the 1830s, a later minister wrote:

> The cream of New York society was gathering in this vicinity when (a previous minister) came ... and up to the time he left this pastorate, the wealthy, the intelligent, the pious were living near.[3]

To this observation, Hageman responded that the decline in the city was a predictable one if our focus was only on the cream of society. For as the elite moved out of the community, our churches declined and finally died because we were not willing to take the risk to minister to a changing city. When we adjusted to a new population, then the church continued to thrive. Hageman points to our experience in Brooklyn as a sign of hope in this regard. When he wrote a brief column about the Classis of Brooklyn in 1983, included in the mix of congregations were three black churches, a Hispanic church, and a congregation that was forming consisting of Liberian Christians. I suspect that a more recent analysis would add Pacific-Asian churches to the rolls of the classis as well.

[2]Howard G. Hageman, "Report on the State of Religion, R.C.A.," *Church Herald* (June 3, 1960): 9.
[3]Howard G. Hageman, "What Happened to the City?" *Church Herald* (June 3, 1983): 30.

In spite of exceptions like Brooklyn, more often than not, the experience of the Reformed church in the city has been a dismal one. In 1969 the Particular Synod of New Jersey celebrated its centennial anniversary and published a history of its ministry in the state. As one would expect, the volume was one that lauded the achievements of the church over the years. In the midst of the story however, there is a subplot that can only be described as depressing. Hageman quotes from the minutes of the Classis of South Bergen in 1903, where it was observed that "immigrants who are often undesirable tarry here instead of moving westward." In another minute recorded just a few years later in 1906, a Jersey City congregation reported, "We hold our own in spite of the fact that Romans, Orientals, and Africans are moving in, causing many to look and move to the hills." This line of response is echoed by the Classis of Raritan in 1914, a congregation in Hackensack in 1923, and even the rural Middlebush church in 1924 complained about "the incursion of foreigners into the community."[4] Hageman did not know if our record was different from that of other denominations, but it makes little difference in the end. Our great distrust of strangers in our midst, a kind of spiritual xenophobia, has marred our ministry in many places and times.

In an article entitled, "Shall the Church Stay in the City?" Hageman acknowledged that the challenge of city ministry is one which calls the church to live out its life on the "edge of the abyss." Quite remarkably, it is only there that we can discover the real depths of God's grace. To the casual observer, such a commitment to the city appears foolish. In response to such a perspective, Hageman wrote:

> As ministers of city churches we are very foolish people engaged in a very silly enterprise in the midst of a world that knows all the answers. That position must always engender nervousness and anxiety in us. But if we are obedient, even when obedience means a cross, there will be a strange confidence undergirding our anxiety. For the Christ of the Cross is the Lord of the world who holds even the city in His hand.[5]

4. Howard G. Hageman, "An Old Reformed Tradition?" *Church Herald* (October 10, 1969): 9.
5. Howard G. Hageman, "Shall the Church Stay in the City?" *Church Herald* (November 9, 1962): 13.

The vision of city ministry is one that can be seen and heard in the first Pentecost when the people of the world gathered in Jerusalem. A mighty wind brought new life to dry bones and tongues of fire inflamed cold hearts. In the streets of the golden city of Jerusalem the curse of Babel met the grace of the Spirit as people of different countries and cultures understood each other. Hageman saw the history of the Reformed church on these shores as a modern illustration of the Pentecost experience. From the beginning, the Reformed Church in America included Christians of different languages and cultures and was served by ministers of remarkable gifts.

It became a kind of crusade for Howard over the years to identify historical circumstances and people that clearly illustrated that the Reformed church was never exclusively Dutch but multilingual and multicultural from the first days in North America. For instance, one of the first ministers to serve the congregations of New Netherlands was a man named Polhemus. Dominie Polhemus began his new world ministerial career in the Dutch colony in Brazil, where he learned Portuguese. When he finally arrived in New Amsterdam in 1651, he had a thorough knowledge of Latin, Greek, and Hebrew and preached in five languages, German, Dutch, Portuguese, French, and English! Howard observed in an article published in 1954:

> Dominie Polhemus had all these arrows in his linguistic quiver, not because language was a hobby or because he wanted to show off, but because in different situations he found people who needed the Gospel in their own language....I wonder what would happen if this doughty old warrior for the faith were alive today, ministering to a church that was being surrounded by Puerto Ricans, Chinese, Italians, or whatever, in one of our great cities. Do you suppose he would suggest to the consistory that they sell out and move to the fashionable heights where the "nice" Protestant families were moving? ...Or would he appeal to the Board of Domestic Missions to send him some foreign language workers?...Not if I know my Polhemus! He would get busy and learn Spanish, Polish, Italian, or whatever the occasion required, and then preach the Gospel in as many languages as there were people to hear it. In this respect, as in so many others, 1954 has something to learn from 1654![6]

[6]Howard G. Hageman, "An Ill Wind That Blew Somebody Good," *Church Herald* (December 24, 1954): 11.

Twenty years after publishing this article describing Polhemus, Hageman wrote a fascinating piece for the *Church Herald* entitled, "Our Dutch Mythology." He gathers into one article the historical observations that he had gleaned over the years to buttress his premise that the Reformed church was always a richly diverse community of faith. He begins by identifying the Heidelberg Catechism as German, while the Belgic Confession is French and the Canons of Dordt were first written in Dutch within an international gathering. Our first elder, Peter Minuit, was a French Huguenot, and the first celebration of the Lord's Supper was shared among both Dutch- and French-speaking Reformed church members. The first minister called to Albany in 1642 was a man named Megapolensis, who Hellenized his German name and learned the language of the Mohawks so he could share the gospel with them. The congregational rolls of the First Church in Albany include Indian names as early as the seventeenth century. From a part of our history that is less than prophetic, we can also claim the inclusion of black slaves on the membership rolls of many of our colonial churches. Finally, by the time of the American Revolution, Hageman claims, no fewer than one third of the *Dutch* Reformed church in this country was German.

The litany continues as Hageman identifies the fact that just after the American Revolution the Reformed church was worshiping in the five boroughs of New York in four different languages: English, Dutch, German, and French. This was unusual; the Anglicans and the Presbyterians were conducting their services exclusively in English. Hageman notes the Scottish heritage of the "father" of the Reformed Church in America, John Henry Livingston, as another clear illustration of our early diversity. This diversity made it necessary for the denomination to look to the Presbyterian and Congregational churches to provide English-speaking ministers for its congregations. Even the "Dutch" immigration in the mid-nineteenth century included a number of German-speaking people especially from the province of East Friesland. It is these folk who created classes like Germania and Pleasant Prairie. Hageman completed the historical survey by noting that he had not even mentioned the significant contributions of families with names like Zabriske and Vermilyea, one Polish and the other Italian, which had fled to the Netherlands for asylum.[7]

[7]Howard G. Hageman, "Our Dutch Mythology," *Church Herald* (November 29, 1974): 10-11.

The point of all of this is that the Netherlands was the freest place in seventeenth-century Europe, and thus it became a melting pot of refugees from a multitude of countries. This tolerance was transported to New Amsterdam, which also included a remarkable diversity of people from its earliest days. Hageman, in view of this, writes, "I think I could easily defend the claim that no church in America has a longer history of ethnic and cultural inclusiveness than ours because of the country from which we came."[8] It is this heritage of tolerance and inclusiveness that Hageman saw as a gift of our past that could bring us into a new and creative future.

Hageman summarizes his historical overview with these words from a column written in 1987 and entitled, "Theme with Variations":

> One of the delightful things about the Reformed faith is the way in which it is a theme with variations....It all makes me wonder what variations our Black, Hispanic and Asian congregations are playing. Our only concern is to make sure that the major themes are there and then we can settle back to enjoy the variations. All of them taken together can make a very rich experience for us as a church. Our problem is to make sure that it is a real theme on which we insist and not on our own variation. Too often in the past that mix-up has cursed our proclamation of the gospel. It is important that Asians, Puerto Ricans, and so on become Reformed, but it is disastrous to insist they become Dutch![9]

Hageman's theme, that of diversity and tolerance, was one that needed to be played out again and again because of the abject failure to hear the gospel melody in our common life as a church and a society. The confrontation with racism in this country moved from simmering to boiling in the turbulent decade of the 1960s. Our churches in the city had a front pew in the conflict and at our best moments were deeply involved in trying to confront evil and seek reconciliation. Howard attempted to play his part by keeping the issue before the church, not as a sociological problem but as a spiritual failure to live out the gospel. When commenting on the marches in the South with Martin Luther King Jr. in the front of the struggle, Hageman pointedly observed that the antagonists, both white and black, claimed to be Christian.

8Ibid., 11.
9Howard G. Hageman, "Theme with Variations," *Church Herald* (January 2, 1987): 31.

He judged the conflict finally as a failure of Protestant Christianity to seek justice in our life together.

The terrible segregation within the church and society had its roots in the experience of slavery in this country. The record of Dutch slave owners is not one for which we can be proud, but by the time of the American Revolution, the newly formed Reformed church included the following article in its original constitution of 1792:

> In the Church there is no difference between bond and free, but all are one in Christ. Whenever, therefore, slaves or black people shall be baptized or become members in full communion of the Church, they shall be admitted to equal privileges with all other members of the same standing; and their infant children shall be entitled to baptism, and in every respect be treated with the same attention that the children of white or free parents are in the Church. Any minister who, upon any pretense, shall refuse to admit slaves or their children to the privileges to which they are entitled, shall, upon complaint being exhibited and proved, be severely reprimanded by the Classis to which he belongs.[10]

Our experience since these words were embraced more than 200 years ago has often been one of regression. Interestingly, the church was an integrated institution until the middle of the nineteenth century in this country and in South Africa. Perhaps it was possible for white and black Christians to worship together under one roof until the emancipation of slaves made the status of both races the same. It was then that we see the tragedy of the church often *leading* each society far deeper into the demonic realm of racism.

In a column published in 1963, Hageman attempted to make some observations regarding what he called the racial revolution. First, he judged that a good portion of the conflict is the direct failure of the church to proclaim justice in the world. He wrote: "We winked at the situation so long, avoided it, compromised with it, rationalized it, or even defended it, that God has finally taken the matter out of our hands."[11] To those who may have been feeling some pride in the role of the church in the racial revolution,

[10]Howard G. Hageman, "What Happened?" *Church Herald* (March 30, 1962): 10.
[11]Howard G. Hageman, "I've Been Thinking," *Church Herald* (October 25, 1963): 9.

Hageman simply observes that we "got there last." Having encouraged the church to be a part of the revolution, Howard was equally clear that he believed that we are called to seek reconciliation in the midst of the pain. Hageman writes: "Of course, there can be no reconciliation without justice, then it would be empty and vague goodwill. But justice without reconciliation is bitter fruit indeed."[12]

Hageman felt deeply the pain of the conflict. Following the terrible bombing of a Birmingham church in which four little girls were killed, he entitled a column, "Were You There." With considerable passion, Howard wrote:

> Were you there when they bombed the Birmingham church? Were you there? Well, I want to suggest that you were there, and so was I. Of course, we should never have done such a thing. But we were there all the same.
>
> All of us were there who still harbor polite prejudice about the African-Americans in our civilized hearts. African-Americans were there who would not want other African-Americans as worshipers in our congregation. All of us were there who feel that the suffering of others is none of our concern and pass by on the other side. Yes, we all were there.
>
> May God grant that those four little girls did not die in vain! Perhaps they will be able to stab our Christian consciences awake to the realization that hatred or indifference against a fellow Christian, however piously concealed, with whatever rationalizations they may be supported, finally comes to this. What more will it take to make us recognize that the religious exercise which God has chosen is "to loose the bonds of wickedness, to undo the heavy burdens, and to let the oppressed go free, and that you break every yoke."[13]

The presence of racism in the church and society was understood by Hageman as a theological problem. Reflecting his dependence on the work of Mercersburg, he tied the sin of racism to an inadequate Christology. The church has far too often been consumed with the atoning death of Christ on

---

[12]Ibid.
[13]Howard G. Hageman, "Were You There?" *Church Herald* (October 4, 1963): 9.

Calvary and ignored the power of love made flesh in the life of the carpenter from Nazareth. It is in Jesus that we begin to understand that God has created a Person in whom we see authentic and genuine humanity. It is a life of acceptance and reconciliation and one that will not ignore the evil which infects the human family. The gospel requires that we confess that the sin of racism is one that the church has not only tolerated but at our worst moments, embraced. Hageman often quoted the words of Thomas Jefferson when he sensed our obliviousness to the raw evil and pain of racism. Jefferson exclaimed, "I tremble for my country when I remember that God is just and that His justice will not sleep forever."[14]

Hageman did see some signs of hope in the church of the 1960s. For instance, he was moved by the response of the Newark community after the assassination of Martin Luther King Jr. In a city that had been torn asunder by riots just a year before, Hageman was profoundly moved to experience a church and city marching together in opposition to violence and in pursuit of peace on a Palm Sunday weekend. Folk who were afraid of each of other locked arms and walked the streets of Newark well into the night so the fires of hatred would not be ignited. At the same time, he remained both surprised and discouraged by the indignation of many who could not or would not believe that white racism was at the root of the riots of the summer of 1967. The President's Commission report, which concluded as much, was received with sneers or snickers by much of the white establishment, which included the churches. Hageman writes contritely and still hopefully:

> The sight of hosts of people rising up in surprised horror to say, "Who, me?" would have been funny were it not so very sad. Because if anything is obvious to even the casual observer, it is the racist assumptions of most of us white people. Perhaps the saddest thing of all is the fact that we are evidently unable to recognize them ourselves....But I still refuse to give up hope because I believe in the transforming power of Jesus Christ my Lord. I believe in Easter.[15]

The struggle with racism in America is just the tip of the iceberg when we begin to explore the sins of our public and corporate life. In the interview

[14]Howard G. Hageman, "I Tremble," *Church Herald* (January 4, 1963): 10.
[15]Howard G. Hageman, "White Racism," *Church Herald* (May 3, 1963): 9.

with Paul Fries just before his retirement, Hageman pointed to his years in city ministry as the time in which he finally came face to face with the systemic existence of evil. He knew perfectly well the temptations of the human heart, but what he learned was that the powers of darkness infiltrate not only the individual but also the systems that we create. In the interview, Hageman recalls an argument he once had with an evangelist through which it became clear that every person in the city of Newark could be "saved" and evil would still exist in the systems of government and business, to name just two of the powers that surround us. This realization drew Hageman closer to an understanding of, and appreciation for, the corporate nature of the church that stands as an alternative to the world.

This theological insight had profound implications for his pastoral ministry in the city of Newark. Hageman was appointed to serve on the Board of Education as the community began to struggle with the ravages of poverty and greed on the nurture of its children. He became an advocate for the poor and the dispossessed as he and his wife lived out in their personal life the gospel of love and justice. In a particularly hard-hitting article published in 1967, which strikes at the heart of what it means to be human, Hageman held up the almost impossible life of those who try to make a future in the city. After lauding the constitutional belief that all children are born free and equal, Hageman writes:

> And then these same youngsters grow up in a place like Newark's Central Ward where their freedom is an open question and even their chance for equality a hollow mockery. There are no jobs, not even for the ambitious. It is a known fact that justice is not color-blind. When the rats that have been plaguing them become the subject of discussion in the Congress of the United States, everyone laughs.[16]

It was the silence of the church concerning the sins of our community that caused Hageman to advocate a more corporate understanding of God's call to be church. When we confess our sins, there is always time and attention given to the struggles of the individual, but we remain strangely oblivious to "injustice, oppression of the poor, racial hatred, national pride, or comfort

---

[16]Howard G. Hageman, "Quork Walker & Co.," *Church Herald* (September 22, 1967): 9.

in material possessions."[17] In a time when the Communist threat was one that caused considerable anxiety among the American people, it was Hageman who observed that we need not look to the godless Communists to see crass materialism, but that our own country was filled with it. As people struggled with the very basics of survival, our economic and political systems had often turned a blind eye and a deaf ear to their plight. Where was the church in the midst of this unholy charade? Hageman pointed to the message of the prophets as the heart of a gospel that needs to act for justice as well as to preach love. As one can sense, the love of the city was a passion that inspired Hageman to see its pain as his own. It was a love which could not be silent in the face of poverty and greed, passive in the presence of pride and selfishness, and insulated from the violence and vice that plagued the life of the city. It was also a love that celebrated the rich diversity of the city and acknowledged the profound resources of our metropolitan centers.

There are some central tenets that undergirded Hageman's view of urban ministry. First, he often encouraged the church to reclaim its parish, the geographical area that surrounds the church, as its realm of responsibility. Both the Reformed churches in the Netherlands and South Africa entered the twentieth century with this European parish system in place. While acknowledging that the church in the United States has clearly become a community of gathered individuals from different parts of a geographical area, Hageman still maintained that the church should assume a special responsibility for the world just outside its doorsteps.

Second, this theology of the church, not only in urban centers but in all locations, is intimately tied to the belief that the community of faith is the body of Christ in the world. Hageman's dependence on Mercersburg theology led him to see the church as an extension of the incarnation in our time and place. Thus, the life to which Jesus was called, one of sacrificial love, is the life of the church in the world. We have been called together in order that we can give our lives so the world may live. The symbol of the cross is not arbitrary but intimately connected to our life of sacrificial mission and ministry in the world.

Third, Hageman understood our concern for the whole person and the whole of society as a natural outgrowth of an incarnational foundation of the church. In 1964, Howard attended a meeting of church leaders in Washington,

---

[17]Howard G. Hageman, "Preacher, Repent!" *Church Herald* (June 12, 1981): 30.

D.C., where the group met with President Johnson. He remembered the president observing, "A religion which has no social concern cannot be truly spiritual."[18] It was John Calvin who once wrote to a friend, "Anybody can stand up in church and sing 'Glory to God' but if we really want to give glory to God, we must get out into his world and obey him."[19] And it was Bishop Tutu of South Africa who responded to the question of why he was involved in politics with these words:

> I'm not in politics. I remain in the church family. Quite plainly, it is because Jesus Christ says it matters whether a person is hungry or not hungry. It matters whether a person is clothed or naked, and he has said that you are going to be judged as to whether you are a bad Christian or a good Christian, whether you go to heaven or to the warmer place, by whether you did fairly secular kinds of things, you fed or did not feed hungry people, you visited or did not visit prisoners.[20]

The church is finally a community in which the whole Christ is offered to the whole person and the whole world. The church is called to make all of life an acceptable sacrifice to God. Thus the offering of our daily work is as important as the worship of our hearts. Indeed, our worship is hollow without the ethical life lived out in obedience to God. It was therefore imperative to Hageman that the gospel he shared was one that met people in this world with a message of hope from the world to come. The struggle for justice and reconciliation is not a struggle for noble ideals but the struggle for the life already won for us in Jesus Christ. With the victory already won, our life as church is one of patient and faithful service to the vision of the cross.

Fourth and finally, Hageman was an early voice for those who recognized in the city the mission of the future. As the world continues to move to the metropolitan areas, tragically the Reformed church continues to be perplexed about our role and ministry in the cities of tomorrow. From the earliest days on these shores, the Protestant church has been in flight from those who are

---

[18]Howard G. Hageman, "The White House," *Church Herald* (May 22, 1964): 9.
[19]Howard G. Hageman, "Orthodoxy and Orthopraxis," *Church Herald* (May 2, 1986): 31.
[20]Howard G. Hageman, "This is My Father's World," *Church Herald* (November 13, 1981): 30.

arriving in our urban centers. In an article entitled "Inner-City Turbulence and the Church," Hageman exclaims:

> Anglo-Saxon Protestantism has been in flight ever since the first non-Anglo-Saxon immigrant arrived on these shores. We ran away from the Irish; we ran away from the Italians; we ran away from the Polish; we ran away from the central Europeans; and now we are running away from the blacks and the Puerto Ricans.[21]

Hageman further observed that our retreat has not been an orderly one but a headlong flight into the places where *they* are not. It is the urban center where the population of the world resides, and it is there that we need to understand how to incarnate the gospel for the citizen of the city. In such a world, the barriers of nation quickly disappear as we discover that there is but one mission in which we are involved. The walls built between domestic and foreign mission are ones that remain only in the paradigms of the past. There is little difference between Chicago and Calcutta, San Francisco and San Paulo, New York and New Delhi. We bring to the city remarkable gifts of theology and polity, of commitment and diversity, of ethics and eschatology, which address not only the individual, but also the society of tomorrow. What limits us are the often confessed fears of the city and those who live there. It is that fear, says Hageman, which has caused us to abandon the city and to stay away. We need to fall in love with the city again.

Following the assassination of Martin Luther King Jr. in the spring of 1968, the city of Newark rallied around and literally walked the streets so that violence would not destroy their community again. The churches were there, at the front of the march for peace on Palm Sunday. On Good Friday of that week, Hageman had been invited to preach at a three-hour ecumenical service. He chose for his text the familiar last seven words of Jesus. Howard had written and published a beautiful volume of meditations on the words of Christ from the cross entitled, *We Call This Friday Good*. But this time he heard the words and saw the scene through the eyes not of a penitent but of a society racked by violence and pain. He stood at the base of the cross as the crucified city and listened for some word of hope. Looking up at the cross, he exclaimed:

[21]Howard G. Hageman, "Inner-City Turbulence and the Church," *Church Herald* (September 19, 1969): 4.

It takes in the rioter and the militant; it takes in the white racist; it takes in Dr. King and it takes in his murderer. The cross is not our private possession. It was erected in the world for the world, to draw all people unto Him.[22]

[22]Sermon Preached on Good Friday in Newark, New Jersey, (1968), Hageman Collection, Gardner Sage Library, New Brunswick Theological Seminary, New Brunswick, New Jersey.

X
Conclusion

> In almost every community where it exists, the Reformed Church is something of a mystery to those who are not part of its life. How many times are we asked from what our church has been reformed, or perhaps wondered it ourselves! Look again then at the full title which our church bears, for it tells the whole story, "The Church of Jesus Christ Reformed according to the Word of God."[1]

Howard loved a mystery! He spent a lifetime exploring the dusty pages of our history trying to make it come alive for the vision which awaits us. He sought out the roots of our common life always struggling to find the fingerprints of the divine in the riches of our heritage. At the same time, Howard had a mystical streak which loved the part of our identity hidden in the depths of God. It was there that he found meaning in a very personal and intimate relationship which could not be dissected. For Howard, the mystery of the Reformed church is constantly evolving as God molds us in new and exciting ways. The community of faith is always on the move finding its identity in the traveling tabernacle rather than the stately temple. Look again, was Howard's cry, as he reminded us to look to our heritage as we charted our future.

[1] Howard G. Hageman, *Our Reformed Church* (New York: Reformed Church Press, 1993): 1.

Howard found that the stories of the past often hold within them the clues which we need to prepare for our journey. History is not the domain of stained-glass saints, but rather the stage where the struggle between good and evil is dramatically and daily played out.

So let the curtain go up! The drama will contain rogues and villains, saints and martyrs, deeds of heroism, acts of cowardice. But even while the story unfolds, this is the question to keep in mind: Is there pattern and purpose in this series of events?[2]

There was a pattern that Howard finally discovered, and it was simply the pattern of the gospel: death and resurrection. Over and over again Good Friday and Easter point to the deepest experiences of the human spirit. The Bible teaches that the human spirit, no matter how technologically sophisticated, will ultimately depend on its pride, greed, and selfishness to produce a cross on which to crucify the good and the gracious. Scripture also teaches us that with God's help, the human spirit is capable of incredible love. This is possible because God is not a spectator in the human drama but a participant who will never let us go. It is at exactly the moment of utter hopelessness that God is able to roll away the heavy stone which blocks our future. When everything seems lost, it is the right time for God to come again in order to call a new community out of the darkness of the tomb. For Howard the pattern of the cross and the empty tomb, of Good Friday and Easter, is the pattern of the Christian life. The purpose is simply to be part of God's new creation.

For Howard it was often the new community, the corporate nature of the church, which had been ignored in the twentieth-century scene. He emphasized the nurture of the church to balance its call to conversion; the corporate nature of the church to balance the often private faith of its members; the sacramental and mystical character of the church to balance the cognitive nature of Reformed faith; the cosmic reach of the gospel to balance the personal focus of our churches; and the rich heritage of the church to balance the pursuit of the new and improved. He clearly saw himself as a man with a mission, which was to nudge the Reformed church back into the mainstream of Western Christianity.

[2]Howard G. Hageman, *That The World May Know* (Richmond, Virginia: CLC Press, 1965): 10.

Only history will judge the impact of this remarkable servant of our Lord Jesus Christ and the Reformed Church in America. For those who knew him, he will be remembered as a faithful pastor, insightful prophet, brilliant scholar, inspiring preacher, and story-filled teacher. But perhaps his greatest gift was to remind us again and again of our name: The Church of Jesus Christ Reformed according to the Word of God. There is a dynamic quality about that name which challenges us when we are complacent, because our very lives are constantly being re-formed by the Word and the Spirit. There is a real sense that once we entrust ourselves into the hands of God we will never be the same again. As Howard once preached, "Old men are made new: cynical and despairing people are transformed into prisoners of hope; the hate is worked out of us, the bitterness seared away, replaced by love and kindness."[3] Consequently, the mystery of the church is that we are in the sovereign hands of God, which are constantly at work remolding and reshaping us into a whole new creation.

Howard looked to a carpenter from Nazareth as the Lord of this new world. It is Jesus who calls us to follow him into a future filled with hope. When Howard visited Geneva he was struck by the fact that Calvin had asked to be buried in an unmarked grave so no future generations would seek to build him a monument. The only monument the Reformed church finally needs is found in the simple life, death, and resurrection of our Lord. For in that life, God mysteriously finds a home on earth.

Of all Howard's writings, there is one which is as eloquent and beautiful statement of his faith as one can find. *We Call This Friday Good* is a reflection on the last seven words of Jesus from the cross. The last word, "Father, into your hands I commend my spirit," inspired Howard to write the following words, which were read at his funeral. They serve as a fitting reminder of Howard's abiding faith in God's unfathomable grace and an appropriate benediction to this work:

> In the darkness, confusion, mystery of our lives, the hand of God is something extended for us to grasp, for us to hold. Sometimes the path is rough. Sometimes the water is cold and deep. We may wonder why it should be that way. But it is that way and there is no

[3]Untitled. Sermon preached on Good Friday in Newark, New Jersey, 1968. Hageman Collection, Gardner Sage Library, New Brunswick Theological Seminary, New Brunswick, New Jersey.

better answer. Yet no matter how rough and dark the path, no matter how chill and deep the stream, there by your side, if you will reach out to grasp it, is the hand of Almighty Love. And if there is anything in life and death of which you may be sure, it is this. That hand is always there and will always be there.

You may not know where you are going. You may not know how you will get there. But this you can always know: the hand of God is stretched out to you in all of his strength. And once you grasp it, he will never let you go—no, not even when you must enter that darkest valley and cross that coldest stream. Even then you can walk without fear, in full confidence that that same hand that has led you all the way will lead you safely across and up into those eternal hills that shine in their glory on the other side.[4]

To God be the Glory!

[4]Howard G. Hageman, *We Call This Friday Good* (Philadelphia: Fortress Press, 1961): 80-81.

XI
Three Lectures
by Howard G. Hageman

For more than thirty years, the remarkable record of a three-part lecture on the history of the liturgy of the Reformed Church in America lay buried in the files of Howard Hageman. In 1966, Hageman had delivered the lectures at a centennial celebration of Western Theological Seminary in Holland, Michigan. Just a few months before, the General Synod had finally approved the twelve orders of the provisional liturgy, a work that had begun in 1950. For sixteen years, the committee on the revision of the liturgy, which included Hageman, had labored and listened, and had finally produced a document which would be published in 1967 as Liturgy and Psalms.

Howard had no idea in 1966 what a dramatic impact the revision of the liturgy would have on the worship of his adopted church. The following lectures presume the general usage of the 1906 liturgy and could not even imagine the dramatic change in language and customs embraced by the Reformed church in the following decades. The value of reproducing these lectures is to share the remarkable history of our worship as it developed in Europe and North America. Hageman stood at a watershed in our liturgical history—looking back with gratitude and forward with hope. For those of us who have been nurtured by the 1966 revision and orders adopted by the General Synod in the 1980s and 1990s, these lectures remain an accurate description of our past and an inspiration to continue the central work of the church, to offer our worship to God.

—G.M.

Introduction

First, I should like to express my gratitude for the invitation to share this centennial celebration with you. Quite apart from all the pleasant things usually said by visitors on these occasions, I have two particular reasons for enjoying this occasion. The first is that it is a good thing to be associated, even for a few days, with an institution which, though celebrating its past, is making such a vital contribution to the life, thinking, and witness of our church in the present. The second is that, if I understand the Reformed view of theological education correctly, I too am a graduate of this institution. Don't gasp; I mean it. The Reformed church has always sought to provide theological education for her sons, whether by means of one institution or two or by instruction in private homes. It is that common theological education which we have all shared, and I believe very strongly that this is how we must think of the interrelationships between our two present seminaries.

Second, a word about the task which lies before us in these three lectures. Since the Reformed Church in America, as of the last General Synod, has completed another stage in its liturgical history (a labor, by the way, in which a member of your faculty made a large contribution), it seemed appropriate to me that in this year of history I might sketch out something of the entire history of the liturgy of the Reformed Church in America. To be sure, it will not be a momentous chapter in either theology or church history. But since, to the best of my knowledge, it has never been collected before, I thought it worth doing not only for its own sake but as well for some of the sidelights which it may throw on theological developments and historical events in the life of our church.

As I set myself to this task, however, it became more and more clear to me that it would have far less meaning did we not give some attention to the origin and development of our liturgy in the Netherlands itself. Admittedly this task has already been rather thoroughly done by a number of competent Dutch scholars and in most instances I shall be doing little more than repeating what they have said. But since their work is nowhere available in English, I may not be wasting time by presenting to you at least a summation of their findings, which will serve as a background for the developments which have taken place in the last 200 years in our own country.

Because of the limitations of time, I shall confine my remarks to those portions of the liturgy which relate to the worship of the congregation of the Lord's Day, i. e., the Sunday service of Word and Supper. In thus limiting ourselves we shall be omitting the form which has over the years created the most excitement, the form for the Sacrament of Baptism. It is interesting to observe that scrapping over it was just as common in the Dutch church of the seventeenth century as it has been in the American church in the twentieth. But since it would really involve an entire study by itself, I leave it to someone in my audience who may have been searching for a good topic for a thesis.

Lecture I

In beginning a consideration of our liturgical origins, I think we do well to remind ourselves that the Dutch church was in every way a Johnny-come-lately upon the Reformation scene. A large variety of understandable reasons accounts for this fact. But we did not, as we so often like to pretend, spring straight from the forehead of John Calvin. In fact the great reformer, himself of the second generation, had been in his grave several years when the first embryonic structure of the Dutch Reformed church appeared in 1568. In other words, by the time the Dutch church had begun to work out its patterns, a number of possibilities, directions, and influences were open to it.

To begin at what might seem to be the beginning, the ancestor of our liturgy was a volume published by Petrus Dathenus in 1566 in the German city of Frankenthal. In this volume were a metrical version of the Psalms, mostly the work of Dathenus himself, a Dutch translation of the Heidelberg Catechism, then only three years old, and finally a section entitled "forms and prayers as they are used by us." Whoever looks at this section of "forms and prayers" will realize that he is looking at the first Dutch version of what are the oldest parts of our liturgy.

But, of course, to get back to Frankenthal in 1566 is to reach only the initial point in the search. Who was Petrus Dathenus? Why was there a Dutch congregation in the German city of Frankenthal? And when Dathenus published his volume in 1566, from where did he get his forms and prayers? Were they his own composition or was he drawing on other sources?

At first the answer to our last question may seem very close at hand. Frankenthal was a city in the Rhine-Palatinate, the dominion of the pious elector Frederick who, to end the strife between Lutheran and Reformed in his territory, had ordered two of his court chaplains to draft a new catechism. It appeared in 1563 and we know it, of course, as the Heidelberg Catechism. That accounts for the appearance of that catechism in Dathenus's little volume of 1566. As a refugee minister in Frederick's territory, he would doubtless have felt obliged to give the elector's catechism every chance, quite apart from its own intrinsic merits.

But it also accounts, at least immediately, for Dathenus's forms and prayers. For it is not commonly remembered that Frederick's forms for unity included not only a catechism but a liturgy and a church order as well. While there are some omissions and a few alterations, even a hasty look will reveal that Dathenus's forms and prayers are mostly nothing but a Dutch translation of a German original, the so-called Palatinate Liturgy, the twin to the Heidelberg Catechism. While he was translating the catechism for the use of his Dutch congregation in Frankenthal, Dathenus obviously continued and translated the liturgy, or large parts of it, as well. As members of the Dutch Reformed church, we have to confess, even though it may hurt our pride, not only our catechetical origins but our liturgical origins as well were in Heidelberg.

But now we have really pushed our original inquiry only one step further back. If Dathenus took his liturgical materials from Heidelberg, where did Heidelberg get them? Were they original or were they reworkings of previous materials? To answer that question we shall have to take a trip through a good deal of sixteenth century Europe. But never fear! We shall return to Frankenthal.

I am sure you are well aware that the first Dutch Protestant congregation in the world was organized in the city of London in 1550. I call it "Protestant" intentionally because its Reformed character was at first not entirely clear. While the southern Netherlands (including a good deal of present-day Belgium) were by this time largely Calvinist, in so far as it was Protestant, the northern Netherlands was still largely Mennonite with some Lutheran thrown in. In any event, about 4,000 of these people fled from the Spanish terror to England, where in 1550 King Edward VI gave them an unused Augustinian monastery in London and allowed them to organize a church.

Though one church, the London group worshiped as two congregations, one French speaking, the other Dutch. The French congregation was led by

Vallerand Pullain who, it may be remembered, was Calvin's successor as minister of the congregation of French refugees in Strasbourg. In fact he had come to London with a good bit of his congregation in 1549 because of Lutheran pressures in Strasbourg. Because the English authorities required complete information about the life and order of these refugee congregations, Pullain presented to them his *Liturgia Sacra* which was nothing more than the same liturgy which Calvin had drafted for the use of the congregation in Strasbourg in the days when he was there.

For the Dutch group, however, the story is a little more complicated and to me, at least, somewhat confused. The leader of the Dutch section was that fascinating Polish nobleman, John Laski. Perhaps I may be permitted to insert a few words about Laski, not only because his greatness is so usually neglected in history but also because of the way in which he illustrates the truly nationless quality of the Reformation. A Polish nobleman by birth, as I have already indicated, he was partly educated in France, where he became acquainted with the work of Zwingli and so learned evangelical theology from the Zwinglian point of view. Returning to Poland, he became dean of Gnesen and ultimately bishop of Vesprin — at least he was elected to the latter office; whether or not he served in it is not quite clear. Forced to leave Poland because of his evangelical views (up to this point, mind you, an announced Zwinglian had been both dean and possibly bishop in the Roman Catholic church!) he crossed the border into Germany in 1540 to serve the congregation in Embden. After a short term there he became superintendent of the church in East Friesland and in 1543 accepted the invitation of the Countess Anna to organize the Reformed Church in Oldenburg. From there he came to London in 1549 at the joint invitation of Archbishop Cranmer and King Edward to take charge of the rapidly growing congregation of Dutch refugees. (And we think our leaders travel today!)

Once again the English authorities required, among other things, the submission of a liturgy. But here the problem was different from that of the French section. The French had a liturgical tradition (if it can be called that) of almost ten years. All Pullain had to do was bring it with him, revise it slightly to fit the English situation, and present it. The Dutch had none. It was one of Laski's first tasks to create one.

The most obvious thing to do would have been to translate the French liturgy in Dutch. *That* he did not do and we can only speculate as to the reasons why. For one thing, I imagine the Dutch section of the church contained a good many Mennonites or sympathizers with that point of view. For them any liturgy was suspect, but that of Calvin was probably too catholic even to be considered. (Incidentally, we shall never understand certain trends in Dutch Reformed history unless we remember that the Reformed church in the sixteenth century carried a great many who had been Mennonites into it where their tradition remained as a leaven in the lump.)

But I think we also have to consider the probable attitude of Laski himself. He was, after all, a confirmed Zwinglian, and, though he never expressed himself on it, he would doubtless have felt that Pullain's liturgy with its emphasis on the frequent celebration of the Supper and its strong theology of the real presence was a liturgical expression with which he could not be happy. In any event, for the Dutch part of the London congregation, without liturgical tradition as it was, he set to work to compose his own liturgy.

The puzzle is to know exactly what it was that the Dutch part of the congregation used. The congregation was scattered after Edward's death in 1553. By that time Pullain's *Liturgia Sacra* had been published in London in 1551. But Laski's work was not published till 1555 and then in Frankfurt. It is an imposing volume entitled, *Forma ac Ratio tota Ecclesiastici ministerii in peregrinorum potissimum vero Germanorum Ecclesia instituta Londini in Anglia*. The liturgical section is of extreme length, long enough to make one wonder whether even in those days it could actually have been used in a congregation. But it could well be that in preparing the work for publication in Frankfurt, Laski embellished and extended what had in actual usage in London been simpler or shorter.

We could assume with Mensinga, the classic historian of our liturgy, that during the London years Laski used only a hand-written copy of his forms (a not impossible suggestion since there was no active congregational participation) which he later, in exile, elaborated for publication were it not for the existence of another volume published somewhere in Germany in 1554, a year earlier than Laski's volume appeared. The author, Martinus Micronius or Maarten Klein, had been an elder in the London congregation. Let me translate the full title page for you.

> Christian Ordinances of the Netherlands congregation of Christ
> which was established in London in 1550 by the Christian prince,
> King Edward VI; faithfully collected and published by M. Micron

with the consent of the elders and deacons of the congregaton of Christ in London; for the comfort and profit of all believers.

Micron's work, like Laski's, is an entire church order. The liturgical portions are obviously a shortened version in Dutch of Laski's longer Latin work. We shall return to it later, but the riddle which has never really been answered is what liturgy did the Dutch congregation in London use during the few years of its existence. Did it use a Dutch translation of Laski's *Forma ac Ratio*, which some historians assert was published in London, though no copy of it has ever been found? Or did it use Micron's abridged form? Or was there only a hand-written Dutch copy of Laski's work, which both Laski and Micron tried to reconstruct after the London congregation had broken up?

Well, whatever the case may be, for the rest of our story Laski's *Forma ac Ratio* remains a museum piece, though a very interesting one indeed. Micron's "Christian Ordinances" is the liturgical tradition which goes with the Dutch congregation into exile. Perhaps we should have a brief look at its liturgical portion before we leave London. The Calvinist (and catholic) character of Pullain's *Liturgia Sacra* may be clearly seen from the first two items in his book; the order of service for Sunday morning; the order for the Lord's Supper. Mensinga's comment on this is a little naive.

The placing of the Communion Liturgy immediately after the liturgy for Sunday morning and not next to baptism is remarkable. It is still the idea of the mass, namely that the Supper ought to be celebrated every Sunday (p. 17).

It seems hard to believe that our nineteenth-century scholar was not aware that is was also the idea of John Calvin and that in laying out his liturgy Pullain was doing nothing more than reasserting the tradition which he learned from his master at Strasbourg!

Micron's Christian Ordinances (reflecting Laski's concepts) show a very different arrangement. The table of contents show a certain logic, but it is hardly Calvin's. The first items relate to ordinations and then they go as follows:

9. The order and way of preaching and common prayer
10. Instruction of children
11. The admission of children to the Supper

12. Prophesying and testing doctrine
13. Baptism
14. The Supper

If Micron's logic was what I think is was, I wonder why baptism is placed after the instruction of children. But that takes us off in another direction. The point to notice is the very Zwinglian way in which preaching and the Supper are separated. Of course, there is nothing strange about it. Laski was Zwinglian, and his liturgy could have been expected to reflect those views. What is amazing, however, is to contemplate that refugee congregation in London, French, and Dutch, using two completely different liturgical traditions under one roof.

And what is more, the congregation took these two traditions with it when it was scattered by the accession of Mary Tudor to the English throne. Its peregrinations are a little difficult to trace, but they seem to have gone about as follows. After a brief and unhappy stay in Denmark and various cities in northern Germany, the refugees were finally welcomed in the German city of Embden. Accommodations proved too small for the entire group, however, so a part moved on to Frankfurt. After seven years there, however, the Lutherans made their lives so miserable (they were not allowed to worship inside the city walls, to vote, to hold office, etc.) that some of them took quick advantage of elector Frederick's offer to settle in his domain and so came—to Frankenthal! So far as I have been able to determine, incidentally, the French group remained in Frankfurt despite the inconveniences. There is still a French Reformed congregation there to this day.

The Frankenthal group was small, two shiploads of about sixty Dutch families, who arrived there in 1562. I am sure you will not be surprised to learn the name of the leader under whose guidance they left Frankfurt and accepted the elector's invitation to settle in Frankenthal. It was Petrus Dathenus.

Now we have gone on this liturgical Cook's tour simply to point out that by the time Ursinus and Olevianus came to prepare their liturgy for the Elector Frederick in 1563, the two liturgical traditions of the Netherland refugees were well known in Germany, if not in the Palatinate. Pullain's *Liturgia Sacra*, representing the Calvinist tradition, was available in Frankfort where it was published both in 1554 and 1555; both Laski's *Forma ac Ratio* and Micron's *Christian Ordinances*, representing the Zwinglian tradition, were also available in German editions. The evidence seems to be that these actually were the sources used by the Heidelberg compilers. Calvin's Genevan service received its first German edition in 1563, the very year the Heidelberg liturgy was published. It would be much more reasonable to suppose that it was Pullain's version which they used for their Calvinistic strain. There is no evidence to suggest that they knew Zwingli's *Church Order,* but the Palatinate liturgy borrows from Micron's *Christian Ordinances* numerous times. (The only other Reformed source used is an occasional line from one of Oecolampadius's early liturgies in Basel which either Ursinus or Olevianus could have had on his library shelf from student days.) We are then faced with the strong possibility that the Palatinate liturgy, the original of the Dutch liturgy of 1566, was a deliberate attempt to fuse both Calvinistic and Zwinglian traditions into a single unity. The possibility becomes all the stronger when we remember the irenic spirit which lay behind the whole endeavor of catechism, church order, and liturgy — the desire to provide forms of unity for a badly divided people.

But when one sits down with the forms and begins to trace out their borrowings from Pullain and Micron, one soon becomes aware of a large block of material which can be traced to neither. The first impulse would be to assign it to the originality of one or both of the authors. But before we do that, we must remember that there were also Lutherans in Frederick's realm. Would it have been possible to include them also by employing something from one of their liturgical traditions?

Knowing the strong liturgical conservatism of Lutheranism even then, that hardly seems possible. But by what can only be called a freak, it was. In the principality of Wurtemburg, the church was something of a maverick (and I understand still is). Strongly Lutheran in its doctrine, it was almost as strongly Reformed in its liturgy. Perhaps that is an unfair characterization, but the fact remains that the liturgy of Wurtemburg has nothing to do with the Lutheran reshaping of the mass, but makes provision for a simple preaching service with an appended Supper, largely didactic in tone. The earliest edition of which we have any record was published in Tubingen in 1561 and must therefore have been available to Ursinus and Olevianus in Heidelberg in 1563. At any rate, in many places they made very generous use of it!

In a moment we shall take a look at this wondrous composition of Lutheran, Calvinist, and Zwinglian strands which is our liturgical ancestor.

But before we leave its history, I would ask you again to consider the strange
way in which liturgies prepared for the refugee congregation in London
became the source for a liturgy in Heidelberg, which in turn became the
original for the liturgy for the same Netherlands church which fifteen years
earlier had tried to establish itself on British soil. A fascinating liturgical
round trip!

II

Before we proceed further with our investigations, however, let us take a
look at what would have taken place in one of Dathenus's congregations. To
give the full picture, we shall assume it is one of the occasions on which the
Lord's Supper was celebrated. Dathenus gives us very little assistance here.
For the worship of the congregation on the Lord's Day, his book contains
only three items, two fairly long prayers, one to be used before the sermon,
the other after it, and the form for dismissing the congregation, in this case
the so-called Aaronic benediction. It should also be noted that the second
prayer, the prayer after the sermon, terminates in the Lord's Prayer.

The order for the Lord's Supper is exactly that which we know in the so-
called unabridged form in our own liturgy. It begins with the recitation of
Paul's version of the words of institution, followed by the long didactic
passage with which some of us have become so familiar. This is followed by
a short prayer and the Lord's Prayer after which the Apostles' Creed is
introduced with a form of prayer. Then comes a paraphrase of the *Sursum
Corda*, the words of distribution, and the actual Communion. The
thanksgiving after Communion is the 103rd Psalm, followed by a short
prayer of thanksgiving and the Lord's Prayer. Presumably a closing psalm
was sung before the benediction was pronounced. Many of you will realize
that I have been doing nothing more than describing the liturgy for the
Lord's Supper on which you were brought up.   We can get a better idea of
the Sunday service in these days, however, from following through the ways
in which various synods dealt with Dathenus's forms down to the great
Synod of Dort, which pretty well fixed things for the next few centuries. It
was 1568 before the first synod of refugee congregations could be held, and
it will perhaps come as no surprise that Dathenus was its moderator. It will
be remembered that Dathenus's liturgical work had been in print as early
as 1566. No synodical action seems to have been taken; probably the

prestige of the editor, together with the already widespread use of the book, already assured its position. It was the synod of 1574, meeting in Dort, which made two alterations that interest us. For one thing, this synod directed that even as worship on the Lord's Day had a fixed ending, so it should have a fixed beginning, the words of Psalm 124: 8, "Our help is in the Name of the Lord who made heaven and earth." These had been the opening words in Calvin's liturgy as indeed in the Roman mass.

(It is rather odd that all later editions of the liturgy omit the Votum, as it came to be called. I rather suspect that its omission in later editions was not intended to say anything more than that its use was so universal as to require no mention. In any event that was the case in the Netherlands right down to the present time.)

The other alteration involved Dathenus's prayer after sermon. Even in that day the synod deemed that the prayer was too long and better suited for days of fasting and penitence. It substituted a prayer from the liturgy of Geneva, and in so doing not only provided a shorter prayer but one of a better character, as we shall see when we come to analyze these forms. (Dathenus must have approved. He was again moderator of the synod which met at Dort in 1578, and the alteration of his prayer was not discussed.)

One liturgical question which repeatedly engaged the attention of all these earlier synods was the relation of the reading of Scripture to preaching. Evidently there were many, and with understandable reasons, who persisted in the use of the ancient Roman lectionaries with epistle and gospel for each Sunday. Lekkerkerker has collected a number of synodical utterances on this question from which I quote a few:

> Dort, 1574: "Regarding the Sunday gospels which are in use in the Church of Rome, it was decided that they shall not be preached in our churches, but an entire book of Holy Scripture shall be useed fully explained in an orderly way...."

> Dort, 1578: "And in places where the Sunday gospels are stil in use, they shall be tolerated until such time as they can be skilfully set aside."

> Middelburg, 1581: "Is it right to use the Sunday gospels to enlighten the people?" Answer. "It is better that an entire book of the Old or

New Testaments, not a piece here or there, be used, provided that
the book chosen is suited to the need of the church."

These synodical actions are interesting in that they reveal two things. One
is the persistent way in which the use of the traditional pericopes hung on,
despite repeated actions by successive synods. I understand that in Friesland
they continued in use right into the nineteenth century. But the more
important observation is the way in which these early Dutch synods
reaffirmed the Reformed concept of the reading and preaching of the Word
as a single act, best carried out by the use of *lectio continua*, the continuous
exposition of a book of Scripture.

It is interesting to observe that these early liturgies omit three items which
you and I would at once connect with our tradition in worship, the Creed,
the Law, and the Salutation. The fate of the Creed is quite easy to trace. All
of the earlier editions of our liturgy place it as the conclusion to the prayer
before the sermon, introduced by words such as these.

> Strengthen us also in the true Christian faith, that we may more and
> more cling to it, whereof we now make confession with mouth and
> heart, saying, I believe etc.

The Synod of Dort removed it from this place in 1619, relocating it in the
afternoon service, which was a teaching service. The synod felt (I think
wrongly) that the Creed was a teaching instrument more than an act of
affirmation and hence the new placing.

The Law is somewhat more difficult to trace. Not only did it occupy a
prominent place in Calvin's liturgy, it can be found in both Zwingli's and
Laski's as well. Indeed, it had a wide use in pre-Reformation Europe,
especially in its Germanic portions, because of the popularity of the *Prone*,
a little devotional service in the vernacular which often served as a preface
to the Mass. In this service the decalogue also played a prominent part. What
therefore happened to it in Dathenus's service book?

Again we know that it was used in worship because the great Synod of Dort
of 1619, which decided that the Creed should be used in the afternoon,
also decided that the Law should be used in the morning. We also have
evidence of its use from an edition of the Bible, Liturgy, and Psalms printed
in Leiden in 1596. (This edition also gives us evidence of something else at
which we shall be looking later.) The editor has inserted a little commentary

on Sunday worship which states very clearly that the Ten Commandments were read or sung as part of the Sunday morning service.

This little commentary leads me to believe that the Decalogue is not mentioned by Dathenus because it was not something which the minister read but something which the congregation sang. Since Dathenus nowhere gives any directions for the singing of the congregation, which nevertheless forms a very significant part of the Reformed liturgy, I assume that so widespread a usage, especially among congregations of a Calvinistic descent, would again have been one of those things which could have been taken for granted.

The salutation has to be the object of another (I hope) educated guess. It has a long history in Christian liturgy where it has always served as a call to prayer. The little antiphony, "The Lord be with thee;" "And with thy spirit," is, I suppose, the best known example. Why Calvin chose to begin his liturgy with the votum, I have no idea. The Palatinate liturgy which served Dathenus as a model begins with a salutation, followed directly, as it should be, by prayer. (In case you have missed my point, the salutation is never a junior grade benediction at the beginning of the service, as it has so often become with us. Its usage always indicated that prayer was about to begin.)

My guess is that in the earliest days of our church both usages were followed to begin the service. Apparently the decision of the synod of 1574 to use the votum exclusively was an attempt to bring some order to the situation, but an attempt which never quite succeeded. I say that because as you know it is the salutation which has survived with us, although in the Netherlands (and in South Africa), the usual custom is to use the votum and the salutation back to back. In that way both of our traditions are present and accounted for.

With this look at synodical actions, records of tradition, and Dathenus's two prayers, we can now begin to reconstruct a service in Amsterdam in 1600. The service begins with the singing of a psalm, led by a voorlezer who holds up a placard on which the number is written. (There were organs in church buildings but at this time they were used only for concert purposes.) During this psalm the domine and the elders enter and take their places. At the conclusion of the psalm, the domine uses the votum or the salutation or perhaps both to call the people to prayer. Thereafter he would use Dathenus's prayer before sermon, a prayer which, as we shall see, is a prayer of confession and for the right hearing of the Word. The prayer would have concluded with the Apostles' Creed, said by the congregation in a kind of low mumble. (I rather suspect that few persons at this time were able to read without forming the words, so that the direction with *heart and mouth* may be quite a literal one.)

At this point, I imagine, the congregation would have sung the Ten Commandments, after which the domine would have given himself to the reading and preaching of the Word. A few months ago I would have said that without any hesitation, but one or two things I have found lately have given me cause to wonder. Here I am afraid I must take you on another digression.

One of the universal marks of Reformed liturgy in the sixteenth century is the use of an act of confession followed by words of absolution and, in many cases, of retention, the liturgical expression of the well-known power of the keys. Usually it comes at the beginning of the service, but sometimes, as in the case of both Laski and the Palatine, it comes after the sermon at the end of the service. Dathenus's first prayer takes obvious account of this usage because it is largely a prayer of confession (in fact, many of its phrases praying for forgiveness are stronger than a good many of the so-called "words of assurance" one hears nowadays), but of an absolution or retention in Dathenus there is absolutely no trace.

Apparently the question was taken up in the early days, since it was on the docket of the synod that met at Middelburg in 1581. The decision of the synod was that the binding and loosing of sins was sufficiently covered in the preaching of the gospel and therefore there was no need for any liturgical form for it. I do not know what lay behind the decision or why the question came up, but I am constrained to believe it was raised by those of Calvinist or French tradition (we must never forget to what extent the early Reformed church in the Netherlands was French) who missed this element in Dathenus's liturgy.

But quite as evidently the decision of the synod made no difference (then as now) to those who were going to do what they were going to do. In any event, our friend the commentator in the Bible of 1596 informs us that in connection with the Decalogue the domine using words of Scripture assures those who repent of their forgiveness and those who refuse that the wrath of God still rests upon them. As late as 1596, therefore, the use of an absolution and retention, though never mentioned in the liturgy, must have been common enough to have warranted this kind of comment. If you ask why it was never set down, I suspect that the answer is that it would have horrified the large contingent of ex-Mennonites still included in the Reformed church at that time (just as its use horrifies the large number of Baptists contained in the Reformed church today!) Liturgical development by accretion regardless of what the book says.

To return to our 1600 service, our domine may or may nor have used such words in connection with the confession and decalogue. But that he read the Scriptures and preached, I am sure. Probably we would be hearing his twenty-third sermon on 1 Samuel, but if he was a stubborn Fries, he might be preaching on the gospel for the day! After the sermon, he would have used Dathenus's second prayer, though the singing of a psalm might have preceded it. That prayer, as altered by the synod of 1574, was one of thanksgiving and intercession, an improvement, as I have said, over Dathenus's original, which contained no thanksgiving but another long confession of sin before the intercessions. Again the Lord's Prayer would have been said much as the Creed had been said earlier.

The Lord's Supper which followed would have been exactly as our unabridged liturgy presents it, with one possible exception. Micron's London book and the Palatinate liturgy give the words of distribution as follows:

The bread which we break is the communion of the body of Christ. Take, eat, remember, and believe that the body of our Lord Jesus Christ was given over to the death of the cross for the forgiveness of all our sins.

The cup of blessing which we bless is the communion of the blood of Christ. Take, drink all of it, remember, and believe that the blood of our Lord Jesus Christ was poured out in death on the cross for the forgiveness of all our sins.

The earliest editions of our liturgy contained these words, the so-called "London aanhangsel." In fact the synod of 1571 allowed the minister to use either Paul's words or the words of Christ, "Take, eat, this is my body," as he saw fit. The synod of 1574, however, took away this privilege and made Paul's words with the London "aanhangsel" obligatory. The strange thing is that there was never a synodical action changing this decision. But in both the editions of 1586 and 1619, the London "aanhangsel" is omitted. Its exact fate will probably never be known.

Before leaving this part of our inquiry, I should like to call attention to the extreme flexibility of Dathenus's provision for Sunday morning worship and to suggest a reason for it. You will have noticed that so far as the requirements are concerned, a Sunday morning service could have consisted of nothing but the opening prayer, the sermon, the closing prayer with the Lord's Prayer, and the benediction, with a psalm or two sung at appropriate intervals. And I do not doubt that many services had no more content than that; a visit to the Zwinglian parts of Reformed Switzerland today would reveal scores of Sunday services built according to precisely the same plan.

On the other hand, by leaving the question of additions to this skeletal form completely open, a congregation which so chose could construct an order of service remarkably like that of Calvin's at Strasbourg or Pullain's *Liturgia Sacra*. I have tried to show from various synodical actions and the words of at least one commentator that many of them did, fleshing out Dathenus's rather meagre provision with votum, law, absolution, etc.

The reason for such liberty, I suggest, goes back to the dual inheritance from the congregation in London. Though that inheritance seems to have followed linguistic lines, the Dutch following Laski and French Pullain, there can be no doubt that there was a good deal of mixing as the church in the Netherlands began to develop. After all, from the very beginning there was a sizeable number of French-speaking churches in the Netherlands, some of which remain to this very day. It is to them, incidentally, that we owe almost all of our forms for ordinations. Though these churches did not use Dathenus's forms but had their own liturgy derived from that of Pullain, their usages were of great influence on some of the Dutch congregations, especially in larger cities. Dathenus's forms, therefore, made it possible for those who wished to be loyal to the fuller tradition of Calvinist liturgy to do so, while at the same time providing equally for those whose liturgical ideas went back from Laski to Zwingli.

I have already indicated several times that the final revisions of Dathenus's work, together with the additions made by later synods, were the work of the great Synod of Dort in 1619. For the most part these were too minor to detain us here, although the greatest revision was the addition of a form for the baptism of adults, which had hitherto not been included. The reason usually given for this addition is that the synod was seeking to make provision for heathen converts in both the East Indies and the West, more commonly called New Netherland. But the Synod of Dort made one addition perhaps unwittingly. When its finished work was published, it was called "The Netherlands Liturgy." I have no idea what led the synod to use this traditional Christian word as the title for its forms for worship. Not even Calvin had made use of it; he had entitled his liturgy, "The Form of Prayers." So far as I can determine, the only Reformation service to make use of the word, in its Latin form, had been Pullain's *Liturgia Sacra*. Whether the French congregations which used Pullain's work had begun to call it their "liturgie" or not I do not know. I wish I could say that the fathers at Dort had some compelling reason which led them to grace the Dutch language with this French word. But I do have to say that I am grateful that it happened, whatever the reason. For however far we may have wandered in these centuries, there staring us from the cover, so to speak, is the everlasting reminder that our forms of worship by their very title claim to be one with the great traditions of Catholic Christendom. I am grateful that thanks to Dort we use not a book of forms, nor a book of worship, nor a ritual, but "The Liturgy."

III

Our final task will be to analyze the sources which Dathenus and his Palatinate original used in compiling their liturgy. Here I must confess that I am relying entirely upon the investigations of Dutch scholars for whom the history of the liturgy has been of interest in a way that has apparently never been the case in this country.

We can dispose of Dathenus's two Sunday morning prayers rather quickly. Nensinga says that the first prayer, the prayer of confession and for a right hearing of the Word, is entirely of Dathenus's own composition. I am sure that this is true, though I cannot help wondering how completely anyone ever composes his own prayer, i. e. whether bits and pieces of other prayers, lodged in the mind unconsciously, do not inevitably find their way into what one supposes to be his own composition.

In passing, I should like to call attention to the fact that the traditional Reformed custom, here evidenced by Dathenus, is to ask for the blessing of the Spirit upon the Word *before* its reading and preaching, not, as has so generally become the case with us, afterward. It may seem a little thing, but I think that if explored it would prove to have fairly large theological dimensions. Dathenus had entitled the prayer after sermon, "A Prayer for the Whole Need of Christendom," a phrase which rather strikingly resembles the prayer "for the whole state of Christ's Church" in the Anglican liturgy.

With some alterations, he had borrowed this from the Palatinate liturgy. The first part, another long confession of sin, had been lifted by the German liturgy almost entirely from a prayer used in Geneva, while the second part, the intercessions, was apparently the work of the Palatine authors, which Dathenus translated and adapted to his own situation.

It will be remembered that the synod of 1574 replaced this prayer with a shorter one taken from Geneva. Not only did this prayer replace the element of confession with thanksgiving, as we have already observed, but it also provided for some variation in the intercessions according to special circumstances. Again, if I may be permitted an observation, our liturgical fathers fully recognized the great part which intercession had to play in the prayer of the church. If there is any outstanding weakness in the worship of the Reformed church today, it is the way in which the prayer of the church has become the prayer of the pastor and intercession replaced by anything running from his own private meditation to a flank attack on the morning sermon. I submit that in the name of free prayer this has been too great a price to pay.

I deal rather hastily with these two prayers because they have almost entirely disappeared from use among us. Vistigial remains of them were to be found in the last edition of our liturgy, though seldom if ever used. Whether even these remains will be found in the new liturgy I do not know. But even though in both language and content the originals have long since become outdated, they still deserve study as examples of what our fathers believed the prayers of the church should contain.

Now I should like to devote our remaining time to an analysis of the origins of our liturgy for the Lord's Supper. Here, again depending upon the scholarship of others, I hope not only to provide you with information but also to dispel some of our mythology. For if the assertion of many among us is to be believed, no greater piece of Calvinism exists than our traditional liturgy for the Lord's Supper. To what extent this assertion is fact and to what assertion it is myth we shall now examine.

To begin with I should like to observe that the entire form is a translation from the Palatinate liturgy of 1563. In translating this form Dathenus made fewer alterations than anywhere else in his entire liturgy, alterations so minor that they need not be mentioned. It is rather an examination of the sources used by the Palatine compilers that begins to turn up some fascinating results.

The form begins with the narration of the events of the Last Supper as given by Paul in 1 Corinthians. In and of itself that may not seem to occasion any surprise. But it does represent a very radical departure from the common usage of Reformed tradition. For consider; this narrative of institution being followed directly by the long didactic passage was obviously meant to be read from the pulpit. In the customary Reformed pattern of the time the narrative of institution were always read at the Table. Here (and I cannot believe it was by accident) they are shoved way back in the service so that they must be read from the pulpit. In fact, if you examine the entire liturgy, the words of institution are never said from the Table. At the time of distribution they are not used, but the Pauline words are substituted. This is the only liturgy never to use our Lord's own words.

The long didactic passage which follows is divided into two parts, the first being a penitential section including a fencing of the Table. Scholars who have gone over this section carefully say that it contains almost nothing original but is in the main a rather skilfull blending of Calvins's *Liturgy* and Micron's *Christian ordinances*. Here for example are some of the phrases from the comparable section of Calvin's *Liturgy*. Do they sound familiar?

> And although we feel we have not perfect faith and do not serve God with such zeal as we are bound, but have daily to strive with the weakness of our faith and the evil lusts of our flesh, nevertheless because the Lord shows us this grace that we have this his holy gospel written in our hearts and that he grants us to live according to his righteousness and holy commandments, so let us be entirely certain that not withstanding the sins and wickedness which remain in us, he receives us and counts us worthy partakers of this spiritual table.

Or how about these words from Micron?

> Nevertheless, we do not say this, beloved brothers, to distress the contrite hearts of believers as though none were worthy to come to the Table of the Lord save those who were free from all sin and perfect in all holiness. For Christ the Lord did not institute his Supper to testify to our righteousness and perfection, but rather to testify to our weakness and unrighteousness.

I could continue with many more examples, but I trust that these few are sufficient to illustrate the fact that this part of the Communion liturgy is simply a skillful editorial combination of Calvin and Micron.

The second part of the form is the theological one, which seeks to explain the meaning of the Lord's Supper. Here the unscrambling of the Palatinate omelette is a somewhat more difficult task. Most of us have heard it read so often that we simply take it for granted. Sheer familiarity has dulled us to the several rather awkward theological shifts which occur within its relatively few paragraphs. My job now is to try to make them clear to you.

The first section of this part is a remembrance of Christ, culminating in the substitutionary atonement of his death upon the cross. It is a beautiful piece of work, making full use of such affecting contrasts as, "He though innocent was condemned to death that we might be acquitted," and, "My God, why hast thou forsaken me? that we might be accepted of God and never be forsaken by him."

Lekkerkerker considers it one of the finest parts of the entire liturgy. Save for an occasional phrase which can be ascribed to Calvin, no original for it can be found. It obviously was the work of one of the Palatinate authors. Mensinga believes that in view of its close theological and literary affinities with the Heidelberg Catechism, especially questions 37 and 38, this section is the work of Ursinus himself and there is no reason to think otherwise.

"The new and eternal covenant of grace and reconciliation" with which this section concludes provides the bridge to the next section, "that we might firmly believe that we belong etc." For this section we do have an original, the Lutheran Agenda of Wurttemberg, which had been widely used by the Lutheran community in the Rhine Palatinate. And it must be remembered that the Elector Frederick sought to include it in his new catechism, church order, and liturgy of 1563. Actually, the Wurttemberg church order was itself based on an even older Lutheran church order, that of Brandenburg in 1534. I say that Wurttemberg was the original for the Palatinate luturgy. That is only half-a-truth. The fact is that what we are about to see is one of the most fascinating liturgical (and therefore theological) swindles anywhere on the record.

I have already mentioned the fact that Frederick's realm contained a goodly number of Lutherans with whom he was anxious to reach an ecclesiastical peace. The liturgy used by most of them was the Wurttemberg church order. It is a fair surmise, therefore, that the compilers of the new liturgy were under royal instructions to do what they could to include a least parts of Wurttemberg. In one sense this did not seem to be difficult, since Wurttemberg, as I mentioned earlier, was Reformed in its liturgical concept.

The trouble was that theologically it was still soundly Lutheran. What our Palatinate friends did at this point, therefore, was to preserve as much of the language of Wurttemberg as possible while completely altering its theological substance. The Lutheran liturgy had several times used the phrase, "By a sure remembrance and pledge." But of what? For the Lutherans the bread and wine of the Supper were a sure remembrance and pledge "that we abide in the Lord Christ and he in us and therefore that we have eternal life." Our authors have altered that to say that the bread and wine of the Supper were a sure remembrance and pledge that Jesus becomes to us the meat and drink of life eternal *on the cross*.

The full meaning of the alteration may not become apparent until we examine the next one. For the Lutherans, the Supper is a sure remembrance and pledge that Christ gives himself to us for food. For the new liturgy it is a sure remembrance and pledge that he feeds and satisfies our hungry and thirsty souls. The difference may not seem great until we ask *how*. The Palatinate product answers our question. Through his death on the cross he has taken away the cause of our hunger, i.e., sin.

It takes little theological insight to perceive that here we are dealing with the basic idea of Zwinglianism, the notion that the only value in the Supper is in making us remember the atoning death of Christ on Calvary. The foundation has been laid in Ursinus's (if it is his) lovely opening section on the atonement. Now here in the Supper we have the instrument by which this remembrance is made possible. What Christ gives us at the Table is a closer view of his death and passion. What satisfies our hunger and thirst is the remembrance that he has died for us. The Lutheran form of words may still be here, but its content has been changed to say something quite different.

Now of course the Zwinglian view of the Supper is a perfectly logical one, but it does not happen to be the official view of the Reformed church. I shall not ask you to compare our liturgy with Calvin's at this point. If you did, you would soon discover that the central element of Calvin's view, the mystical union of the living Christ with his people, has completely dropped out. I shall simply ask that you compare our liturgy with the most truly Calvinist of our theological standards, the Belgic Confession.

Article 35 of that document presents a very different theology from that of our liturgy. Christ is the heavenly bread coming down from heaven to be the true nourishment of the believer who receives him by faith, the eyes and mouth of the soul, even as he eats the bread and drinks the wine. The whole imagery of John 6, which both Zwingli and our liturgy carefully reject, is the background of this chapter. In fact, our confession states that the godless receive the sacrament to their damnation—as nearly Lutheran a statement as anything to be found in any Reformed confession. No, the didactic portion of our liturgy, the explanation of the meaning of the Supper, is as thoroughly anti-Calvinist and as completely pro-Zwinglian as any Reformation document can be. Calvin used only on margins—theological heart is Zwingli.

We should be grateful to the Wurttemberg Lutherans, however, for it is to them that we owe the last paragraph of the passage, the exhortation to true brotherly love among the communicants. The Palatinate form lifted this almost bodily from the Lutheran original, and we can be glad that it did.

Having been critical of the composition of the didactic part of the liturgy, let me say two things in praise of its Communion prayer. So far as I am aware, it is the only Communion prayer of the sixteenth century to bring out two elements strongly implicit in Calvin's eucharistic theology but nowhere expressed in Calvin's own liturgical forms.

The first is the Holy Spirit as the agent of the "miracle" (if that be the word) of the Supper. Calvin never wearies in repeating that in the Supper it is through the power of the Spirit that the living Christ is made present to the believer, whether, as he sometimes says, he is brought down or, as he elsewhere says, the congregation is lifted up. In either case, it is only the power of the Spirit that unites those who are separate.

With such strong emphasis upon the presence of the Spirit in the Supper in all of his writings about the Supper, one would expect to find this faith expressed in Calvin's liturgy. Surprisingly enough the Communion prayer contains not a word to this effect, nor does any liturgy of the Calvinistic family, except that of John Knox in Scotland. On the continent it is only our Palatinate-Dutch liturgy that contains a true epiclesis, invocation of the presence of the Spirit, in its liturgy for the Supper.

The other noteworthy emphasis in this prayer, the work of the Palatine authors, is an eschatalogical one. "And in all our suffering with uplifted head to look for the coming of our Lord Jesus Christ from heaven when he shall make our mortal bodies like unto his glorious body and take us to himself in eternity." The eschatalogical side of the Supper is an aspect which has come into consideration only very recently. How did it find its way into our liturgy in the sixteenth century?

It would be comforting to think, as Lekkerkerker suggests, that our liturgical authors got their idea from a passage in Micron's *Christian Ordinances*. As part of the thanksgiving after Communion in that form the minister says,

> I also hope that you who are sitting at the Table of the Lord have seen with the eye of faith that holy sitting together which is to come with Abraham, Isaac, and Jacob in the kingdom of God; and that you are certain of it through your faith in the righteousness, merit, and victory of Christ the Lord, just as we all have sat together at this table of the Lord.

There is certainly no similarity in language, but it is possible that Micron, whom our authors certainly knew, suggested the idea which they used in another way.

Dr. Beardslee of New Brunswick Seminary has made an alternate suggestion, which I also find attractive. I have several times referred to the fact that both in the Netherlands and in the Rhine Pallatinate the Reformed church had, for a variety of reasons, attracted a number of right-wing Anabaptists whose influence can never be forgotten. He feels that the inclusion of this eschatalogical passage, so untypical of most Reformed liturgies, is one of their contributions to our liturgical tradition. In any event, I call your attention to the way in which both the short didactic passage and the Communion prayer in our new liturgy have sought to emphasize this part of our heritage.

The remainder of the liturgy can be briefly dealt with. The final exhortation after the Creed, "That we may now be fed with the true heavenly bread Christ Jesus etc." has been taken almost verbatim from Calvin, though the authors have somewhat moderated the polemic quality of his language. Incidentally, one has only to think about it briefly to realize that it speaks a totally different view of the meaning of the Supper from that contained in the longer didactic passage.

I have already spoken about the words of distribution. Perhaps I need to say a word about the posture in receiving the Supper. The custom of coming to sit at the Table was, so far as I know, first used by Laski in London and has continued to be the custom of the Dutch church to this day. In other Reformed churches the custom is to stand around the Table (German) or to kneel before it (French). It was Zwingli's custom to have the elements distributed to the congregation as they sat in their pews, a custom adopted by English Puritanism and finally in the late nineteenth century (much to my regret) imitated by most of the congregations of our Communion.

Our liturgy concludes with a double thanksgiving, the reading of a part of the 103rd Psalm (with some additions), and a brief prayer. The prayer bears some resemblance to one in the Genevan liturgy, and the theology is centainly Calvinist rather than Zwinglian. The interesting thing, however, is that in both the original Palatinate version and in Dathenus's translation, the psalm and the prayer are present as alternates. Between them very clearly are printed the words *or this*. Somewhere along the line (and I must apologize for not being able to say exactly where) the words *or this* were dropped out. Was this merely a printer's error or was it by deliberate design? Again, I must leave the riddle unsolved.

This was the Sunday service which our fathers brought with them to the new world. In fact, nine years after its final revision by the Synod of Dort, it was used in a loft over a horse-mill in New Amsterdam for the first celebration of the Lord's Supper in the Reformed church. I have no doubt that it was similarly used by Van Raalte whenever the Lord's Supper was first celebrated in western Michigan, for not even the great reorganization of the Dutch church in 1816 changed it. Its usage in North America and South Africa, long after it had fallen into disuse in the land of its birth as well as the land of its adoption, probably makes it the oldest Reformation liturgy continously in use; yet, so far as I know, its 400th birthday in 1963 passed unnoticed.

May I summarize its pedigree? The liturgy of the Dutch church was German in origin, composed of elements drawn from the liturgies of the French church in Strasbourg, the Dutch church in London, the Lutheran church in Wurttemberg, woven together by a compiler whose theological cast was overwhelmingly Zwinglian.

But the story does not end there. Soon after its official adoption by the Dutch church, it was translated into English, and that started it on an entirely new career. Tracing the course of that career will be our next task.

Lecture II

A few years before the liturgy of the Reformed Church in the Netherlands was given its final form by the great Synod of Dort in 1619, political and ecclestiastical events in Great Britain were conspiring to give it a second career in another language. The pressures of King James to unite the churches in his two realms of England and Scotland had made a number of people in both countries unhappy. Partly for this reason and partly also for reasons of commerce, a number of English and Scottish Presbyterians began to take up residence in the Netherlands, then almost the commercial capital of the world. In a fairly short time in the early years of the seventeenth century, a little classis of seven English-speaking congregations was formed in the Reformed church in the Netherlands. It may be a matter of passing interest to note that two of these congregations, Amsterdam and Rotterdam, survive to this day and that some of the most prominent Dutch commercial families still belong to them. The most prominent of these congregations was that in Amsterdam, which was given the chapel of a Roman Catholic convent for its house of worship. The nuns still occupy the convent, while the English Presbyterians still use the chapel.

One of the conditions imposed upon this group of refugee congregations, however, was the full use of the liturgy of the Dutch Reformed church. This requirement necessitated a translation into English, which was made under the auspices of the Amsterdam consistory and used by the other six congregations. Interestingly enough, therefore, the English version of our liturgy is almost as old as the Dutch, although until the latter years of the eighteenth century its use was confined to the seven English-speaking Reformed congregations in the Netherlands.

In 1764 the consistory of the church in New York decided to bow to the inevitable and to open a place of worship in which the services should be entirely in English. To serve this North Church, as it came to be called, the consistory called Dr. Archibald Laidlie, the minister of the English Reformed Church in Vlissingen, one of the seven congregations to which reference has been made.

Dr. Laidlie took up his work in New York on the first of April 1764 and as early as the first of May was appointed chairman of a committee to prepare and publish an English translation of the Dutch liturgy. The fact that his committee was able to report on the fifth of June indicates that the work was really not very strenuous. As the committee report stated, the work had been prepared from existing translations. In other words, the commitee had simply made use of the translation which Laidlie already knew from his ministry in Holland, making such substitutions in the prayers of intercessions as the change from Dutch to British sovereignty required.

Details of publication proved troublesome, however, and it was not until late in 1766 that the first edition of the 1,800 copies was ordered from the printer, John Holt. Most of the delay seems to have resulted from the difficulty in getting the printing for the music notes for the psalter. This work was done by the firm of Daniel Crommelin in Amsterdam, since no facilities for printing music notes were at that time available in New York. While 1767 marks the first official appearance of the English translation of the Dutch Reformed liturgy, there are several reasons for thinking that it had enjoyed an unofficial career for some time previously. One of the early ministers in New Amsterdam was Domine Samuel Drisius, who came out in 1652 and remained until his death in 1673. Drisius was sent in response to a special request from Governor Stuyvesant for a domine who could preach in English. Most of his career before coming to this country seems to have been spent in ministering in the English congregations in the Netherlands; in fact, his most glowing testimonial came from the English church in Amsterdam.

There is no record that Drisius ever preached in English in this country, although he did act as Stuyvesant's emissary to several of the English colonies. There is good probability, however, in view of the governor's request, that he did hold many English services, especially in Long Island where the English population was increasing steadily during the later years of Stuyvesant's administration. In that case, he would certainly have used the English translation of the liturgy for the Sunday prayers, a translation which he would have known well from his earlier ministry in Holland. Or consider the case of Dr. John Henry Livingston, virtually the founder of the American Reformed church. How did someone with so Scottish a name come to be so closely identified with the Dutch church in the Hudson valley? His great-great grandfather was minister of the Scots church in Rotterdam, and the Livingston family came to the new world via the English-speaking Reformed churches in the Netherlands. It seems entirely likely, therefore, that the English liturgy, psalmbook, and catechism must have been known to the young Livingston from the family library, especially since English was his native language and Dutch a second language which he learned only in order to minister to his people. Such things may be only speculations; but there is the hard fact that when, after the Revolution, the Reformed church decided to cut all ties with the Netherlands and set up housekeeping for itself in the English language, the liturgy provided no great problem. The English translation which had been made for the churches in the Netherlands and taken over with slight revisions by the New York consistory was there to be used.

The committee, of which Dr. Livingston was chairman, brought in its final report to the synod of 1793, the minutes of which record the following:

> Professor Livingston, in the name of the committee reported to the body that the (task) had been happily completed, and exhibited the book containing the Liturgy and Government of the Church.... Synod received the same with full approbation and with thanksgivings to the Lord Jesus Christ, on whose shoulders is the government of the church and who has hitherto blessed and preserved the Reformed Church and enabled its members to present their constitution in a manner which they regard acceptable to Him; and not without expectation that the same will be contemplated with satisfaction by other persuasions, being convinced that it will subserve the promotion of piety and good order in the respective congregations.

Though it is true that the liturgy published in 1792 was almost a literal translation of the original Dutch, Livingston's preface to it makes it clear that the liturgical attitude of 1792 was quite different from that of Dort in 1619.

> Firmly believing that the gifts of the Holy Spirit for the edification of Zion in every age are promised and bestowed, the Reformed Dutch Church judges it sufficient to show in a few specimens the general tenor and manner in which public worship is performed and leaves it to the piety and gifts of her ministers to conduct the ordinary solemnities of the sanctuary in a manner they judge most acceptable to God and most edifying to his people.

The language is gracious, but the meaning is unmistakable. The good doctor is saying that the liturgy herewith published is not to be taken seriously except as a general indication of what might be called liturgical etiquette. The concept of liturgical prayers to be used by the congregation in its worship every Sunday, quite clearly the concept of Dort in 1619, was completely unacceptable to him. His liturgical forms were printed (as another Reformed synod was to say quite frankly) only as models for the beginner until he could get the hang of the thing himself.

This difference in basic liturgical outlook between the original Dutch liturgy and its American counterpart almost two centuries later requires a few words of explanation. This is not the place for a detailed consideration of the developments in Dutch theology during the eighteenth century. It was essentially the story of a struggle between two contending parties, and, with either of them, the liturgy was the loser. The left wing, with its theology of rational enlightenment, clearly the ancestor of what today we should call liberalism, despised the antiquated theology of the liturgical forms. The right wing, heavily influenced by the Puritan theology of the covenants and strongly tinged with pietism, regarded the liturgy as a useless crutch for those who were weak in the faith.

It is significant to remember that Dr. Livingston's own education was at Yale and Utrecht, the former a center of New England Puritanism, the latter the stronghold of a similar viewpoint in Dutch theology. It is also significant to notice that, unlike its Dutch original, the American version contains no reference whatever to the Christian year. We learn from another source that Livingston's identification with the Puritan point of view was so complete that he disapproved of the prevailing Dutch custom of observing the major Christian festivals, such as Christmas, Good Friday, Easter, etc., and expressed the hope that it would soon be discontinued in the Reformed Church in America.

Why then did Livingston even bother to publish a liturgy when the American church became independent? One great reason was the fact that not every one in the Reformed church shared his aversion to forms. It can be said with certainty that the conservatives who had adhered to the Conferentie party in the dispute that had split the church earlier in the eighteenth century would have treasured the historic Dutch liturgy and its usage, if for no other reason than to distinguish them from the pietists whom they so greatly detested. The leading congregation in the church, that of

New York, also had a strong attachment to the historic liturgy that had come from the land of their fathers.

But even Dr. Livingston and his group, much as they disliked formal prayers, had a definite attachment to the two forms for baptism and the Lord's Supper. The larger part of these forms was didactic in character, and in these didactic sections, rightly or wrongly, they saw clear expositions of that convenant theology which was to them almost the central article of the faith. They would surrender these only with the greatest reluctance, believing that they represented a genuine safeguard against the intrusion of alien theologies. The rest of the liturgy, since it did represent orthodox theology, could be tolerated as a model, if not ignored.

The point is important because the Reformed Church in America, the real birth date of which is 1792 and not the date of the formation of its earliest congregation in 1628, was liturgically stillborn. Perhaps that is too extreme a statement; but certainly it was born with a set of quasiliturgical formularies, mostly didactic in nature, which were highly valued for their doctrinal content, and a collection of prayers which only a small minority of the church had used or thought of using for at least fifty years previous. In short, our birth as a church came in the full flood of American pietism.

Another fact must be added here. The emergence of the Reformed church as an English-speaking denomination in 1792 (the last Dutch service in the church was held in 1808) put us into direct contact with two other denominations which fully shared the nonliturgical stance of American pietism, the Presbyterian family of churches and New England Congregationalism. The rapid disappearance of Dutch and the need for English preachers forced us to make almost wholesale importations in the years from 1795 to 1810. Without making a detailed census, here is a cursory listing of calls issued and accepted during that period. In 1787, William Linn, a Presbyterian, was called to the church in New York. In 1805, the church in Albany called John Melanchthon Bradford, a New England Presbyterian. Selah Strong Woodhull became minister of the church in Brooklyn in 1806. His education and previous ministry had been both Congregational and Presbyterian. James Matthews, an Associate Reformed Presbyterian, became minister of the South Church in New York in 1809. William McMurray, also Associate Reformed Presbyterian, was called to the church in Rhinebeck in 1812.

No one wishes to imply that Congregationalists and Presbyterians took over the Reformed church in the early years of the nineteenth century; but in the vacuum created by the lack of English-speaking preachers, a large number of these brethren came, most often to the more influential congregations of the denomination. Their point of view, together with that of the leaders of the Dutch church, pretty well removed the liturgy from any serious role in the life of the church, except when children were baptized or the Lord's Supper was celebrated.

Not before 1835 have I been able to discover any protest against this state of affairs. In that year George Washington Bethune, one of the most colorful figures ever to serve in our ministry, delivered an address entitled, "Reasons for Preferring a Union with the Reformed Dutch Church." Dr. Bethune was the son of one of the leading Presbyterian families in New York and was presenting in this address his own reasons for having united with the Reformed church. It was also a kind of apologia for the Reformed church in an area in which at the time it was not well known or firmly established.

One of Bethune's reasons for preferring union with the Reformed church was its liturgical position, even though he had to admit that that position might indeed exist more on paper than in fact.

> The Reformed Dutch Church has a liturgy adapted to all the offices and occasions of worship. It is perhaps to be regretted that its disuse has become so common among us, perhaps from a weak desire to conform to the habits of other denominations. Certainly there are occasions when the forms of prayer are at least as edifying as many extemporaneous effusions we hear from the desk, and it is evident that the wise fathers of the church did not intend that they should remain a dead letter in our books.

It is not difficult to make some deductions from Bethune's remarks. Obviously extemporaneous prayer, often of an inferior character, was the order of the day in the Reformed church in 1835. Equally obvious is the fact that he had discovered the liturgical prayers of the church and had made use of them in his own services. Finally, it is clear that Dr. Bethune did not believe that the liturgical state of affairs prevailing in the church in 1835 was what the reformers had intended.

There seems to be no evidence as to how widely these views were shared in the church at that time. Bethune was still a young man when he delivered this address. He became one of the most influential ministers in the Reformed church. Perhaps it is an indication of the spread of his feeling in this matter and the growth of his influence that the question first came to some kind of official attention in 1848.

In the previous year the synod had appointed a committee of nine persons, of whom Bethune was one, to study the whole state of the church and make definite recommendations for new policies and directions that would advance its growth. The report which the committee presented to the synod of 1848 was a large document of more than forty printed pages covering almost every aspect of the life and work of the Reformed Dutch church. It was by no means a superficial survey.

One wonders whether it was Bethune's influence that accounts for items VIII and IX in the committee report, "Liturgy and Church Music." Item VIII begins by calling attention to the "prevailing unseemly diversity" which prevails in the liturgical observances of the Reformed church. Not even the treasured forms for baptism and the Lord's Supper

> ...receive that uniform marked observance that may be claimed for them, in view of their being labored, careful expositions of the mysteries of the faith in their connection with sealing ordinances and necessary to be understood in order to guard against their abuse.

Item VIII also calls attention to the growing demand in the church for a burial service, which the old liturgy did not contain.

Item IX concerns itself with the decline in congregational singing. It views with great alarm the alleged practice in some churches

> ...of employing the attaches of theatres and other places of mere worldly amusement and that no recognition of such as conductors of a branch of sacred service can be made by the Synod because tending to sink a service whose savor before God is melody of heart to a mere professional artistic performance, to encourage levity, and to introduce the spirit of mere amusement into the sanctuary.

Item IX is not really germane to the case, but as one of the few pronouncements on the subject of church music ever made by a General Synod, it is perhaps worth quoting. Even as early as 1848 some of the more affluent congregations were evidently employing professional soloists and quartettes and synod, quite ineffectively, decided to be rid of them before they became a habit.

The part of the report which dealt with the liturgical situation in the church clearly indicated that by 1848 the same liturgical chaos which has plagued the life of the church at other times had pretty well set in. Not only were the prayers in the liturgy still being ignored, but now even the sacred sacramental forms themselves were being tampered with to suit individual tastes. In the committee's opinion, the only solution (how little times have changed!) was the appointment of another committee "to find means to secure greater uniformity in the use of the liturgical forms contained in our books."

Exactly what the committee had in mind in recommending the appointment of another committee is not clear. It must have intended something more than merely getting the classes to ride herd on those who were playing fast and loose with the existing liturgy. That could have been accomplished by mere synodical resolution. It seemed probable that what was intended was a recommendation that in view of the chaos, the whole liturgy be made the object of study and revision, but that the committee did not think it politic to say so.

In any event, a special committee was appointed with instructions to report to the next synod. That committee must also have felt that it was expected to get into the touchy subject of liturgical revision. At the meeting of the synod in 1849, however, the chairman, John Garretson, presented the following report:

> The undersigned...begs leave to state that he has made several attempts to convene the committee and has failed in every instance to secure the attendance of the members. Two of them stated, soon after their appointment, that it would be impossible for them to attend any of the meetings. The other two had no doubt the very best reasons for not attending.

The implication is that on at least one occasion Brother Garretson sat waiting for two committee members who neither appeared nor sent any excuse for their absence. Evidently the special committee was not about to pick up the hot potato which the Committee on the State of Religion had tried to throw it the year before. It seemed wiser to ignore the whole question and let matters stand *in statu quo*.

But apparently the mood of the church was developing in such a way that that attempted solution to the problem would no longer work. At the synod meeting in 1853, the question came up again and this time it had to be dealt with. Toward the close of the session the following resolution was introduced from the floor. Unfortunately the record does not state the name of the proposer.

Resolved, that a committee of ten be appointed to take into consideration the whole subject of the Liturgy of our Church and report such modifications as they may deem proper to the next General Synod; provided, however, that no alterations shall be made in the doctrinal sentiments contained in the forms now in use in the Church.

The resolution was hotly debated and a division of the house was called for. It carried by a vote of sixty to twenty-four. A look at the names found in both the affirmative and negative columns does not seem to reveal any consistent pattern in the voting, with one exception.

That exception, however, is worthy of comment, casting, as it does, the shadow of things to come. The synod of 1853 was the first to which the Classis of Holland, representing the new Dutch immigrants in the Midwest, had been able to send a delegate, even though they had been affiliated with the Reformed Church in America since 1850. The single delegate was Albertus Van Raalte, the leader of the Michigan colony. His was one of twenty-four negative votes cast when the question of liturgical revision was raised. We shall defer to a later time a consideration of the liturgical attitudes and practices of the immigrant churches of 1847, because it was not until later that these really became determinative. But at this early date it is significant to note where the leader of the Michigan churches stood.

Before beginning the story of the results of the work of the committee appointed in 1853, we may pause briefly to consider some of the factors which made the issue an important one at that time. Trends like these are always impossible things to document but are rather caught in the impressions of prevailing moods.

First of all there was the vexing question of the strained relations between the Dutch and the German Reformed churches, a question which came to a head at this very synod of 1853. Little more than a difference in language had kept the two churches apart in 1792, and for many years after that date the relationship between them had been very close. Indeed there was a body called the "Triennial Convention" which, as its name suggests, met every three years to discuss matters of mutual interest and concern between the two churches. Though the convention had no power, it provided a place for fellowship as well as the discussion of mutual concerns which the delegates were then able to report back to their respective synods.

Even before 1853, however, theological developments within the German church, today known as "Mercersburg Theology," had begun to distress some of the Dutch brethren. They had earlier distressed many members of the German church, so much so in fact, that the leader of the anti-Mercersburg movement in that church, failing to obtain a satisfactory response to his complaints, had seceded to the Dutch church with a good portion of his Philadelphia congregation. Once safely in the Dutch fold, Joseph P. Berg continued his attacks on Mercersburg, persuading other Dutch leaders to join him. Naturally, the German church resented such activities on the part of its Dutch cousins, accused them of fishing in troubled waters, and the resulting situation was unhappy to say the least.

By 1853, however, Dr. Berg and his party had persuaded the Dutch synod that it was time to act. A resolution was presented protesting "in the most decided and unequivocal manner...against all those sentiments of a Romanizing character and tendency which are technically known as 'Mercersburg theology.'" The resolution, which was carried, further directed that any and all fraternal relationships with the German church be discontinued. The mere passage of such a resolution did not mean that the entire Dutch church was in agreement with it. There remained a strong undercurrent of sympathy with the German church on the part of a number of leaders who did not think that Mercersburg was quite so black as painted. This was especially true in the sphere of influence of Union College in Schenectady, which traditionally tended to oppose the directions taken by New Brunswick. We also tend to forget what a large percentage of Reformed Church in America at this time was German in background, especially in the Mohawk and Schoharie valleys. Long associations such as these were not easily disturbed by Dr. Berg's summons to a theological crusade.

It is significant to notice, however, that just a year before this in 1852, the German synod had appointed a committee to revise its liturgy and that this committee was made up almost entirely of Mercersburg sympathizers. The mere existence of such a committee probably posed something of a threat to some of the leadership of the Dutch church. It made them realize that they could no longer ignore the question in their own Zion but had better get on with it before their admitted liturgical chaos was confronted with a full-blown Mercersburg liturgy which, given the ethnic composition of the Dutch church, was bound to be influential. At any rate, it is difficult to believe that it was only coincidence that led the Dutch to begin their liturgical project just a year after the Germans had started theirs.

A second factor which was always lurking in the background in this era was the simple existence of the Episcopal church. In the mid-nineteenth century, the principal strength of the Dutch church was in the Hudson Valley from New York to Albany and on Long Island. In this same area the seepage from the Reformed church into the Episcopal church was considerable. Over in the New Jersey garden of the Dutch church, the situation was less acute, but in the New York area the continued loss was a source of worry. Among the old Dutch families living in this same area today, members of the Episcopal church outnumber by far those of the Reformed Church in America.

To be sure, this seepage was something that had begun much earlier, as a direct result of the refusal of the Reformed church in the eighteenth century to come to terms with the English language. But the distressing fact was that even after the church had Americanized itself, the exodus still continued. Family after family, which by long tradition had belonged to the Reformed church, became Episcopalian. In fact, in the city of New York, at least one Episcopal church was literally built on the bones of the Reformed church.

Today we recognize that sociological and economic factors were deeply involved in this denominational change. But in 1850 men did not think of religion in those categories. For them the real reason had to be something in the life of the church and to many that something had to be liturgical. They would have been impressed by the testimony of a man like George Templeton Strong, who had come from a long Reformed church background, but became one of the leading laymen in the Episcopal church in New York. Strong said that he much preferred the simple decencies of the Anglican Prayer Book to the longwinded, extemporaneous effusions of the Dutch Reformed pulpit. How many others there were like Strong we do not know. But evidently there were enough to convince a number of leaders in the Reformed church that something had to be done.

There were at least two other factors which were in the air at this time. This was the Gothic age, a time when such things as the liturgy had a special fascination because it represented a reaction against an era of which the world was tired. Georgian meeting-houses with their clear glass and spare decor were out; Gothic lines, stained glass, dark colors, and heavy decorations were in. An architectural historian might find it interesting to assemble a collection of pictures of church buildings erected by the Reformed church in its major centers after 1850. Almost without exception they would be imitation Gothic or imitation Renaissance.

Even when no new building was possible, old buildings were radically altered in a romantic direction. The white pews were stained dark, the clear glass replaced by stained glass. The building which Potter designed for the First Church in Schenectady in this era, or the one designed by Renwick for the South Church in New York, each replacing a typical early American ediface, illustrate the point. The traditional Reformed stricture against pictorial art held in each. The windows and the decoration contain nothing but symbols. But with this exception, these buildings are good specimens of the Romantic Revival, the attempt to rebuild the Middle Ages in nineteenth-century America.

But the very erection of such a building will greatly influence what will go on inside it. The simple clerical monologue which had seemed an appropriate liturgy in the old building does not seem right in the new one. Vestments, organs, choirs now have a new necessity. In this era a Reformed church minister can write about "the notes of the organ sounding through the shadowy arches," a sentence which Dr. Livingston would have found it almost impossible to understand. A close analysis of that vote of sixty to twenty-four could reveal that it was the Gothic men in the growing cities versus the meeting-house men in the small towns and rural areas.

Finally, however, we must face the fact that by 1853 men in the Reformed church were tired of liturgical chaos (and that not for the last time in our history). Unfortunately for the historian, weekly bulletins were not printed at this time, so we have no record of its peculiar experiments as another generation will have of ours. But from the continual complaining about them, liturgical experiments must have been numerous. Even the sacred liturgies for baptism and the Lord's Supper were not exempt. I have in my library the copy of a liturgy which belonged to a minister at this time. In it are penciled in his omissions and additions and they are numerous. The

Gothic men improved in one direction; the meeting-house men in another. Many felt that it was past time for the church to seek some kind of uniformity in the whole liturgical question.

After such a build-up, the results achieved as a result of the action of 1853 may seem feeble. In fact, Edward T. Corwin, the standard historian of the Reformed church, rather contemptuously dismisses them by saying that "the only result was the correction of a single grammatical error." Though technically correct, Corwin is badly mistaken in his evaluation of the matter. Though less did happen than might have been hoped for, a summary of the next five years of discussion and study will reveal that they were by no means a waste of time.

The committee appointed in 1853 took its task seriously. It met seven times during the year with almost full attendance and was able to present a very full report to the synod of 1854. In fact, copies of a proposed liturgy were circulated among the delegates to synod, although I have never been able to locate one of them. The committee reported that they had prepared a full series of prayers for Sunday morning worship, "drawn in large measure from the existing forms, but adapted to the prevailing usage among us." It also reported a recommendation to reverse the position of the prayers in the service so that the longer prayer would come before the sermon and the shorter one after it. The form for the Lord's Supper had been abridged and some of its parts transposed.

The immediate determination of the question was that the revision was recommitted to the same committee for further work in the light of the remarks and criticisms that had been made during the discussion on the floor of the synod.

The committee's report to the synod of 1853 begins with some fairly strong language.

> We cannot forget, and would not if we could, that we are strictly and truly a liturgical church. The Reformed Church of Holland, with which our own is identified, recognizing certain great principles of doctrine and order as unmistakably and immovably established, very early adopted a Formulary, containing a clear and comprehensive expression of them. In the same spirit has our own church acted and thus, in her constitution, has this great fact been conspicuously set forth, and all who unite under her banner are solemnly bound practically to recognize it.

The report went on to state that the committee had met a number of times during the year, revising its own revision, as synod had directed. In submitting it again to the synod, it politely stated that it had done all it could do and did not want the subject recommitted to it again.

Most of the discussion seems to have centered in the form for the Lord's Supper. At the end of the day the proposed revision was turned over to a special committee of five persons, who were given the impossible task of studying it over night and reporting their findings the next morning. Even though this special committee gave its approval, the discussion was so prolonged that further consideration was postponed to a special session of synod to be held in October. But when the October meeting came, the synod had bigger fish to fry and all that happened was that everyone was asked to give the question further study for discussion in 1856.

By 1856 the committee had begun to grow weary. At least this is what I hear in the opening lines of its report.

> The Committee appointed by the General Synod of 1853 to revise the liturgy of the church beg leave to submit a final report of their labors. This Committee has now been in existence for a period of three years. They have held in all fourteen meetings and have bestowed upon their work all the care and diligence which its importance demanded. Having submitted to two previous Synods partial reports of the progress of their labors, and deriving, so far as they were able, both from Synodical action and from private conferences with individuals, a knowledge of what seemed most necessary to be done toward perfecting the Liturgy of the Church and adapting it to our present denominational necessities, the Committee have assiduously aimed to incorporate into the revision the understood wishes of the Church.

Synod apparently appreciated the committee's weariness. It decided to send down the proposed alterations in the forms for baptism and the Lord's Supper to the classes for their approval and to postpone discussion of the rest of the question till 1857.

The results of the voting, however, were disappointing. Of the thirty classes, five approved, eight disapproved, while seventeen abstained from voting. Ordinarily that would have ended the matter. But the synod was not content to let it rest there. It authorized the publication and use of the committee's report as a provisional liturgy for an indeterminate period, after which the question should be taken up again. In the meantime it requested the various classes to submit their suggestions for changes in the sacramental forms.

The action, however, was precipitate. At a special session in October, synod rescinded its action in June as being unconstitutional and ordered that the book which had been published should be voted on by 1858. Once again a majority of the classes took no action and synod of 1858 declared the whole project legally dead. The single exception was the fact that a number of classes had suggested that the phrase in the form for the Lord's Supper, "that He was innocently condemned" should be altered to read "that He, although innocent, was condemned." This alteration was proposed to the classes, received their approval, and was enacted by the synod of 1859.

Despite the technical correctness of Corvin's verdict on the five years from 1853 to 1858, what happened in those five years cannot so easily be dismissed. Even though the synod had to remove its *imprimatur*, a book had been let loose in the church. Copies of it were not recalled but were circulated and used. Not only is the copy which I possess well worn, but it is carefully edited with a number of pencil marks and a few insertions by its owner. It was a book of ninety-six pages, the first liturgical book that the Reformed Church in America had ever possessed. Before this time the liturgical forms had simply been printed as an appendix to the hymnal. In addition to the traditional forms, it contained a small selection of prayers for various occasions and the Nicene and Athanasian creeds. Two features are worthy of special mention. Bucer's adaptation of the litany was included as well as a table of scripture lessons for morning and evening services every Sunday. The committee claimed that it had taken this lectionary from an old Holland Bible, but nothing more than that is known about its source. No attention was paid to the Christian year. For example, in the morning table the first two lessons are from Genesis 1 and John 1, while in the evening they are taken from Isaiah 1 and Acts 2. Evidently, the intention of the lectionary is to present a sampling of the historical books of the Old Testament and the gospels in the morning and of the prophets and the other books of the New Testament in the evening.

This provisional liturgy of 1857 also contained an Order for Public Worship, the first in our history. Hymns are not mentioned; presumably they were to be inserted as local custom demanded. The service began with an invocation and salutation, followed by the reading of the Law. It was suggested that after the Law a brief scriptural response could be chanted. Then came the reading of the scripture lessons, followed by the long prayer before the sermon, the sermon, a brief concluding prayer, and the benediction.

Several comments about this order of worship are necessary because, whether or not synod approved it, it clearly represented the committee's effort to set down and regularize what was current practice in many Reformed church congregations at the time. Notice the use of a prayer of invocation at the beginning. None of the historic Reformed liturgies was aware of such a practice. In fact, an opening prayer beseeching God to be present with his worshiping people would probably have seemed to our Reformed ancestors to be totally unnecessary, since God had promised to be present and it was on the basis of that promise that they assembled. "Our help is in the Name of the Lord who made heaven and earth" indicated a very different attitude from, "O Father of our Lord Jesus Christ, graciously regard us thine unworthy servants." Research on the origin of our widespread use of the prayer of invocation is indicated, but it seems likely that the origin was pietistic and its general use in the Reformed church the influence of Presbyterian and Congregational neighbors.

What followed, however, indicated the influence of Anglicanism. While the use was permissive, the suggestion that a scriptural chant would follow the reading of the Law was certainly a look in the direction of the prayer book. Even more strongly so was the suggested use of two scripture lessons in the service, one from each Testament. In the Reformed churches in Europe, two lessons were sometimes used, but always from the epistles and gospels. The use of Old and New Testament lessons was entirely taken from the Anglican services of morning and evening prayer to which our revisors were evidently anxious to pay some attention.

But the most Anglican feature of the revision, the effects of which are still with us today, was the reversal of the order of prayers. In the classic Reformed liturgies, the only prayers before the sermon are those of confession and for a right understanding of the Word, and they are relatively brief. The longer prayer of thanksgiving and intercession always followed the sermon. This arrangement was still indicated in our first liturgy of 1792. But the Anglican service of Morning (or Evening) Prayer has a different rationale. As originally conceived, these were daily offices, simple services of psalms, lessons, and prayers. When these services came to be used as the principal acts of worship on Sunday, they had to be supplemented with a sermon and some closing devotions. Thus, quite by accident, in Anglican usage the prayers of thanksgiving and intercession came before the sermon. In our 1857 liturgy this order of things was picked up and has been pretty well standard ever since. Indeed when the liturgy of 1967, a century later, sought to restore the classic Reformed order, placing the major prayers after the sermon, it ran into considerable resistance, especially from conservatives who, though they little realized it, were at this point defending the Anglican prayer book against historic Calvinistic liturgies! The only relic of earlier days in this matter in the 1857 book was the retention of the Lord's Prayer at the end of the service.

Another permanent result of Anglican imitation may be noticed. Because morning or evening prayer were independent offices to which a sermon had been attached, the sermon did not, as in Calvin's usage, directly follow the reading of the scripture, but was separated from it by a number of liturgical items. For the first time in Reformed church history, this unhappy arrangement was sanctioned by the liturgy of 1857. Again, we can see that whether the liturgy in question was approved or not, it certainly set the pace, because this separation of sermon from scripture is the order that almost all of us remember from our youth.

A student of this order for public worship will be struck by the omission of any reference to the offering. We can only make an educated guess as to the reason for this, but probably even in 1857 there was no offering. The support of the local congregation was doubtless raised by pew rents, while the deacons stood at the door after the service to receive gifts for benevolent purposes. This was true, incidentally, in all the older denominations of the time. Only despised groups like the Methodists and the Baptists in this era sought to support the local congregation by voluntary free-will offerings.

Except for a single phrase, the Lord's Supper remained unchanged. However, many private revisions of it there were in use. It is interesting to note that the Reformed church had not yet yielded to the common Congregational and Presbyterian practice of serving the elements in the pews, but was still preserving its own tradition of gathering around the Table. In our friend Bethune's *Lectures on the Heidelberg Catechism* the following words occur:

> Our church…sets before the people a table crowned with the holy elements and invites the true disciples of Christ to separate themselves from the world and gather themselves together about the table that they may sit together as a family of God….
>
> The table should be as large as possible, and no other seats occupied, but when it is filled. The aged or infirm may very well be allowed to keep their previous places for the gospel requires no painful ordinances; but others have no such excuse and ought not to lose any benefit of the instructive figure. If the table be not large enough for all, those who cannot find places should at least change to others that they in outward act as well as in thought go to the holy table.

Incidentally, it is interesting to find Dr. Bethune in the same lecture stoutly defending the use of wine in the Supper. It indicates how early that tradition came to be questioned and ultimately changed.

More evidence could be cited, but this should be enough to indicate that the provisional liturgy of 1857 accomplished far more than the technical achievement of one grammatical correction. It established entire patterns which became intimately woven into the life and worship of our church, for better or for worse, and, though never authorized, gives us some clear indication of the direction in which things were moving.

But most significant of all is the fact that it was not too long before the question came up again; in fact, it was just ten years. In the minutes of the synod of 1868 under the lemma, "Customs and Usages," we find the following:

> Resolved, that a committee be appointed to revise our Liturgy so that it may more fully meet the wants of the church. Such committee to report to General Synod at its next session and to have power to print their report, provided it can be done without expense to Synod.

Many members of the Reformed church must have thought, "Here we go again." But the fact is that we had never stopped going. The ferment of the earlier discussion had continued during the decade. In fact, in Sage Library there are several private revisions of the liturgy printed during this era, one an edition containing musical responses at various points in the service, the other a curious combination of our liturgy and the Episcopal prayer book. The question had be no means been resolved by the action (or lack of it) ten years earlier.

There was obviously one person who felt that he did not want to get back on the merry-go-round. The Rev. Dr. Elbert S. Porter had been secretary of the previous committee, and synod appointed him convener of the new committee appointed in 1868. In 1869 the committee simply reported progress, but in 1870 the only report was a request from Dr. Porter to be relieved of any further duty. Obviously one liturgical chairmanship in a lifetime was enough! Synod accepted Dr. Porter's request and appointed in his place the Rev. Dr. Mancius Smedes Hutton, minister of the Washington Square Church in New York. It was therefore really 1871 before the committee appointed in 1868 got off the ground and made its first report.

That report, which was probably largely the work of Dr. Hutton, represents a kind of landmark in our liturgical history. It shows what the leadership of the eastern church felt about the question and clearly indicates the direction in which they wished to move. It also shows a good deal of historical knowledge, which in that era was not frequent. It is too long to quote in its entirety, but we can summarize it and offer some comments by the way.

Dr. Hutton's first point was that the great lack in contemporary Reformed worship was its lack of congregational participation; it had too much the character of a monologue. Here is his happier way of putting it.

> We consider it desirable that it be made more obvious not merely that the gospel minister is not by virtue of his office a priest, but that the people themselves are a royal priesthood with all the power and privilege of prayer. It is also supposed that if the people take a more active part in the worship of the Sanctuary, a happy influence will be exerted...by enlisting their personal interest in the services.

The report went on to state that if the Reformed church were to remain aloof from reunion with the Presbyterian family of churches, it must make the marks which distinguished it more pronounced and prominent. One of these was:

> our historical position as that of a Reformed Presbyterian and Liturgical Church, neither falling into the formality of episcopacy or the baldness of Puritanism.

The committee therefore saw its task in this light.

> ...if our grand and ancient liturgy can be placed in a more practical
> and attractive form, a more perfect freedom will be given to those
> who desire to make this feature more prominent than it now is.

Thirdly, Dr. Hutton commented that we enjoyed a great advantage in this task since our liturgical prototype is the Strasbourg liturgy of Calvin. Dr. Hutton went on to claim that the Dutch liturgy was simply an adaptation of Calvin's Strasbourg service, which, as we have seen earlier, was hardly the case. But his point was still valid. In the task of restoring the Reformed Church in America to its position of a liturgical church, the committee was not indulging in innovation but simply returning the church to its own best traditions.

It is necessary to spend a few moments examining the context in which this report was made. Students of American church history will know that in 1867 the two principal branches of northern Presbyterianism, Old and New School, had reunited. In the ensuing years there began to be mounting pressure for the Reformed Church in America to become part of this re-united Presbyterian church. Although the question did not come to a head until 1874 (when it was defeated by a vote of 58 to 52), it was a lively topic of discussion from 1869 on.

Whatever else it accomplished, it forced the Reformed Church to do some serious thinking about its future role in the Presbyterian family of churches. If the Reformed church was staying out, it should have reasons for staying out, and to many people the liturgical reason seemed an attractive possibility. Some of them, like Dr. Hutton, were evidently sincere. The sincerity of others was apparently questionable. Writing in 1876, after the question had been decided in the negative, Dr. Chester Hartranft of New Brunswick pulled no punches.

> Why do we continue to publish a liturgy, with its formal prayers, its
> confession of sins, its litany, its creeds, as well as its orders, if the
> tyranny of the free spirit virtually allows no option whatever as to
> its use, and if every form which the constitution does not compel
> us to use be considered empty of spirit?
>
> It seems very childish for the General Synod to appoint
> committees now and then to undertake the severe task of

revision…only that the ministry and the people may remand it to as complete oblivion as its predecessor. Possibly the Synod commands so apparent superfluous an exercise in order to show out of what miserable gelatinous masses we have been evolved, how magnificent our development has been out of such crude forms into the elegent subjectivities of our extempore prayers and confessions; to afford a sort of evidence to the world of how little there is in our present appearance that would indicate even a remote connection between our present hoof and our then five-toed foot, and to reveal the protoplasms out of which we have attained our plastic way of dealing with the traditions.

Dr. Hutton's report and Dr. Hartranft's rather biting comments are separated by five years. But both are cited because they belong in the same era and the same struggle. The leadership of the church had decided that if there was to be a Reformed Church in America distinct from other Presbyterian churches, the liturgy had to be played out to the full as one of the principal marks of distinction. Dr. Hartranft's satirical remarks give some indication of the difficulties which were going to be involved in bringing the Reformed church to this view of itself. But here, as men generally saw it in the 1870s, was the choice. Either join the Presbyterian church or else work out a position which will give a distinct place in the Reformed and Presbyterian family of churches.

The results of this rather clear challenge will be examined in the next chapter. But to complete this part of the story, we need a few comments about an aspect of our liturgical history which to this point has been neglected — our hymnody.

The English liturgy first used in New York in 1764 also contained the 150 psalms, translated into English and set for the most part to the traditional Dutch or Genevan tunes. After the American Revolution, however, tunes like these rapidly lost their popularity. Desiring to demonstrate its Americanism, the Dutch church wanted to sing the same tunes as its Presbyterian and Congregational neighbors. As early as 1787 Dr. Livingston was appointed chairman of a committee to prepare an English psalm book.

In 1788 the committee reported that it was planning a mosaic of psalms using the version of the New York Church, the metrical psalter of Tate and Brady, and the psalm paraphrases of Isaac Watts. A further recommendation of the committee was that the new book should contain a supplement of some "well- composed spiritual hymns." So far as can be determined, this abandonment of the historic Reformed principle of using only the psalter in worship was carried without a single dissenting vote. Quite probably ours must have been one of the first Reformed churches in Christendom to allow the use of hymns in public worship. By 1790 the collection had been published and was beginning to be in general use. In addition to the 150 psalms it contained a supplement of 100 hymns, fifty-two on the Lord's Days of the catechism, the remainder on the sacraments or miscellaneous subjects.

By 1812 a need for revision began to be felt, and synod asked Dr. Livingston again to serve as chairman of the committee. The revision which was completed by 1814, left the 150 psalms unchanged, but added 173 hymns. The 100 hymns of the previous collection remained unchanged even as to their numbering. The new 173 hymns were simply added as a supplemental collection to the earlier one. It may be noted in passing that the publication and sale of the book was entrusted to private printers with the understanding that General Synod was to receive six cents for every copy published, these royalties to be used to support needy students in the seminary. This process of revision by accumulation, as it might be called, received a further assist in 1831 when by synodical action what was called "the second book of hymns" was added. This was another collection of 150 hymns, which was simply tacked on to the previous collection of 273 and indeed, for those who chose, could be obtained in a separate volume. The psalm and hymnbook of the Reformed church was now in three layers, the original 150 psalms and 100 hymns, the additional supplement of 173 hymns, and the second book of 150 hymns. The numberings never changed from 1787; they were simply added to. It was an interesting solution to a continuing problem. New hymns could always be added at the open end, so to speak, and none of the old favorites were lost.

By 1846 the question was up again. A committee appointed at the previous synod recommended the addition of 350 more hymns. Acknowledging that this would make a very large book, some 1,100 hymns and psalms in all, the committee also pointed out that since the Reformed church permitted no congregation to use any but the authorized book, it was necessary to produce a book large enough to allow for a fairly wide variation in taste. The committee did, however, feel that adding a supplement to a supplement to a supplement would produce a book in which it would be difficult to find things, since hymns on the same subject would be found in different supplements. Accordingly the committee requested permission to rearrange all of the psalms and hymns by subjects. The book that appeared in 1848, therefore, contained the entire collections of 1787, 1814, and 1831, as well as the 350 hymns, but now arranged in a fairly workable table of contents.

If the synod believed, however, that it had solved the problem, it was in for some surprises. In fact by endorsing so large and unwieldy a volume, it was opening the way for that hymnological chaos from which, more than a century later, we still suffer. In 1858, for example, a "Book of Selections" was authorized as a shorter version of the larger hymnal adopted a decade earlier. But the real break in the dyke came four years later in 1862. The synod's rule was that no hymns could be sung in a Reformed church without the approval of synod. Up to this point that had been taken to mean that no hymnbook could be used without synod's approval. But in 1862 a new interpretation was tried. The sponsors of the "Fulton Street Hymn Book" approached synod for approval, contending that of the 326 hymns in their collection, 304 had already been approved, since they appeared in previous books authorized by the synod. All that was required, therefore, was synodical approval for the remaining twenty-two hymns and, so the sponsors believed, theirs could become an authorized book.

The synod took the bait, without quite realizing where this hymn-by-hymn approval could lead. They soon began to discover. In 1866 the Board of Publication brought out an edition of the authorized hymnal which was entitled, the *Book of Praise*. But just two years later in 1868, no fewer than three hymnbooks were presented to the synod, each one claiming approval on the hymn-by-hymn basis. One of these was a collection which the South Classis of Long Island proposed to publish under its own masthead, probably the only hymnbook which was ever prepared by a classis.

Actually the classis had not really worked very hard at the task. Just the year before the Church on the Heights in Brooklyn had called to its pulpit the Rev. Zachary Eddy, a New Englander who had already served in the Cumberland Presbyterian, the Presbyterian, and the Congregational ministries before he entered the Reformed church in 1867. At the first classis meeting which he attended, Dr. Eddy heard complaints about the official hymnal of his newfound home. It just so happened that hymns were his hobby, and he had a proposed collection of hymns on which he had been working for a number of years. It was this collection that the classis was now asking synod for permission to publish.

None of this is meant to be disrepectful to the Rev. Eddy, for he knew his business when it came to hymns. The synodical committee appointed to inspect his collection, along with the other two, was obviously impressed by its merits and also saw the chance to end the confusion and dissatisfaction which had been growing ever since 1848.

In their report, therefore, they recommended that synod accept Dr. Eddy's collection, as proposed by the South Classis of Long Island. It is just as well that the principle of accumulation was abandoned at this point, since the Eddy collection contained 600 hymns never before approved by synod. If, following their former custom, these had been added to the existing collection, the result would doubtless have been the most voluminous hymnal in Christendom. But only some 350 hymns of the former book were retained and the rest were consigned to oblivion.

The new book was presented to the church in 1869 under the title, *Hymns of the Church*. In reporting its publication, the committee in charge acknowledged that it had used some few hymns beyond those which had already received the *imprimatur* of synod. In some cases this had been the result of publication necessities, but the committee added slyly that a few had been inserted at the special request of brethren or were written specially for this work (by whom is not stated). Synod did not seem to mind, and the work was enthusiastically approved. At last, thanks to the fortuitous arrival of Dr. Eddy in the South Classis of Long Island, the Reformed church had a hymnal which made its "poetical liturgy" second to none.

That claim was not exaggerated. It was an excellent book and one which was used by many other denominations in preference to their own. Its use continued for a long time in our communion; in the North Church in Newark, New Jersey, for example, it was in the pews until 1906. It was certainly the best hymnal the Reformed church had ever produced and, unfortunately, the last. As such it deserves a brief look.

For one thing it was the first Reformed church hymnal to be printed with music. That is not so strange as it may at first sound. For long years the custom was to print only the words in a hymnal, indicating their meters. The tunes to which they were fitted were the business of the precentor or, where there was one, the organist. The early psalter published for the New York Church did contain the melody line, but that was a European custom which was dropped when the church published its first hymnal in 1792. It was also the custom for singing masters to publish books of tunes from which the musical leader could make his selections. While these contained many standard melodies, they also contained compositions by the singing teacher, who thus was able to introduce his own work to the public. Many of our celebrated hymn tunes of today came into use in this way. But as organs and choirs became more prevalent and congregations became more sophisticated musically, the system was gradually abandoned in favor of the one which we know today, that of printing melody and accompaniment as well as the words. We were among the last, if not the last, major church in America to make the change. Not only did the editors of the 1869 hymnal print music as well as words, they secured a musical editor in the person of Dr. Uzziah Burnap, one of the leading church musicians of the time.

Another marked change was the dropping of the psalms as a separate section. The 1869 hymnal still contained a number of metrical psalms or psalm paraphrases, though by no means the entire psalter. While these were clearly indicated, they no longer formed a separate section but were placed under whatever section their content indicated. Thus, for example, Psalm 121 occurs under the section "God the Father Almighty"; seventy-two under "Missions," etc. It is debatable whether this development was a blessing or a curse; certainly it marked the beginning of the end of our history as a psalm-singing church. The arrangement of the book tried to follow the order of the Creed. The first section is entitled, "The Trinity," followed by a second, "God the Father Almighty, Maker of Heaven and Earth." The section, "Jesus Christ our Lord," is broken into subsections beginning with "His Advent" and continuing through "Ascension," "Glory," and "Intercession." After the hymns based on the articles of the Creed there follow a few miscellaneous sections, and the book concludes with a surprisingly large number of chants and responses, including quite a few prose psalms pointed for chanting.

Looking through the list of authors, one finds most of the standard hymn-writers, with Watts, Wesley, and Montgomery leading the list. What is surprising is to discover a large number of mediaeval Latin hymns, for the most part in excellent English translations. Here, for example, is a stanza or two from the great Latin eucharistic hymn, *Ad regnias Agni*.

1. At the Lamb's high feast we sing/praise to our victorious King,/
Who hath washed us in that tide/flowing from his pierced side.

2. Praise we Him whose love divine/gives his sacred blood for wine,/
Gives his body for the feast,/Christ the Victim, Christ the Priest.

The theology indicates that somebody had been reading his Calvin rather
than his Zwingli. In all cases the translator of these Latin hymns chooses to
remain anonymous, but there is good reason to think it was a member of the
synod's committee, Dr. Alexander Ramsay Thompson, then minister of the
21st Street Church in New York, well known for his gifted translations of
Greek and Latin hymns.

A final feature worth mentioning is the inclusion of a fair number of
hymns by Reformed church ministers. Several are by Dr. Eddy himself, as
we might expect. But his is by no means the only name represented. While
these Reformed church compositions are not great hymnody, they are
certainly as good if not better than many of the things sung in the Reformed
church today. Here is an example, a few stanzas of a hymn written by Dr.
Harvey Ganse, minister of the Northwest Church in New York.

1. Lord, I know thy grace is nigh me,/though thyself I cannot see;/
Jesus, Master, pass not by me;/Son of David, pity me.

2. While I sit in weary blindness,/longing for the blessed light,/
Many taste thy loving-kindness;/"Lord, I would receive my sight."

3. I would see thee and adore thee,/ and thy word the power can give;/
Hear the sightless soul implore thee,/let me see thy face and live.

It is too bad that our own tradition of hymnwriters has now entirely been
lost, except for Dr. Wortman's hymn written for the centennial of New
Brunswick Seminary, "God of the Prophets." Perhaps someone could
provide us with a monograph on "Hymn-Writers of the Reformed Church
in America." They were not great, but then, few hymnwriters are. But they
represent a side of our tradition too little known and certainly too little
valued.

The hymnal of 1869 was a volume of which the church could be and was
proud. Dr. Hutton's manifesto indicated the desire of his committee to
provide the church with a companion liturgy, which would give the church

leadership in this field, as it now had it in the field of hymnody. His successes and his failures must be our next topic for investigation.

Lecture III

After our long digression of yesterday afternoon, let me begin this morning by reminding you of the things Dr. Hutton, in his report to the synod of 1871, said that his committee hoped to accomplish. It was their aim, he said, to restore the Reformed church to its place as a liturgical church in the Presbyterian family, to make provision for larger congregational participation in public worship, and to use as a guide the liturgical tradition exemplified by Calvin's Strasbourg liturgy.

The committee was ready to report to the synod of 1873 but its report was somewhat handicapped by the fact that the printer had failed to deliver copies of the proposed liturgy in time for the synod's meeting. All that was possible, therefore, was to describe the work and wait for any judgment until copies were available later in the year. This was an unfortunate beginning but synod accepted it and asked the committee to get a copy of the proposed revision to every consistory as soon as practicable.

What is more unfortunate for us is the fact that the minutes of General Synod do not contain a copy of the committee's report. All that we have are abstracts and summaries of it from other places, which leave us with a number of unanswered questions. For example, the reports say that the committee had prepared a highly liturgical form of service, which, after much discussion, it had decided not to present to the synod. What did it look like? Did anybody keep a copy of it? Another report states that the committee suggested that synod consider the possibility of adopting the Episcopal *Book of Common Prayer* as the liturgy of the Reformed church, except for sacramental forms. Was this actually proposed and seriously discussed by the synod? Another account has it that the committee's report included an ample discussion of the history of our form for the Lord's Supper — but whatever history was presented is, of course, lost to us, unless the report is still lying in the bottom of a picnic basket in one of our libraries.

What we can judge, however, is the proposed revision which, though not there in time for synod, was distributed in the church later that year. A handsomely bound volume of 128 pages appearing over the imprint of the

Board of Publication, 34 Vesey Street, New York, its hard covers and gold-edged pages indicate that whoever prepared it for publication thought of it as something more than a pamphlet for study. Suppose now we examine it briefly.

It begins with an order of scripture lessons identical with the one in the liturgy with which we are familiar. The Christian year is divided into three seasons, with Old and New Testament lessons for every Sunday in each season. Furthermore, each season is headed with a rubric enabling one to locate it in terms of the calendar year. In addition to the Sunday lessons, there are also lessons for Christmas, Circumcision, Good Friday, Ascension Day, as well as days of humiliation and thanksgiving, ordinations, etc.

This is quite a different lectionary from the one presented in 1857 from an old Holland Bible, as you may recall. This lectionary quite obviously follows the Christian year and includes the seasons of Advent and Lent, though not mentioned by name. It also takes account of the so-called Dominical Festivals, quoting Post-Acta of the Synod of Dort as warrant for their inclusion. Was this lectionary a creation of the members of the committee or did they borrow it from some other source?

The answer seems to be a little of each. In the last lecture I alluded briefly to the beginning of liturgical renewal within the German Reformed church. After many wrangles, that liturgy won at least a limited approval in 1866. Its opening page contains a Table of Scripture Lessons for all the Sundays in the Church Year. Even a hasty inspection will reveal that with exceptions so minor as to be negligible, this is the source that was used by our committee for its "Order of Scripture Lessons for use in Public Worship on the Lord's Day."

But the borrowing was not quite that simple. The German Reformed original simply lists all the Sundays and festival days from the first Sunday in Advent to the Sunday before Advent with the appropriate lessons opposite. It fully retains the traditional titles of all Sundays, including such names as Epiphany, Septuagesima, etc. It also recognizes the first Sunday after Pentecost as Trinity Sunday and then proceeds to number the Sundays following as "after Trinity."

Dr. Hutton's committee did some rather creative revising of this lectionary. First it broke the year into three parts, the Season of the Advent of our Lord, the Season of the Death and Resurrection of our Lord, and the Season of the Mission of the Holy Comforter, using the three great New Testament feasts of Christmas, Easter, and Pentecost as its pivotal points. Next it removed all names which might frighten Dutch Reformed people into seeing popes under committee reports. The First Sunday after Epiphany becomes the Third Sunday after Christmas, Septuagesima is now the Ninth Sunday before Easter, etc. The words Advent and Lent are never used.

But perhaps most importantly, in the third season the Sundays are numbered after Pentecost and not after Trinity. I think that most liturgical scholars today are agreed that this is the better arrangement, since it is Pentecost that really governs the character of the season and not Trinity, a johnny-come-lately in the Christian year anyway. I wonder whether Dr. Hutton knew that he was adopting a numbering which was used, at that time, only by the church of Rome. I rather suspect he did!

The order for public worship on the Lord's Day morning begins with the by now familiar invocation and the Lord's Prayer. The invocation that is suggested is the well known Collect for Purity from the prayer book, "Almighty God unto whom all hearts are open, all desires known, etc." The service is prefaced with a rubric which directs that the people shall unite audibly in the Lord's Prayer and in the AMEN at the close of every prayer. This is the first time such a direction has appeared in print and was obviously a result of the committee's desire to secure greater congregational participation in worship. Such a rubric, incidentally, still stands in our liturgy before morning worship, though I doubt that more than one in 100 of our people have ever seen it or know it is there.

The service which follows pretty much follows the order prescribed in the provisional liturgy of 1857, which shows how thoroughly that liturgy, approved or not, had become part of the life of the church. The only variation is the inclusion of the responsive salutation, "The Lord be with you. And with thy spirit" as an alternate to the more customary form.

A response is suggested after the reading of the Law and a "suitable chant" is indicated between the Old and New Testament lessons. The principal prayer which comes before the sermon "will ordinarily be free." But Bucer's Litany, first proposed in 1857, is indicated as an alternate with appropriate responses by the people.

"The Thank-Offering of Alms" is placed directly after the sermon. Notice that it is still a benevolent offering. In 1873 as well as in 1857 the support of the local congregation is still by pew rents and, in the case of many churches, land rents. But the benevolent offering has been moved from the church door to a place in the service. Four collects, all from the Anglican prayer book, are suggested as appropriate possibilities for the closing prayer, which is followed by the benediction. The order for evening worship is almost identical save for the omission of the Law and the inclusion of the Creed after the New Testament lesson.

It is not difficult to see in this order of service that even though the committee may not have been serious in proposing the Anglican prayer book as suitable for Reformed church worship, it was greatly indebted to it. The only omission which strikes one as strange, especially in view of the committee's declared knowledge of classical Reformed patterns of worship, is the omission of any prayer of confession and words of assurance. Not only are they there in the prayer book, but they are there in those Calvinistic originals which the committee was anxious to reproduce. The reason for their omission can only be a matter of speculation.

For the Lord's Supper, however, the committee was much more conservative—or appeared to be. The didactic portion was broken into two parts, with the suggestion that the first part be used at the preparatory service. In both parts there were generous abridgements, though the major abridgements suggested were in the preparatory section. For the rest there was no alteration, except for the introduction of a rubric requiring the audible recitation of the Creed by both minister and people. The 103rd Psalm at the close ended with the phrase, "Like as a father pitieth his children," etc. and bracketed all the rest, beginning with "who hath not spared his own Son." Here also we find another rubric directing that the psalm be said responsively. Before this time it had been said by the minister alone or, as is still the case in some of our older congregations, by the entire congregation.

I said a moment ago that the conservatism of the committee regarding the Lord's Supper was more apparent than real. I should now explain that remark. The original American constitution of 1792 strangely enough made no mention of any required use of the liturgy for the celebration of the Supper. The revised constitution of 1833 sought to remedy that omission by including the following article.

> Every Church shall observe such a mode in the administration of the Lord's Supper as shall be judged most conducive to edification; provided, however, after the sermon and usual public prayers are

ended, the form for the administration of the Lord's Supper shall
be read, and a prayer suited to the occasion shall be offered before
the members participate of the ordinance.

At this late date it is difficult to interpret what was meant by this article.
Patently, there is a suitable prayer in the form itself and has been since 1566.
It is possible that the article means that either the prayer contained in the
form or some other may be used. I doubt that, however, because I think it
likely that in 1833 and after, "The Form for the Administration of the Lord's
Supper" meant the entire service. A more likely explanation, I think, is the
supposition that the entire form through the paraphrase of the *Sursum
Corda*, "That we may now be fed with the true heavenly bread," etc., was
read from the pulpit, prayer and all. Remember that there were no
permanent Communion tables in our churches at this time. There were only
the long tables for the congregation set up for these sacramental occasions.
After the form had been completed, the minister came down from the pulpit
to distribute the elements; this is the next thing indicated by the liturgy.

But I dare say that to many, especially in the hey-day of Puritan pietism,
this seemed an abrupt transition. It was at this point in the Presbyterian and
Congregational churches that the minister poured out his soul in some great
devotional urtterance. Yes, a Communion prayer had already been offered
in the pulpit, but a short one, a formal one, a read one. So the custom grew
up of having what amounted to two liturgical prayers, a short liturgical one
from the form in the pulpit and a longer extemporaneous one at the Table,
a custom which by 1833 had become so prevalent that it became
constitutionalized. I have read just enough descriptions of Reformed
Communion services from the era to believe that my explanation is the
correct one.

But correct or not, this is the device by which the committee sprang a real
surprise on the church. Over on page 109 of the proposed revision, tucked
in among such items as prayers for the opening of consistory or at the
meeting of the deacons, the casual reader is suddenly startled to find the
words, "Eucharistic Prayer." The rubric beneath cites the constitutional
article which I have already quoted and then goes on to state, "The following
is submitted as a suitable prayer which may be used in compliance with this
direction."

The suitable prayer that follows is nothing less than a beautifully traditional
canon of the mass, beginning with the historic "it is very meet and right"

continuing through the Sanctus and Benedictus Qui Venit, which are printed in capitals to indicate congregational participation whether sung or said. Then come an epiclesis and oblation, both taken bodily from the prayer book, followed by a thanksgiving for the faithful departed and a declaration of the eschatological hope with which the prayer concludes. I hope you are as surprised as I was when I first ran on to the thing a number of years ago. Evidently someone had decided that it was impossible ever really to revise the form for the Lord's Supper in a genuinely liturgical direction and so thought it best to make an end run around it. Picking up a fairly innocent article in the constitution he uses it as the excuse to introduce a prayer which is as completely catholic in its structure and its concepts as anything in the prayer book or, for that matter, the Mass book.

If only the wretched clerk of synod had published that committee report we might know how the thing happened. Instead we shall have to content ourselves with analyzing its content which is an amazing little story in itself. It begins with a strange little group in England, the Catholic and Apostolic Church, more commonly known as the Irvingites, whose history in itself would require several lectures. In the mid forties this group had published one of the most truly remarkable liturgies in Christendom, the product of much research, more certainly than had ever been done up to that point, into the liturgies of both western catholicism and eastern orthodoxy.

It is a known fact that the revisers of the German Reformed liturgy in this country had a copy of the Catholic and Apostolic work before them and made considerable use of it. But so far as I can see it was not the German Reformed liturgy that our committee had before it in this case. It was rather a volume entitled *Euchologion,* which had been published in Scotland in 1867 by the Church Service Society, an unofficial group dedicated to doing something about the deplorable conditions of worship among Scottish Presbyterians.

A close study of the two prayers indicates that *Euchologion* for the most part represents a rather careful abridgement of the much longer eucharistic prayer in the Catholic and Apostolic liturgy. Let me illustrate. Here is the Catholic and Apostolic original:

> Thou hast ransomed us from eternal death and given us the joyful hope of everlasting life; through Jesus Christ, who, being very and eternal God, dwelling with thee before all time in glory and

blessedness unspeakable, came down from heaven in perfect love, from perfect love, and became very man for our salvation.

This is the Scottish abridgement:

.. hast ransomed us from eternal death and given us the joyful hope of everlasting life, through Jesus Christ Thy Son; who came down from heaven in perfect love, and became man for us men and for our salvation.

Permit me one more illustration of the way in which the Scots cut back the rather expansive model of the Catholic and Apostolic church. The earlier book read as follows:

We bless thee for the giving of the Holy Spirit; for all the sacraments and ordinances of thy church; and for the most blessed communion of all saints in these holy mysteries. We bless thee for the hope of everlasting life and of the glory which shall be brought unto us at the coming and in the kingdom of thy dear Son.

The Scots reduced it to this:

We bless thee for the giving of the Holy Spirit; for the sacraments and ordinances of the church; for the great hope of everlasting life and of an eternal weight of glory.

I realize how difficult it is to make judgments in this kind of thing without being able to see the text. But perhaps these samples are sufficient to indicate that the eucharistic prayer of the Scottish *Euchologion* from the beginning through the sanctus and benedictus qui venit is simply an abridged form of the corresponding prayer in the liturgy of the Catholic and Apostolic church.

The remaining parts of the Scottish prayer, the epiclesis and the oblation, are of different origin. The epiclesis begins in imitation of its Anglican counterpart but then shifts ground to alter the theology. The Anglicans pray that "through the power of the Holy Spirit we may be very partakers of his body and blood with all his benefits," which the Scots have altered to, "That the bread which we break may be to us the communion of the body of Christ and the cup of blessing which we bless the communion of the blood of

Christ." The oblation seems to have no original and was probably the work of the Scottish compilers.

When we look at the Eucharistic prayer presented by Dr. Hutton's committee in 1873, its dependence on the Scottish prayer is obvious. Perhaps even as I was making the few quotations a moment ago, they had a familiar ring in your ears. If you could lay the two prayers side by each, you would see almost instantly the dependence of the one upon the other. In fact it is not improbable that Dr. Hutton or some member of his committee possessed a copy of *Euchologion*. At this time generally there was a great deal of interest in worship in Presbyterian circles, and this early Scottish attempt at reform had probably found its way into many an American library.

The interesting thing is to make close comparisons between *Euchologion* and our proposed liturgy. At the risk of being tedious, I should like to try to do that now. In the first paragraph there are only editorial changes. A phrase or two has been omitted, perhaps in the interest of further abridgement. The phrase "our bounden duty" has been changed to "above all things." Perhaps the only change of any significance is the one which alters the language about the incarnation. Following the Catholic and Apostolic original, the *Euchologion* reads, "Who came down from heaven in perfect love and became man for us men and for our salvation." Speaking with a more theological accent, our version reads, "Who, being very and eternal God, became man for us men and for our salvation."

Paragraph two is identical in both prayers. In paragraph three we have added a phrase. The Scots bless God "for the sacraments and ordinances of the church," while the Reformed add, "For the communion of Christ's body and blood," which is an original addition not copied from any other source.

The paragraph leading up to the sanctus and benedictus is the same. In the Scots original, these two ancient hymns are printed in such a way as to indicate that they were to be said by the minister. In our version the type-face indicates that they are to be said or sung by the congregation. And sure enough, in the new hymnbook of 1869, #963, there is a musical setting waiting for any congregation or choir willing to try!

I have already indicated that the Scots used only part of the Anglican epiclesis, preferring to avoid the phrase, "very partakers of his body and blood." Evidently the Reformed were not afraid of it but used the entire

Anglican prayer and went on to use the Anglican oblation rather than the one the Scots had devised.

The Scottish model ended there, but the Reformed did not. It went on to include one final prayer which I should like to quote to you in its entirety.

> And rejoicing in the communion of thy saints, we bless thy holy name for all thy servants who have departed in the faith and who, having accomplished their warfare, are at rest with thee; beseech thee to enable us so to follow their faith and good example, that we with them may finally be partakers of thy heavenly kingdom — when, made like unto Christ, we shall behold him with unveiled face, rejoicing in his glory, and by him we, with all thy church, holy and unspotted, shall be presented with exceeding joy before the presence of thy glory. Hear us, O heavenly Father, for his sake to whom with thee and the Holy Ghost be glory for ever and ever.

It is interesting to observe that our committee felt the need of adding to their Scottish model a thanksgiving for the departed and a prayer of eschatological hope. If it be asked where they got it, the answer is simple. I shall not bore you with my proofs, though I could easily demonstrate it. They got it by putting together bits and pieces from the eucharistic prayer in the Catholic and Apostolic liturgy. We cannot escape the conclusion that the committee was not only working with the Scottish book, a thing relatively easy to maintain, but also had before it the Catholic and Apostolic liturgy, a thing which it must have been fairly difficult to obtain. If you ask for the sources of this eucharistic prayer (I think even the title is worthy of some notice in our circles) which the committee rather smuggled in, the answer is the liturgy of the Catholic and Apostolic church and its Scottish abridgement in *Euchologion*.

Personally I should give a great deal to know whose work this was, but of course there is no way of telling. Looking down the membership of the committee, I can come up with only two candidates. One is Dr. Hutton himself. As Corwin describes him, "Six feet and four inches in height, robed in cassock, girdle, bands, and gown," he sounds like the kind of person whose interests might well run in a liturgical direction, although none of his few publications were on this subject. The other prospect is Dr. John Bodine Thompson, although during the two years from 1871-1873 he was serving a church in Italy. During his previous pastorate in the First Church in

Tarrytown, however, he had made a number of liturgical experiments, some of which may still be seen in print. While he could not have met with the committee while it was preparing its revision, he may have left behind materials of his own compiling of which the committee made use.

It may seem to you that I have spent an inordinate amount of time on a single prayer. My reason is that this single prayer is terribly important. It was somebody's attempt to put Reformed liturgy into the mainstream of catholic liturgical tradition. Did you notice how the committee deliberately stressed by its emendations that the Sacrament is the communion of Christ's body and blood. Since this happened twice, once through the addition of a phrase and once by using the Anglican rather than the Scottish original, I have to think it was deliberate. And I have to think it was an attempt to offset the rather Zwinglian stance taken by our didactic section which the committee knew it could not attack directly.

But more importantly, this back door method succeeded. Despite all the vissicitudes through which the proposed revision had to go, this prayer stuck. In fact, in the later revision of 1906 it was actually moved over, in part, to the abridged form itself. It still lasted in the first revisions of the present committee and finally succumbed only last year in response to the church's demand for greater brevity. Personally, I rather mourn its passing.

But it is time to return to the main thread of the story. When synod met in 1874, it had already had this proposed liturgy before it for study for some months. The record tells us that there was a full discussion of the whole subject but again fails to tell us what was said or by whom. The motion which was finally put was so dangerously like the one put about the former attempt at revision that one wonders that there was the courage to try it again. It reads as follows.

> Resolved, that this Synod approve of so much of the Liturgy
> reported by the Committee as is not inconsistent with or forbidden
> by the Constitution and give permission to use the same, this
> resolution not sanctioning any change in the baptismal form or the
> form for the Administration of the Lord's Supper.

The intent of the motion, I think, was clear. With the exception of the two sacramental forms in which all of the judicious bracketing which the committee had done was to be discarded, the rest of the liturgy was approved. Most of it was not of constitutional authority anyway and therefore required no classical vote.

I think we must also admit, however, that it was a slovenly motion. By its very language it raised the possibility that some of the approved material might be inconsistent with or forbidden by the constitution, which was a pretty silly thing to do. Additionally, synod was putting its seal of approval on minor modifications in the ordination forms which were constitutional and therefore should have been sent down to the classes.

But it was not the first foolish motion a General Synod has made, nor will it be the last. At least the majority of brethren present thought it would do and passed it by a vote of eighty-two to forty-one. Since the *ayes* and *nays* were recorded, we can have a glance at the voting pattern. Middlewestern representation at the synod was from five classes, Michigan, Illinois, Holland, Wisconsin, and Grand River. Michigan and Illinois were entirely composed of the few English-speaking churches which the Reformed church had been able to start across the Alleghanies, although the Pella churches were attached to Illinois. Holland, Wisconsin, and Grand River were entirely composed of Dutch churches from the second immigration. In the voting, the delegates from Michigan and Illinois, the English classes, voted entirely in the affirmative, while those from Holland and Wisconsin, the Dutch classes, voted entirely in the negative. Lest this be interpreted as the beginning of the east-west tension, however, I hasten to add that the three delegates from Grand River, also a Dutch classis, voted solidly in the affirmative. Since Holland and Wisconsin had only four delegates between them, their voting was not very influential anyway. The revision of the liturgy in 1874 was still a question for the eastern church to decide.

The Classis of New York spotted the rather wobbly character of the action of this synod and presented the synod of 1875 with a lengthy overture demanding that the action of the previous year be rescinded. The New York overture took a ground which synod accepted, though its implications seem rather startling. It argued that although many liturgical items were not mandatory but given only as specimens, even as specimens they had constitutional authority and therefore could not be altered or introduced except as amendments to the constitution. Since the book of 1873 had not only altered several specimen forms but introduced a number of new ones such as public reception of members, laying of cornerstones, etc., all of these, according to the classis, had to be sent down as amendments to the constitution.

Synod accepted this logic, and the whole book was sent down to the classes with the omission of any changes in the two sacramental forms. Voting was slow; it was not until 1878 that all classes were heard from with the necessary two-thirds majority. For some reason or other the Board of Publication took its time with the publishing task, and it was not until 1882 that synod was informed that the book was now available.

But the report contains one curious feature. The report to the synod of 1882 announces the availability of the revised liturgy with appended psalms for responsive reading. Perhaps you do not find the announcement so startling. But it raises the question; who authorized this appendix? After the fussy way in which the Classis of New York persuaded the synod that nothing, but nothing, should be included in the liturgy even as a suggestion, without the two-thirds approval of classes, it is rather surprising to find so important an addition to Reformed church worship as a responsive psalter appearing without so much as a syllable of synodical action, let alone classical approval, to support it. But there it is, obviously a case of liturgical reform by board action and nothing else. There have been others like it, but this is the best example I know and should be of interest to anyone studying the rise of the influence of boards in the life of the Reformed church. Not only is the responsive version of the psalter appended to the book, but in the order of worship the following rubric has been inserted without so much as anybody's by your leave.

If desired, one of the Lessons may consist of a portion from the Psalms, read responsively by the Minister and People.

A whole field of inquiry has been opened up here about which something needs to be said. Even a slight acquaintance with the Reformed churches in Europe will tell you that the responsive reading of the psalter is a custom of which they have never heard. To the Reformed European, be he Dutch, French, German, Swiss, or Hungarian, psalms are things to be sung in metrical versions to recognizable tunes.

The responsive use of the psalter was something which grew up in the Middle Ages in monasteries where the psalms formed the principal part of the so-called daily offices. The monks gathered in stalls facing each other (the origin, by the way, of the popular divided chancel of today) and read, or more probably chanted, the psalms antiphonally. The antiphony, it should be noted, was not between leader and people but from side to side.

At the time of the Reformation, the Church of England reduced these medieval offices to two, morning and evening prayer, retaining the antiphonal use of the psalter as part of the service. Obviously Thomas Cranmer and the compilers of the prayer book intended these as daily services of devotion, but through an involved history which we shall not trace here, morning prayer became the principal Sunday morning service in many Episcopal churches as it still continues to be in some places.

As the singing of metrical Psalms declined in the Reformed church in the nineteenth century and as fascination with Anglican worship increased, Reformed people became impressed with the chanting of prose psalms, as they were called. The 1869 hymnal, as I have already mentioned, contains a number of psalms set this way. But imitation of the Anglican practice, using reading instead of chanting, was already growing in other Protestant groups, and by 1882 the Board of Publication had obviously decided that a little responsive psalmody would not hurt us either.

But by the time the custom was introduced among us, the real meaning of it had already been lost. Psalms, as any Sunday school child knows, are hymns, and in the Middle Ages or the Episcopal church they were sung as acts of praise, exactly as their metrical counterparts were sung by Reformed people in Europe and Scotland. But notice that by 1882 they are no longer hymns; they are a first Scripture lesson. "If desired, one of the lessons may consist of a portion of the psalms, read responsively by the Minister and People."

From there, it is only a short distance to the lunacy in which we are presently involved. If a responsive psalm is not an act of praise, but a lesson, why should the lessons be only from the psalter? Why not anywhere in scripture? And so in the back of many a hymnal today you find all kinds of scriptural passages cut up into stove-wood lengths to be tossed back and forth between the minister and the congregation in what is clearly the most meaningless exercise in public worship. If our liturgical revision committee today wants to do us a favor, it can stop fooling around with trying to provide another responsive psalter, toss the whole thing out, and provide us with a body of psalmody which we can sing. That clearly is our tradition. Perhaps the Board of Publication of 1966 could atone for the sins of the board of 1882 and forget to print the responsive readings from any future hymnal or liturgy!

While I am on this subject, I may say a few words about something which though it does not directly bear on our history may serve to clear up some confusion. Early along in Christian history, a little hymn was developed called the "Gloria Patri." Its origins are so far back we cannot trace them, but the hymn was developed as a concluding piece to any longer hymn of praise, to give it Trinitarian baptism, so to speak. Thus in the Middle Ages the Gloria Patri was always sung at the end of every psalm, a custom which many of our churches have retained to this day.

When English hymnwriters began their work at the time of the Reformation and after, they continued the pious custom of concluding every hymn with an additional stanza of praise to the Trinity. They could not use the Gloria Patri as such, but had to fit it into metre. These concluding stanzas or metrical Gloria Patris came to be called "doxologies." One of the greatest of English hymnwriters was Bishop Thomas Ken, whose two most famous hymns are his morning and evening hymns, "Awake My Soul and With the Sun" and "All Praise to Thee My God This Night." Each hymn concludes with the same doxology, written in what is commonly called "long meter." The words, as you may have already guessed, are "Praise God from whom all blessings flow."

Now for reasons which utterly elude me, this concluding Gloria Patri in meter from Ken's two office hymns has been canonized in American Protestant usage as though there were no other. I suppose it never occurs to the average American Protestant, clerical or lay, that the Gloria Patri and the Doxology are simply variants of the same thing. I suppose it occurs to him still less that while not entirely without meaning by themselves, they were intended to be and still serve their best function as a finale to something else. The development is not an important one, but it interests me as a good illustration of the way in which things can become highly traditional which represent nothing more than somebody's misunderstanding or even ignorance.

Before we leave the liturgy of 1882, I should like to make two final observations about it. Although the skeletal forms were bound up with the hymnal, 1882 was the first liturgy to be printed as a separate book. With its forms, its prayers, its lectionary, and its psalter, it could well have been used in the home as a book of family devotions. To some degree I am sure it was. But in that format it served another subtle purpose. In appearance it was not unlike the Episcopal prayer book and could worthily take its place alongside the hymnal in the pew. The custom is disappearing in my part of the world (I don't think it ever obtained in yours), and I am sorry to see it go. But there was a time when it was very easy to tell the congregation whose minister had at some point had a liturgical inclination. In his church the complete liturgy would have been found in the pew as well as the hymnal, a subtle reminder to all who might still be hankering after the strange gods of episcopacy that they too were members of a liturgical church.

The other observation about 1882 is a piece of Anglicanism which I should have noticed before. In all classical Reformed services, the use of the Lord's Prayer was the great and final act of prayer, following the great prayer of thanksgiving. Even in the revision of 1857, though the final prayer had been reduced to a brief prayer for blessing on the word, the Lord's Prayer still held its traditional place at the end. But in 1882 the surrender to the Episcopal pattern of morning prayer is complete and the Lord's Prayer is relocated to follow the invocation, just as in the prayer book it follows the opening prayer of confession and the words of assurance. Once again I have to say that the committee's suggestion that the prayer book service might do for Reformed worship may have been more seriously intended than we should like to believe.

But even before the revised liturgy had left the press, new questions began to be raised. Since these questions which occupied the attention of synod for the next decade or so do not relate to that aspect of the liturgy in which we are interested but had largely to do with the liturgy for baptism and other related offices, we can pass the discussion by, simply noting that much of it was an increasing warning to the synod that the day was coming when the two sacred offices of baptism and the supper would have to be seriously re-examined because they were saying things with which Reformed church people were finding it increasingly difficult to live. Synod could and did add footnotes and explanatory material to try to make some of the sticky phrases more palatable. But these were stop-gap measures that merely postponed the coming of the day when the nettle that no previous revision had dared to touch would have to be grasped courageously.

That day came with the turning of the century. Taking notice of a liturgical discussion which had been going on for at least twenty years, the Committee on the State of the Church recommended to the synod of 1900 that a special committee be appointed to prepare certain new liturgical orders and to revise the baptismal forms which had come to be the sorest spot in the whole book. Since baptism is not in our present field of interest, I shall merely summarize the result by saying by the synod of 1902 though it was evident that the proposed revisions had not received classical approval, it was also evident that a majority of the classes were unhappy with the present situation and wanted some kind of change.

Synod therefore appointed a committee not simply to deal with the sore spots but to revise the entire liturgy. The mandate under which it was appointed was as follows:

1. That the revisers seek simplicity, dignity, and brevity, rather than elaboration in their revision.

2. That they have their revision ready for presentation to the spring meeting of classes where it may be discussed before action by the synod of 1903.

Having served as a member of a committee to revise the liturgy, I shuddered when I saw the mandate. But evidently it did not bother the committee, and they went to work at once, presenting a lengthy report to the synod of 1903. When one examines their report, however, it is not difficult to see why it could be done with such dispatch. I trust that I shall not be considered unkind if I say that the committee viewed its job simply as one of using the pruning shears.

The cat comes out of the bag early along in the report. After all, synod had charged the committee with brevity and they had taken that charge seriously. With a good deal of satisfaction, the committee announced that had been able to reduce the size of the liturgy by one-quarter to one-half. Furthermore the task had been simplified by the committee's decision to leave the Sunday morning services and the collection of prayers as they were.

The Lord's Supper, however, had received a few changes beyond mere abridgement and these may be worth some notice. First of all, the committee noted that it had received repeated requests that the reading of the form should begin with some form of prayer. This had seemed to them a reasonable request, and so they provided an opening prayer which they considered mandatory, since they prefaced it with the rubric, "The minister shall say."

And what prayer did they use? They took the epiclesis section from the eucharistic prayer that had first appeared in 1873, boiled it down a little, and used it as the prayer with which to begin the reading of the form. I do not think their condensation was particularly a happy one, but it was of sufficiently little consequence, since the old Anglican prayer from which it was taken is still clearly visible. I shall say something more about the use of this prayer in a few moments, but let us continue with the story.

The narrative of institution with which the old form began has been eliminated on the ground that it is read a second time in the didactic part of the form itself. The abridgements made in the form itself look a great deal like the abridged form with which most of us are familiar, although there are some minor differences.

The next change is the offer of an alternative to the old prayer which had been contained in the form since the beginning in 1566. To be sure that ancient prayer was still printed as a second choice, but now there was a first choice. And that first choice was — the prayer of oblation from the old eucharistic prayer of 1873! So now we have two bits of prayer, hacked off and replaced in this liturgical proposal of 1903.

In the body of the report itself the committee did acknowledge that it had made use of the richer parts of a Communion prayer already in the earlier part of the liturgy among the special prayers. Since the chairman of this committee was Dr. Mancius Holmes Hutton, son of Dr. Mancius Smedes Hutton, the chairman of the prevous committee, one is tempted to think that perhaps the son was trying to secure a better place for the work of his father. But it must be said that the son was not the man the father was, at least not liturgically. Anyone with even an elementary liturgical education knows that to take the epiclesis and the oblation out of a eucharistic prayer and strew them around a service is to commit a kind of liturgical mayhem. Obviously Dr. Mancius Holmes Hutton did not know it and was not interested in finding it out. His one desire was to make things shorter!

But we still have to ask why it was that when the committee of 1903 came to look for suitable prayers with which to begin the form or to provide an alternate to the prayer in the form, they chose to look at the old eucharistic prayer of 1873. I can only conclude that the prayer of 1873 had not lain in the pages of the liturgy as a dead letter but to one degree or another had been used in the church. Otherwise, I see no real reason why the committee should have felt obliged to use two chunks of it for its new liturgical requirements, for which a number of other prayers could have been found which would have been equally suitable, or for which new ones could have been composed. These must have been forms of words which to a recognizable degree had found their way into the life of the church, so that the committee wanted to give them further status.

There were only two other abridgements. The Lord's Prayer, which up to this time had occurred twice in our form, was eliminated after the first prayer and retained after the post-Communion prayer of thanksgiving. I think we all would sympathize with the elimination of what would seem to be a useless repetition, but I also think I could argue, if challenged, that the committee eliminated the Lord's Prayer from the right place and kept it in the wrong one. Also the "Who hath not spared his own Son" section at the end of the 103rd Psalm was shortened to the version we know today.

Perhaps you will have gathered that I do not think the revision of 1903 was a very great piece of work. The church did not think so either, though I suspect its rejection of the revision was for very different reasons from mine. Indeed I have been informed by those who remember the occasion that the real reason for the rejection was what had been done to the form for the Sacrament of Baptism. Eighteen classes rejected the proposal, some outright, some with qualifications.

Here the classical voting does take a pattern. At that time there were eight classes in the Midwest. Of these, seven voted a total disapproval of the revision. The only middle-western classis to be an exception was Pleasant Prairie, which voted a qualified disapproval. Quite evidently by this time, the middle-western church was pretty definitely against revision of the liturgy. In a short time we shall be enquiring why.

The General Synod of 1904, feeling that despite the failure of revision some kind of revision was still the desire of the church, appointed an almost totally new committee and sent the whole problem back to it. I say *almost* new; two members of the previous committee, Dr. John W. Beardslee of this seminary and Dr. Ferdinand Schenck of New Brunswick, were placed on the new committee, I suppose to provide some kind of connection with the work already done. The rest of the personnel was totally new. The new committee was ordered to take the work of the old, submit it to still further revision, and get their report out in time for the spring classes at their 1905 meetings.

At this date I could wish that the synod had given a different kind of mandate, for there were some able people on this new committee. If the committee had been given the power to start afresh and the time to do some creative work, something of significance might have resulted. As it was the committee was simply told to take the hack work of its predecessor and fix it up so it could get past the classes. I am putting it crudely, but it is not hard to read between the lines of synod's instructions. Synod was anxious to get the thing done and didn't much care at this point what it took to do it.

In its proposals to the synod of 1905, the committee made some drastic changes in its predecessor's recommendations for baptism, but very few in the two areas which interest us. Again it was decided to do nothing with Sunday morning or the collection of prayers. So far as the Lord's Supper is concerned, it continued the use of a prayer with which to begin the form. But this committee used the entire prayer down through the epiclesis (and this time the epiclesis was not boiled down), omitting only the sanctus and benedictus. But this time the committee was resolved to use as much of that famous eucharistic prayer as it could. To be sure, it was indicated that everything down to the epiclesis could be omitted, and even the epiclesis could be replaced by another prayer of a similar kind. But since the committee continued to use the oblation as an alternate for the old prayer in the form, all of Dr. Hutton's or Dr. Thompson's great work except for the thanksgiving for the departed and the eschatological hope were now officially represented, though again in odd positions. The other abridgements suggested by the previous committee were retained, except for the narrative of institution, which was restored to its position at the beginning of the form.

The results announced in 1906 indicated that everybody (or almost everybody) had wanted to get it over with this time. Twenty-four of the thirty-five classes voted to approve and the work was finished! The minutes of 1906 do not tell us the names of the classes which were opposed, but I have a strong feeling that they were no different from those opposed in 1904, which is to say most if not all of the Midwest.

Now I do not want to seem to be castigating the middle-western church in this business. Personally I do not think the liturgy of 1906, our official liturgy for more than half a century, was any great shakes. But I do not think that my dislike of it was for the same reasons as the Midwest's. They had their own stance and at that stance we ought now to have a brief look.

I should like to submit that the church which came here with Van Raalte in 1847 and following came with a liturgical point of view not unlike that with which Dr. Livingston returned to New York from Utrecht. In the struggles of the Dutch church after 1816, struggles which finally resulted in the separation of 1834, the liturgy clearly became a badge of orthodoxy. In the Holland of that era, Van Raalte and his followers would have been stout defenders of the liturgy against their liberal opponents.

But again we must be careful to define our terms. To the Bethunes, Thompsons, and Huttons of the Reformed church the term *liturgy* meant the entire worshiping pattern of the church. To Van Raalte, the word *liturgy* meant the theological statements in the forms for baptism and the Lord's Supper and, to a lesser degree, ordinations and excommunication. The rest had so completely passed out of usage in the orthodox Reformed Netherlands that when Dr. Kuyper discovered it and wrote an excellent book about it much later, it was considered quite a shock.

And why should Van Raalte and his followers have valued the litanies, confessions, prayers, and collects of a full liturgy? He and his entire movement were children of the Reveil, an evangelical revival which had swept throughout the continental Reformed churches, a movement which was totally pietist in its basic attitudes. People always wonder why the psalm singing Dutch so easily began to sing the worst productions of gospel picnic music (and in many places still do). Part of the reason probably lies in the desire to identify with the prevailing American cultural pattern, which was camp-meeting and not psalmsinging. But the larger reason is simply that this is the way they were headed even before they landed here. To be sure, theirs was a much healthier pietism than what came later; but it was pietism all the same.

The result of all this was not only that in these discussions the word *liturgy* was being used in two senses. In the way in which the leaders of the eastern church were using it, it was wrong. It was wrong to have books of prayer and litanies and all that kind of thing. Men filled with the Holy Spirit should pray from the Spirit. The rest was not only unnecessary but dangerous. And in so far as the eastern church was attempting to play around with those theological formulations contained in the liturgy, this was wrong too. Here were the classic statements of covenant theology, of as high an authority as the Confession and Catechism themselves. Who were these upstarts from New York and Albany who wished to deal lightly with the sacred traditions of the fathers?

Again it cannot be an arguable point, but I wonder to what extent the language difference at this point helped open the gap. It is bad enough to have a form in English to begin with (I learned that when I was in South

Africa. English, they told me, can never be the language of Calvinism). But when English is not one's native tongue, it is, I submit, much easier to believe that the form is being robbed of its essential content when it is altered or shortened in any way.

In proof of my contention I offer the following evidence. The midwestern church insisted that the liturgy published in 1906 must retain the old unabridged forms in all their fullness. They are still there, but today I do not know of a single congregation which employs them. As the change came from Dutch to English, as Americanized middle-western churches demanded shorter services, the transition came imperceptibly. Today the children are perfectly happy with forms which in 1905 their fathers denounced as utterly unacceptable and subversive. It makes one wonder what will happen fifty years hence with certain forms from 1906 which still will be carried over into our new liturgy.

But back to the 1906 liturgy. I shudder to think what it might have been had it not been for a hasty action taken by the synod. A small committee, headed by Dr. Edward B. Coe, minister of St. Nicholas Church in New York, was given almost carte blanche to make a selection of prayers to be printed in the new liturgy for optional use. Shades of the Classis of New York which in 1875 had argued that even the options had to receive a two-thirds majority in the classes! Now the synod handed all the options over to a committee of four men who had complete power and never needed to report to synod.

Dr. Coe was an extremely gifted person, and the liturgy of 1906 could have been a far inferior product to what it was had it not been for him. In putting the book together he retained all of the best features of 1882 and added some excellent ones of his own. Familiar as you may be with that book, I call your attention to the addition of a number of canticles to the psalter, the fine set of daily morning and evening prayers for use in the family, the collects for the Christian year (including All Saint's Day), and the little table of psalms appropriate for the seasons of the church year. I shall not conceal my opinion that Dr. Coe had a pretty poor piece of work to deal with, but I also cannot conceal my admiration for the excellent liturgical material with which he surrounded it. To be sure, he was in the enviable position of being able to do almost anything he liked without having to report to synod. And even for that unprecedented action we may be grateful. His work was well received. Within ten years the Board of Publication had sold 17,000 copies of the pew edition alone, to say nothing of the many more that were bound up in hymnals.

One change is worth mentioning as an indication of the movement of the times. In the order of worship in 1857, you may recall, there was no offering indicated, or rather the offering was received at the door. In 1882 the offering had moved into the service and was received after the sermon. In 1906 it has moved to a position before the sermon, although a rubric indicates that it may be received after the sermon if desired. The trend to moving the sermon as far down in the service as possible so that almost nothing can interfere with its magic words has at last overtaken the Reformed church.

I can spare you the rather detailed study of hymnals in which we were involved last time for the very good reason that never again did we have one official hymnal. For a number of years, synod refused to endorse any number of hymnbooks which were presented to it, even on the hymn-by-hymn basis. But as *Hymns of the Church* became less and less popular and the demand for a new hymnal more and more clamorous, the synod of 1889 weakened and gave endorsement to the collection of a private publisher, the *Church Hymnary*. The *Church Hymnary* happens to have been an excellent book for its time, but the door had been opened. To trace out the story of endorsements from that point on would require an entire lecture. I know little about it, but I am sure that it would in many ways prove to be an amusing story.

We now enter the period of the long silence. Synod after synod passes by and there is no mention of the liturgy. This is not surprising. The nineteenth century interest in liturgy, reflected in our own discussions of 1857-1882, had subsided in almost all denominations. Christian concern had moved into other directions. I do not think that this argues that everyone was entirely satisfied with the liturgy of 1906. I think it argues quite simply that nobody much cared.

But we cannot dismiss what I have called the "long silence" quite that easily. As you will have noticed, from 1853 to the end of the century, the Reformed church was in almost continuous liturgical ferment. From 1906 to 1950 the question was never raised or, as we shall see, raised in only a rather desultory fashion. I think it is fair to ask why.

There would be many reasons, I am sure. But I am sure that one great reason was the nature of the 1906 revision itself. Its predecessors had, for us, been quite daring. Little as was actually approved by the synod, the mere issuance of those provisional books of 1857 and 1873 put forth numbers of new liturgical ideas. Even though synod recalled its approval of them, it did not collect the books together and burn them. The books were out where people read them, studied them, and used them. It is very significant to see how much material put forward experimentally in one is used in the next.

But the 1906 revision contained nothing new. It was a very conservative revision made almost solely in the interest of brevity. There was nothing in it to create ferment, raise questions and discussions. I suggest, therefore, that it had a mummifying effect on the liturgical situation in our church. There was not, as there had been previously, an experimental residuum about which people could think and debate. There was simply the reduction of what we had always had. That kind of work does not make for a creative future in any field. It would, of course, be interesting to enquire why this kind of revision suited the mood of the church in the opening years of the twentieth century. But that would be a chapter in that badly needed but never written history of the Reformed Church in America since 1792.

To complete the record, I should mention a few events during this period. The special committee appointed to revise the liturgy, though in no serious way, brought in a report to the synod of 1932 suggesting a number of minor alterations in the ordination forms. When the committee had completed its report, a motion was introduced from the floor by Dr. John Warnshuis of Staten Island. (By this time the clerk was keeping better records.)

> Resolved - that the General Synod continue the special committee on Revision of the Liturgy with a view to the publication, at a suitable date, of a new edition of the Reformed Church Liturgy, which shall incorporate recent revisions and additions together with such additional changes as the committee may find necessary or desirable; that the President of General Synod be empowered to name additional members to increase the committee to a membership of ten; and that this committee report within three years.

The motion was carried, and Dr. Warnshuis and two other ministers were added to the committee.

The committee was not heard from until 1936, but it is not difficult to imagine what was happening behind the scenes. Chairman of the committee was Dr. William H. S. Demarest of New Brunswick to whom the liturgy, save for an occasional comma or semi-colon, was almost canonical. It could not be revised. Obviously the new members of the committee (and some were old) found themselves in a deadlock with Dr. Demarest. When Dr. Demarest reported to the synod of 1936, his report contained such phrases as these:

> Impressed with the general excellence of the Forms in the Liturgy and reluctant to propose any changes...the Forms in general commend themselves so highly that they deserve most careful conserving.

Dr. Demarest did promise, however, that the committee would submit a proposed revision to the following synod, but he asked to be relieved of the chairmanship. The Rev. Dr. Edgar F. Romig of New York was appointed to replace him.

No report was ready for 1937, however, and synod, calling attention to the liturgical stirrings that were taking place in other Presbyterian churches, rebuked the committee and virtually commanded it to come in with something in 1938.

Not anxious for another rebuke, Dr. Romig's committee had something ready for the synod of 1938. It was far from the complete revision indicated by Dr. Warnshuis's motion in 1932, but it was a fairly well thought out revision of the liturgy for the Lord's Supper. The didactic portion was noticeably shortened by the elimination of whole paragraphs. None of the remaining language was disturbed, but the omissions were extensive.

Dr. Romig's committee also tried to put back the pieces of the old eucharistic prayer which the revisers of 1904 and 1906 had scattered. The entire prayer, from "It is very meet and right" through the epiclesis, omitting the use of the sanctus and benedictus, was indicated for use as the prayer at the Table, while the oblation was inserted after the words, "That we may now be fed," etc., before the actual Communion, a somewhat novel but not entirely inappropriate place. Apart from these, there were no changes.

Synod passed the revision and sent it down to the classes. If it had been carried there, it would have become a third possible form, published as an abridgement. But the proposal died in the classes where only 14 classes voted approval, while twenty-four registered their disapprobation. It is clear that Dr. Romig's revision fell between two stools. As a rather drastic shortening of an already shortened form, it aroused the ire of the conservatives. As a rather tame revision of only one form, it made no appeal to the liberals.

In 1938 the chairmanship of the committee had passed from Dr. Romig to Dr. Frank Fry of Staten Island. Almost as though he guessed what was going to happen to the 1938 proposal, Dr. Fry was ready for the synod of 1939 with a second proposal, certainly one of the most curious synod had ever laid eyes on. It was called, "A Devotional Order of the Holy Communion," and bore absolutely no resemblance to anything in our tradition.

Beginning with a short exhortation to worthy Communion, it went on to a catena of scriptural passages from both Old and New Testaments, concluding with a cutting from John 6. This was followed by a confession of sin borrowed from the German Reformed liturgy. As the table was uncovered, the rubric suggested that the choir sing the *Ave Verum* or the *Sanctus*. The words of institution, a kind of consecration prayer from the Presbyterian *Book of Common Worship*, and the Apostles' Creed follow in that order. After the singing of the hymn, "Just as I Am," or some other suitable selection, the Communion takes place, followed by a post-Communion thanksgiving taken from the Anglican prayer book.

In anybody's language it was a liturgical curiosity, but in our setting it was something worse; it was a joke. For the next ten years or so the memory of this thing cursed any attempted renewal or revision. Dr. Fry may perhaps be excused for it. His entire training and previous ministry had been in the German Reformed church. He simply did not know Dutch Reformed tradition or the mood of our church. But how the other members of the committee, including one theological professor and three mid-western ministers, ever let the thing get to the floor of synod is hard to say. Perhaps it was a case of a committee with a headstrong chairman. I do not know. But synod would not even pass this one on to the classes. The form was defeated by a vote of synod.

After that the committee, understandably, marked time. But at the synod of 1942 they were back again. Recommending the enlargement of the membership to twenty (which was approved), the committee also presented a "Brief Order of the Holy Communion for use in emergencies." Incredibly, it was almost the same form that had been presented and turned down in 1939. The only visible difference was that that form had been devotional; this one was brief. This time synod was a little kinder to Dr. Fry and his committee. This time their proposal was laid on the table.

Following these two fiascos, Dr. Fry left the committee chairmanship and Dr. Stephen James assumed it. In response to the committee's suggestion in 1944, two committees were created. The old committee of twenty remained under the leadership of the Rev. Theodore Brinckerhoff, while Dr. James took the chairmanship of a special committee of six, which had been authorized to make a thorough study of the liturgy of the church looking toward its complete revision. One finds it difficult to understand what this doubling of committees was intended to achieve. Possibly it was thought that a small committee of six could work more expeditiously than a large committee of twenty (and perhaps less expensively). But synod accepted the suggestion and appointed a second committee on liturgical revision.

The clumsiness of the arrangement became apparent in a short time, and the following year we find the committees recommending that the two committees of twenty-six be consoladated into one committee of ten. At the risk of being critical of some who are still living, I must say that not much happened as a result. A few desultory reports can be found in the minutes of synod until 1948, when the committee was discharged in view of the impending union with the United Presbyterian church.

That properly is where my story ends, though I recognize that I am ending it not with a bang but a whimper. Of course the impending union with the United Presbyterian church never took place and the Reformed church once again was called upon to consider reasons for its separateness. Once again as in 1873 the possible position of the church as a liturgical church was taken up as one reason, and the synod of 1950 appointed a committee of four persons to begin the task of liturgical revision anew. Since it is sometimes alleged that the committee then appointed went far beyond the mandate given it, let me conclude by quoting the first report of the committee to the synod of 1951, which report synod approved.

> Your committee recommends that General Synod authorize the Committee on Revision of the Liturgy to proceed with a comprehensive revision of the liturgy in its various offices, making needed corrections, clarifying confusing procedures, providing more adequate materials for use both in public and private worship, and in general to provide within the liturgy a more adequate

expression of the living tradition and teaching of the Reformed faith as a guide to our corporate and private worship.

From this point on, the story must be told by someone else, and someone else fifty years from now when the accomplishments of the committee have had the chance to find their way or lose their way into the life of the church.

I suppose our story is not really a very important one. In telling it this briefly I am conscious of how many chapters in it might have been expanded into much fuller detail. But in this ecumenical age in which liturgical renewal is so prominent, perhaps it is not so unimportant as it may seem. The well nigh universal story of Reformed liturgies is the same. They proliferated in the sixteenth century, died in the seventeenth, and were buried in the eighteenth. So far as the churches of continental origin are concerned there are only three exceptions to this statement: the liturgy of the church in Neuchatel in Switzerland which enjoyed a brief resurrection in the eighteenth century; the liturgy of the German Reformed church, now part of the United Church of Christ; and the liturgy of the Reformed Church in America. Though there have been periods of neglect followed by disappointing decisions, we can still say that from 1792 till now, in the Reformed Church in America the liturgy has been a living tradition. I have my own opinions about the liturgy of 1966. But I trust that the liturgy may continue to be such a living tradition among us that it will not be sixty years before we revise it again.

A. A Brief Chronology of the Life and Ministry of Howard G. Hageman

1921   Born April 19 in Lynn, Massachusetts.

1923   The Hageman family move to Albany, New York.

1937   Howard's father dies in a boating accident on Lake Champlain.

1938   Graduates from the Albany Academy.

1942   Graduates from Harvard University.

1945   Graduates from New Brunswick Theological Seminary.
        Licensed by the Classis of Palisades and ordained by the Classis of Newark to be the minister of the North Reformed Church of Newark, New Jersey.

1947   Attends Princeton Theological Seminary, 1947-1948.

1950   First visit to Holland; attends the laying of the cornerstone of the new Austin Friar's Church in London as a representative of the R.C.A.; begins his service on the Commission on the Revision of the Liturgy, 1950-1967.

1953   Publishes *Lily Among the Thorns*.

1955   Lecturer at New Brunswick Theological Seminary in Liturgics, 1955-1957.

1956   U.S. State Department Visit to South Africa as a lecturer in theology.

1957   Honorary degree (D.D.) from Central College.

1959 President of General Synod in 1959-1960.

1960 Stone lecturer at Princeton Theological Seminary.

1961 Publishes *We Call This Friday Good;* lecturer in liturgics at NBTS from 1961-1973.

1962 Publishes *Pulpit and Table* and *The Book That Reads You;* member of the Committee of twenty-four on Church Union with the Southern Presbyterian church 1962-1969.

1963 Publishes *Predestination;* RCA delegate to the Faith and Order Conference of the World Council of Churches in Montreal.

1964 RCA delegate to the nineteenth General Council of the World Alliance of Reformed and Presbyterian Churches in Frankfort, Germany.

1965 Publishes *That the World May Know.*

1967 Treasurer of the Societas Liturgica, 1967-1973.

1970 Retreat master for the Armed Forces in Berchtesgarden, Germany.

1972 Appointed to the Newark Board of Education, 1972-1973; Named dominie of the Holland Society.

1973 President of New Brunswick Theological Seminary, 1973-1985.

1974 Publishes *Easter Proclamation;* return visit to South Africa.

1975 Honorary degree (L.H.D.) from Ursinus College; honorary degree (Litt. D.) from Hope College.

1976 Named editor of *de Halve Maen,* 1976-1989.

1977 Honorary degree (D.D.) from Knox College in Toronto; cofounder of the doctoral program in liturgical studies at Drew University.

1980 Lecturer at Westminster Choir College in Princeton, New Jersey.

1982 Inducted as Commander of the Order of Orange Nassau by Queen Beatrix of the Netherlands.

1983 Receives Medal of Honor from N.S.D.A.R.

1984 Publishes *Two Centuries Plus;* helps found the Mercersburg Society and serves as president until his death; receives the

Medal for Outstanding Service from the St. Nicholas Society of New York City.

1985   Receives Medal of Service from the Holland Society of New York City.

1986   Named minister emeritus of the North Reformed Church; helps found the Friends of New Netherlands and serves as president until 1992; serves as visiting lecturer at New Brunswick Theological Seminary and Drew University from 1986-1990.

1988   Serves as lecturer at Princeton Theological Seminary; named president emeritus of New Brunswick Theological Seminary.

1992   Dies the fourth Sunday of Advent.

B. Publications by Howard G. Hageman

Articles published in the *Church Herald* from 1946-1990

Articles not part of a column:

"What Church History Teaches Us," 12/27/46, p. 16.

"Recent Churchmen Who Risked Much," 1/3/47, p. 16.

"World Churches Present A United Front," 1/10/47, p. 14.

"The Bankruptcy Of The World's Best," 3/26/48, pp. 8-9.

"How Shall We Sing the Lord's Song?," 4/23/48, p. 12.

"The Crime of Efficiency," 11/5/48, pp. 12-14.

"The Office of the Ministry in the RCA," 2/4/49, pp. 12-13, 20.

"The Other Side of the Cross," 4/15/49, pp. 12-13.

"I Serve a Risen Savior," 4/17/49, p. 16.

"An Easter Doxology," 4/18/55, p. 12.

"Every Man's Ministry," 5/13/55, p. 12.

"Begin at the Beginning," 12/30/55, p. 4.

"The Theology of the Urban Church," Part I, 11/7/58, p. 4.

"The Theology of the Urban Church," Part II, 11/14/58, p. 13.

"The Theology of the Urban Church," Part III, 11/21/58, p.10.

"The Theology of the Urban Church," Part IV, 11/28/58, p. 10.

"On Giving Things Up For Lent," 2/6/59, p. 6.

"Ash Wednesday," 2/6/59, p. 6.

"A Word About Anniversaries," 2/6/59, p. 7.

"The Lord Reigneth," 1/22/60, p.4.

"Let the Earth Rejoice," 1/22/60, p. 4.

"Report on the State of Religion, RCA," 6/3/60, p. 4.

"Annuit Coeptis—Norus Ordo Saeculorum," 12/30/60, p. 4.

"The Greatest Issue Facing the Reformed Church in America," 4/21/61,
    pp. 12, 23.
"Shall the Church Stay in the City," 11/9/62, p. 12.
"The Story of Our Two Churches," 4/5/63, pp.12-13, 23.
"The World Reformed Alliance at Frankfurt," 9/25/64, p. 15.
"Songs For a Small Planet," 1/29/65, p. 4.
"Fraternal Greetings," 7/9/65, p. 11.
"The Riots: A Report from Newark," 8/11/67, p. 14.
"B.C. in A.D.," 4/12/68, pp. 2-4.
"To Unite or Not To Unite," 1/24/69, p. 10.
"A Plea for Understanding," 5/23/69, p. 20.
"Inner-City Turbulence and the Church," 9/19/69, p. 4.
"Easter and Your Closed World," 3/27/70, p. 18.
"So I Send You," 4/24/70, pp. 4-5, 20.
"When Christendom Flourished," 3/19/71, p. 4.
"The Disappearance of Christendom," 3/26/71, p. 12.
"Church School," 5/28/71, p. 8.
"The Imponderables," 5/28/71, p. 8.
"The Irish Question," 11/26/71, p. 4.
"Christmas Eve in Newark," 1/14/72, pp. 20-21.
"New Look at Apostolic Succession," 7/27/73, p. 12.
"Our Dutch Mythology," 1/29/74, p. 10.
"The Old Order Changeth," 1/10/75, p. 6.
"Easter Is not an Island," 3/21/75, p. 10.
"South Africa Revisited," 5/30/75, p. 10.
"The Need and Promise of Reformed Preaching," 10/17/75 p. 6.
"The Gift of Office," 9/30/77, pp. 16-17.
"Office as Ministry," 10/14/77, pp. 10-11.
"Where's the Foundation of Life?," 1/2/84, p. 6.
"NBTS: Reformed Theology in an Urban Setting," 9/21/84, pp. 6-7.
"Make Me a Captive, Lord," 4/5/85, p. 8.
"Reformed Worship is Corporate, Liturgical, and Sacramental," 6/6/86,
    p. 11.
"Our First Ecumenical Encounter," 1/89, p. 21.
"Who Follows in His Train?" 2/89, p. 21.
"Dutch Wasn't Much in His Ministry," 3/89, p. 23.
"Answering the Call," 1/90, p. 28.
"Changes Along the Way," 9/90, p. 49.

"This Reformed Church of Ours" (column):

"Why We Are Here," 9/6/46. p. 9.
"What We Believe," 9/13/46, p. 9.
"How We Worship," 9/20/46, p. 13.
Part One: "The Recovery of Our Heritage," 10/7/49, p. 10.
Part Two: "The Gateway to the Knowledge of God," 10/14/49, p. 12.
Part Three: "An Accident that Changed a Life," 10/21/49, p.4.
Part Four: "The Band of Peace," 10/28/49, p. 10.
Part Five: "The Spirit of the Catechism," 11/4/49, p. 9.
Part Six: "A Confessing Church," 11/11/49, p. 10.
Part Seven: "Churches Under the Cross," 11/25/49, p. 14.
Part Eight: "The Belgic Confession," 12/2/49, p. 11.
Part Nine: "The Reformed Battlecry," 1/13/50, p. 13.
Part Ten: "Reformed Reading," 1/20/50, p. 8.
Part Eleven: "The Romance of the Liturgy," 2/3/50, p. 13.
Part Twelve: "The Liturgy of John Calvin," 4/14/50, p. 13.
Part Thirteen: "The Liturgy of John Calvin," 4/21/50, p. 9.
Part Fourteen: "The Liturgy of the Heidelberg Catechism," 5/5/50, p. 11.
Part Fifteen: "The Dutch Liturgy," 5/12/50, p. 5.
Part Sixteen: "A Reformed Service," 5/19/50, p. 8.
Part Seventeen: "Nec Tamen Consumebatur," 5/26/50, p. 5.
Part Eighteen: "The Reformed Church Through the Centuries," 7/21/50,
    p. 7.
"Becoming What We Are," 9/29/50, p. 11.
"Our Liturgical History," 5/4/51, p. 12.
"Enriching the Church of Jesus Christ," 9/5/52, p. 4.
"Discerning the Body of the Lord," 9/12/52, p. 11.
"Preaching the Word," 9/19/52, p. 5.
"Completing Christ," 9/26/52, p. 5.
"Let's Build Reformed Churches" I, 1/11/52, p. 9.
"Let's Build Reformed Churches" II, 1/18/52, p .8.
"Let's Build Reformed Churches" III, 1/25/52, p. 8.
"On Naming Churches," 2/1/52, p. 11.
"After the Shadows, Light," 2/22/52, p. 5.
"Post Tenebras Lux," II, 3/14/52, p. 9.
"Post Tenebras Lux," III, 4/18/52, p. 9.
"Post Tenebras Lux," IV, 6/6/52, p. 5.
"Post Tenebras Lux," V, 6/20/52, p. 13.
"Post Tenebras Lux," VI, 7/4/52, p. 5.

"Focus on the World" (column):

1961

"An Interrupted Conversation," 11/10/61, p. 10.
"When is a Dutch Reformed Not Dutch Reformed?" 11/17/61, p. 10.
"Can the Church Be Redeemed?" 11/24/61, p. 8.
"May Their Tribe Increase," 12/1/61, p. 8.
"It Happened in Holland," 12/8/61, p. 8.
"Et Tu, Brute," 12/15/61, p. 10.
"The Unsaved Suburb?" 12/22/61, p. 8.
"Some Reflections on Councils," 12/29/61, p. 8.

1962

"Has Calvinism Lost Its Nerve?" 1/5/62, p. 8.
"Hamlet Without the Prince of Denmark," 1/12/62, p. 8. "Moscow
    Missions," 1/19/62, p. 8.
"Strange New Europe," 1/26/62, p. 8.
"Hedging the Holy Spirit," 2/2/62, p. 8.
"What's In a Name?" 2/9/62, p. 8.
"The Shape of Things to Come," 2/16/62, p. 8.
"What's Behind the Curtain," 2/23/62, p. 8.
"Oh No!" 3/2/62, p. 8.
"A Forgotten Doctrine," 3/9/62, p. 8.
"The City of God?" 3/16/92, p. 8.
"On Rocking the Ark," 3/23/62, p. 8.
"What Happened?" 3/30/62, p. 10.
"A Forgotten Anniversary," 4/13/62, p. 10.
"Growing Pains All Over," 4/27/62, p. 8.
"A Sense of Solidarity," 5/4/62, p. 8.
"A Forgotten Feast," 5/18/62, p. 8.
"A New High in Silliness," 6/1/62, p. 8.
"It Does Make a Difference," 6/8/62, p.14.
"Focus on the World," 6/15/62, p. 8.
"Let's Fight Fairly," 6/29/62, p. 12.
"Realignment in Spain?" 7/13/62, p. 8.
"We'd Better Start Thinking," 7/27/62, p. 8.
"Suburbs in Heaven?" 8/10/62, p. 8.
"Another Geneva," 8/24/62, p. 8.
"A Conspiracy of Silence," 9/7/62, p. 10.
"And We Are Not Saved," 9/21/62, p. 8.
"You Are Thine," 9/28/62, p. 8.
"A New Song," 10/5/62, p. 8.

"A Different Approach," 10/12/62, p. 8.
"Well, We Should Hope Not," 10/19/62, p. 8.
"But Do They Know What We're Saying?" 10/26/62, p. 8.
"The Itch to be Modern," 11/2/62, p. 8.
"Keep Them on the Farm?" 11/9/62, p. 10.
"The More it Changes," 11/16/62, p. 8.
"More on the Vatican Council," 11/23/62, p. 10.
"Representative Government," 12/7/62, p. 8.
"Fact or Fad?" 12/14/62, p. 8.
"Stop Talking and Listen!" 12/21/62, p. 10.
"The Christian Year," 12/28/62, p. 8.

1963

"I Tremble," 1/4/63, p. 10.
"The National Pastime," 1/11/63, p. 8.
"The New Altar," 1/18/63, p. 8.
"Where Are We?" 2/1/63, p. 11.
"Did You Know?" 2/8/63, p. 10.
"What Shall We Talk About?" 2/15/63, p. 9.
"Let's Face It," 2/22/63, p. 9.
"The Dimensions of Our World," 3/1/61, p. 9.
"Leave It To the Dutch," 3/8/63, p. 9.
"A Dangerous Shorthand?" 3/29/63, p. 11.
"I Didn't Quit the Ministry," 4/5/63, p. 11.
"More Conversations," 4/12/63, p. 9.
"A New Look at Spain," 4/19/63, p. 9.
"South Africa Again," 4/26/63, p. 9.
"A Case of Mistaken Identity," 5/3/63, p. 11.
"To Think About," 6/7/63, p. 15.
"Speaking in Tongues," 6/14/63, p. 9.
"A Bilingual Dutch Church," 6/28/63, p. 23.
"Theology By TV," 7/12/63, p. 8.
"An Ecumenical Sour Note," 7/26/63, p. 8.
"Reflections After Montreal," 8/23/63, pp. 9, 30.
"Honest to God," 9/20/63, p. 8.
"And the Word Was Scarce," 9/27/63, p. 9.
"Were You There?" 10/4/63, p. 9.
"Too Much and Too Fast?" 10/11/63.
"When Is a Saint Not a Saint?" 10/18/63, p. 10.

"I've Been Thinking," 10/25/63, p. 9.
"For Conscience's Sake," 11/1/63, p. 11.
"Pulling Down the Temple," 11/15/63, pp. 9, 21.
"Reflections," 12/13/63, p. 9.
"Rethinking Seminaries," 12/27/63, pp. 9, 23.

1964

"A Lost Cause?" 1/3/64, p. 9.
"Members One of Another," 1/3/64, p. 9.
"Time For Study," 1/3/64, p. 9.
"A New Investigating Committee," 1/17/64, p. 9.
"The Deputy," 1/17/64, p. 11.
"The New Morality," 1/24/64, p. 9.
"What Next?" 1/24/64, p. 9.
"Minister in the White House," 2/7/64, p. 9.
"You Figure it Out," 2/7/64, p. 9.
"South Africa Again," 2/7/64, p. 9.
"Layman's Sunday in Chile," 2/14/64, p. 9.
"Pardon Me While I Explode," 2/14/64, p. 9.
"A Dirty Word," 2/14/64, p. 9.
"In Twenty Years," 2/21/64, p. 9.
"Ecumenical Relations—Dutch Style," 2/28/64, p. 9.
"And Irish Style," 2/28/64, p. 9.
"And American Style," 2/28/64, p. 9.
"The Coming Great Church?" 2/28/64, p. 9.
"Every Man a Minister," 3/6/64, p. 9.
"Lenten Thoughts," 3/6/64, p. 9.
"The Nassau Scandal," 3/6/64, p. 9.
"The Mass in English," 3/6/64, p. 9.
"It's Up to Us," 3/13/64, p. 9.
"It's Up to Us," 3/27/64, p. 9.
"Where Do You Live?" 3/27/64, p. 9.
"Luther's Will," 3/27/64, p. 9.
"The Reign in Spain," 3/27/64, p. 9.
"What Gospel?" 4/3/64, p. 9.
"What Next?" 4/3/64, p. 9.
"Restoring Our Heritage," 4/3/64, p. 9.
"A Sunday in Geneva," 5/1/64, p. 9.
"As Others See Us," 5/1/64, p. 9.

"The Woes of the House of Orange," 5/8/64, p. 9.

"Gossiping the Gospel," 5/8/64, p. 9.

"Unity—A New Dimension?" 5/8/64, p. 9.

"The New Immortality," 5/15/64, p. 9.

"A Confusing Story," 5/15/64, p. 9.

"We Went Down to Washington," 5/22/64, p. 9.

"Wanted—A New Record," 5/22/64, p. 9.

"The White House," 5/22/64, p. 9.

"Where Have We Been?" 5/22/64, p. 9.

"A Disappearing Theory?" 6/5/64, p. 15.

"It's an Ill Wind...," 7/10/64, p. 9.

"A Tale of Two Cardinals," 7/10/64, p. 9.

"Point of Order," 7/24/64, p. 9.

"A Wasteland of Irresponsibility," 7/24/64, p. 9.

"Time For an Explosion (Again)," 8/7/64, p. 11.

"A Footnote," 8/7/64, p. 11.

"The Los Angeles Story—Chapter II," 8/7/64, p. 11.

"Time For A Change?" 8/21/64, p. 8.

"Cross-Fertilization," 8/21/64, p. 8.

"It Happened!" 9/4/64, p. 9.

"Stop the World!" 9/4/64, p. 9.

"Well, Which?" 9/18/64, p. 9.

"The Vice of Religious Conformity," 9/18/64, p. 9.

"Your Statistic is Showing," 9/25/64, p. 12.

"A New Song," 9/25/64, p. 12.

"Broadcasting Biblical Illiteracy," 9/25/64, p. 12.

"Now It's Their Turn," 10/2/64, p. 9.

"Behind the Bamboo Curtain," 10/2/64, p. 9.

"Cathedrals on Wheels," 10/2/64, p. 9.

"When Will We Learn?" 10/9/64, p. 9.

"A New Song," 10/9/64, p. 9.

"Biblical Ventriloquism," 10/16/64, p. 11.

"The Sickness of Theology," 10/16/64, p. 11.

"As Others See Us," 10/16/64, p. 11.

"I've Changed My Mind (Well, Almost)," 10/23/64, p. 9.

"We Still Don't Know," 10/23/64, p. 9.

"On Drawing Conclusions," 11/6/64, p. 9.

"Shalom," 11/6/64, p. 9.

"What's Irrelevant," 11/13/64, p. 9.

"Breaking the News Barrier," 11/13/64, p. 9.

"Speaking of Unity," 11/13/64, p. 9.
"What About Us?" 11/27/64, p. 9.
"The Fine Art of Pre-Judgment," 11/27/64, p. 9.
"A Word About Preaching," 12/4/64, p. 9.
"Answer, 1964," 12/18/64, p. 9.
"Question, 1964," 12/18/64, p. 9.
"McCarthy in South Africa," 12/18/64, p. 9.
"A Word For Christmas," 12/25/64, p. 9.
"Behind the Iron Curtain With the Heidelberg Catechism," 12/25/64, p. 9.
"Have You Ever Rented the Church Herald?" 12/25/64, p. 9.

1965

"A New Seminary," 1/15/65, p. 9.
"A Question of Motion," 1/15/65, p. 9.
"The Two Cultures," 2/5/65, p. 21.
"Happy New Year!" 2/5/65, p. 21.
"Well, What Would You Do?" 2/19/65, p. 9.
"Lift Your Sights," 2/19/65, p. 9.
"Who Said It?" 2/19/65, p. 9.
"Whither Rome?" 2/26/65, p. 9.
"An Angry Old Man, 2/26/65, p. 9.
"It Was News to Me," 3/12/65, p. 9.
"Focusing on the Church," 3/12/65, p. 9.
"(!)" 3/19/65, p. 9.
"What Are You Building For," 3/19/65, p. 9.
"Sunday in New York," 4/9/65, p. 9.
"God-Fearing People," 4/9/65, p. 9.
"On Bringing Luther Up to Date," 4/9/65, p. 9.
"An Apology," 5/28/65, p. 9.
"On Asking the Right Question," 5/28/65, p. 9.
"My Annual Plea," 5/28/65, p. 9.
"Toumliline," 6/4/65, p. 15.
"The CTM," 6/4/65, p. 15.
"A Dangerous Division," 6/11/65, p. 9.
"Well, What Do You Think?" 6/11/65, p. 9.
"Author Wanted," 6/25/65, p. 21.
"Women Again!" 6/25/65, p. 21.
"A Protest Against Labels," 7/9/65, p. 9.
"A Chance for Distinctiveness," 7/9/65, p. 9.

"Do They Mean What They Say?" 7/23/65, p. 9.
"The Age of Anonymity," 7/23/65, p. 9.
"Recovery," 8/6/65, p. 9.
"Civil Disobedience," 8/6/65, p. 9.
"On Changing Confessions," 8/20/65, p. 9.
"Our Favorite Whipping Boy," 8/20/65, p. 9.
"The Third Church," 9/3/65, p. 9.
"Postscript on Luci," 9/3/65, p. 9.
"On Team Ministry," 9/3/65, p. 9.
"Concluding Unscientific Postscript," 9/17/65, p. 9.
"How to Be a Sect," 9/17/65, p. 9.
"Where the Battle Lies," 9/17/65, p. 9.
"On Knowing Your Neighbors," 9/ 24/65, p. 7.
"1984," 9/24/65, p. 7.
"Are We Using Our Potential Ministry?" 10/1/65, p. 9.
"In the Book Corner," 10/1/65, p. 9.
"The Importance of Announcements," 10/8/65, p. 9.
"Transatlantic Union?" 10/8/65, p. 9.
"A Footnote on Law and Order," 10/8/65, p. 9.
"The International Politics of Calvinism," 10/15/65, p. 11.
"The Other America," 10/15/65, p. 11.
"Hurrah for the Social Gospel," 10/22/65, p. 9.
"From Behind the Bamboo Curtain," 10/22/65, p. 9.
"BOMFOG," 10/29/65, p. 7.
"That Shall Never Call a Retreat," 10/29/65, p. 7.
"The British Methodists Again," 11/5/65, p. 9.
"Jesus in Magnitogorsk," 11/5/65, p. 9.
"When is an Episcopalian Not an Episcopalian?" 11/12/65, p. 9.
"Getting Behind the Facts," 11/12/65, p. 9.
"No Comment," 11/19/65, p. 9.
"Guess What?" 11/19/65, p. 9.
"Advent," 11/26/65, p. 7.
"Unfinished Business," 11/26/65, p. 7.
"Why?" 12/3/65, p. 7.
"Will Anyone Help?" 12/3/65, p. 7.
"Some Notes on the Death of God," 12/10/65, p. 9.
"Whatever Happened to Heaven?" 12/10/65, p. 9.
"The Two Cultures," 12/17/65, p. 7.
"Speaking of Tensions," 12/17/65, p. 7.
"School of Religion," 12/24/65, p. 11.

"Let Us Go Higher," 6/3/66, p. 9.
"If Only," 6/3/66, p. 9.
"Whither COCU?" 6/10/66, p. 9.
"Vita Brevis Est—Ecclesia Longa," 6/10/66, p. 9.
"Man Is Dead," 6/17/66, p. 7.
"The Dutch Do It Again," 6/17/66, p. 7.
"Let's Get at the Root," 6/17/66, p. 7.
"Separation of Church and State," 7/1/66, p. 21.
"Less than Human," 7/1/66, p. 21.
"An Evangelical Front," 7/15/66, p. 9.
"Another Birthday," 7/15/66, p. 9.
"On a World Come of Age," 7/29/66, p. 11.
"Happy Birthday [Karl Barth]," 7/29/66, p. 11.
"Caritas Pro Armis," 8/12/66, p. 9.
"In Praise of Chesterfield," 8/12/66, p. 9.
"The Orange and the Green," 8/26/66, p. 11.
"The Church in Gulpen," 8/26/66, p. 11.
"The Middle-Class Hood," 8/26/66, p. 11.
"More on the Death of God," 9/9/66, p. 9.
"Good Old American Religion," 9/9/66, p. 9.
"Another Word on COCU," 9/23/66, p. 9.
"A Freudian Slip?" 9/23/66, p. 9.
"Back to the Pulpit," 9/30/66, p. 9.
"They Have It Too," 9/30/66, p. 9.
"In the Streets!" 9/30/66, p. 9.
"No Ecumenical Traps," 10/7/66, p. 11.
"You Can't Win Them All," 10/7/66, p.11.
"Lies, Half-Truths, and Statistics," 10/14/66, p. 9.
"Peruvian Deacons," 10/14/66, p. 9.
"Whose Day?" 10/21/66, p. 9.
"Acting, Not Talking," 10/21/66, p. 9.
"As Seen From 3000 Miles," 10/28/66, p. 9.
"Who Said It?" 10/28/66, p. 9.
"The Downlash," 11/4/66, p. 11.
"Hierodoxy," 11/4/66, p. 11.
"The New Immorality," 11/25/66, p. 9.
"Enlarging the Gospel," 11/25/66, p. 9.
"Are Protestants Dead?" 12/16/66, p. 9.
"From Parish to Congregation," 12/16/66, p. 9.
"A Brief Essay on Four-Letter Words," 12/23/66, p. 13.

"Two Funerals," 12/23/66, p. 13.

1967

"Where We Stand," 1/13/67, pp. 9, 12.
"Unfinished Business," 1/13/67, pp. 9, 12.
"Reflections on a New Year's Eve," 1/20/67, pp. 11, 30.
"Focus of Our Focus?" 1/20/67, pp. 11, 30.
"Fly Now, Gloria," 2/3/67, p. 13.
"Reach for the Heart," 2/3/67, p. 13.
"Our State of Religion," 2/10/67, pp. 9, 22.
"With Apologies to Salem," 2/10/67, pp. 9, 22.
"For Your Bedside Reading," 2/17/67, pp.9, 22.
"Ferment in the Faith," 2/17/67, pp. 9, 22.
"In MEMORIAM," 2/24/67, p. 11.
"The Shape of the Future?" 2/24/67, p. 11.
"The Good Old Hymns," 3/3/67, pp. 9, 22.
"Those Naughty Dutch," 3/3/67, pp. 9, 22.
"McLuhanism and Reformed Theology," 3/10/67, p. 9.
"A Common French Bible," 3/10/67, p. 9.
"Lent—Spanish Style," 3/17/67, p. 11.
"From My Corner," 3/17/67, p. 11.
"Union on the Right," 3/24/67, pp. 16, 30.
"Sign on the Line," 3/24/67, pp. 16, 30.
"Ecclesiastical Boycott," 3/31/67, pp. 9, 20.
"Which Way?" 3/31/67, pp. 9, 20.
"An Aging Cynic," 4/7/67, p. 9.
"What's In a Name?" 4/7/67, p. 9.
"History's Oldest Question?" 4/21/67, p. 9.
"Ministers in Politics," 4/21/67, p. 9.
"The Dutch (Again)," 4/28/67, p. 9.
"Is Anything New?" 4/28/67, p. 9.
"Not Always Greener," 5/5/67, p. 9.
"When Is a Church Not a Church?" 5/5/67, p. 9.
"The New Science," 6/2/67, p. 9.
"America—Land of Mission," 6/2/67, p. 9.
"Whither COCU?" 6/9/67, pp. 7, 37.
"The Dutch Best-Seller List," 6/9/67, pp. 7, 37.
"Signs of the Times?" 6/16/67, p. 10.
"In Tribute," 6/16/67, p. 10.

1968

"Neatness Counts," 1/26/68, p. 11.
"Ecumene, Where Art Thou?" 1/26/68, p. 11.
"It Also Has to be Faced," 2/2/68, p. 7.
"Please Explain," 2/9/68, p. 9.
"Of Sermon Titles," 2/9/68, p. 9.
"'Tis the Season for Bishops," 2/16/68, p. 11.
"Heard It All Before?" 2/16/68, p. 11.
"New Directions," 3/1/68, pp. 9, 21.
"What is a Classis?" 3/1/68, pp. 9, 21.
"A World come of Age?" 3/8/68, p. 9.
"The New Mars Hill," 3/15/68, pp. 7, 21.
"Iconoclasm, Anyone?" 3/15/68, pp. 7, 21.
"Which Paper Do You Read?" 3/22/68, p. 12.
"Another Dutch Experiment," 3/22/68, p. 12.
"Please, No!" 3/29/68, p. 9.
"Which Way America," 3/29/68, p. 9.
"Second Summer, Anyone?" 4/5/68, pp. 9, 21.
"If You Don't Want To," 4/5/68, pp. 9, 21.
"Isn't Something Wrong?" 4/5/68, pp. 9, 21.
"What Bible Do You Read?" 4/12/68, pp. 15, 32.
"The Bankruptcy of the Protestant Ethic," 4/12/68, pp. 15, 32.
"The Newark Story," 5/3/68, p. 9.
"White Racism," 5/3/68, p. 9.
"To Baptize or Not to Baptize," 5/10/68, p. 9.
"Pick Your Friends and Your Family!" 5/10/68, p. 9.
"The Protestant Hang-up," 5/17/68, p. 9.
"A Word on Law and Order," 5/17/68, p. 9.
"The Blind Spot," 6/14/68, p. 13.
"Our Disorder of Service," 6/14/68, p. 13.
"The Story of Two Churches," 6/28/68, p. 19.
"No Hiding Place," 6/28/68, p. 19.
"Of General Synods," 7/12/68, pp. 13, 31.
"A Word on Racial Questions," 7/12/68, pp. 13, 31.
"The World Turned Upside Down," 7/26/68, p. 13.
"God in the Netherlands," 7/26/68, p. 13.
"Thank God Our Time is Now!" 8/9/68, pp. 9, 28.
"A Lutheran Postscript," 8/9/68, pp. 9, 28.
"The Reformed Church and the Urb," 8/23/68, p. 9.

"Department of Roman Affairs," 8/23/68, p. 9.
"The Latin Reformed Church," 9/6/68, p. 9.
"News and Notes From Rome," 9/6/68, pp. 18, 30.
"Why don't They Read the Bible in the Bible Belt?" 9/20/68, p. 9.
"Send Me a Letter," 9/20/68, p. 9.
"The Hermit," 9/27/68, pp. 9, 21.
"From Peter's Seat," 9/27/68, pp. 9, 21.
"It's Their Problem Too," 10/4/68, p. 9.
"Ecclesiastical Blackmail," 10/4/68, p. 9.
"Change and Decay," 10/11/68, pp. 7, 22.
"The Brethren in Poland," 10/11/68, pp. 7, 22.
"Creeds and Confessions," 10/18/68, pp. 9, 21.
"It Works Both Ways," 10/18/68, pp. 9, 21.
"First Prize for Pessimism," 10/25/68, p. 9.
"Rome In the Inner City," 10/25/68, p. 9.
"The Burning Ecumenical Question," 11/1/68, p. 21.
"Where Else?" 11/1/68, p. 21.
"Reflection After Hearing the Needs of the Committee on Church
    Extension, Retention, Etc.," 11/8/68, p. 9.
"From the Churches of Czechoslovakia," 11/8/68, p. 9.
"The Paperback Stand," 11/15/68, pp. 11, 29.
"For Ministers Only," 11/15/68, pp. 11, 29.
"Death of a Magazine," 11/22/68, pp. 9, 21.
"Happy to be in Church!" 11/22/68, pp. 9, 21.
"Some Irish Eyes Aren't Smiling," 11/29/68, pp. 9, 21.
"On Reading the Word," 11/29/68, pp. 9, 21.
"What Shall We Sing?" 12/6/68, p. 9.
"Another Look at Those Good Old Days," 12/6/68, p. 9.
"Anniversary Time," 12/13/68, p. 7.
"A Word About Beards," 12/13/68, p. 7.
"Give Me More," 12/20/68, p. 13.
"Other Routes to the Ministry," 12/20/68, p. 13.
"A Comment on Law and Order," 12/27/68, p. 7.
"Footnote," 12/27/68, p. 7.

1969

"Christians and Color," 1/3/69, p. 9.
"Undisciplined Affluence," 1/3/69, p. 9.
"As Others See Us," 1/10/69, p. 9.

"Follow Me!" 1/10/69, p. 9.
"In the Nice Suburb," 1/17/69, p. 19.
"Column Right?" 1/31/69, p. 11.
"Building Poor," 1/31/69, p. 11.
"Homage to Karl Barth," 2/7/69, pp. 11, 28.
"Dissension in the Ranks," 2/7/69, pp. 11, 28.
"Count Me Out, Your Eminence!" 2/7/69, pp. 11, 28.
"Hope for the Secular City," 2/14/69, p. 9.
"The Dirty Offering Plate," 2/14/69, p. 9.
"Is Lent Spent?" 2/21/69, pp. 9, 21.
"Let's Celebrate!" 2/21/69, pp. 9, 21.
"Focused in a Dutch Paper," 2/28/69, p. 9.
"A Layman Looks at Preaching, Now It's Official," 2/28/69, p. 9.
"Help Wanted," 3/7/69, p. 9.
"A Word on Those Irish Protestants," 3/7/69, p. 9.
"What Can We Afford?" 3/14/69, pp. 9, 20.
"Too Complicated to Live," 3/14/69, pp. 9, 20.
"Who in the World Listens?" 3/21/69, p. 9.
"A Small Footnote on the American Way of Death," 3/21/69, p. 9.
"It Wonders Me!" 3/28/69, p. 11.
"Who Needs It?" 3/28/69, p. 11.
"A Word About Church Music," 4/4/69, p. 11.
"A Day of Recollection," 4/4/69, p. 11.
"What Next?" 4/11/69, p. 7.
"Who Will Do the Chores?" 4/11/69, p. 7.
"More About Science," 4/25/69, p. 9.
"For Whatever it May be Worth," 4/25/69, p. 9.
"Down With Ecclesiastical Tyranny," 5/2/69, p. 13.
"Merger Problems," 5/2/69, p. 13.
"Shekels, Anyone?" 5/2/69, p. 13.
"The Tax Question Again," 5/9/69, p. 9.
"Student, Quo Vadis?" 5/9/69, p. 9.
"Those Rambunctious Dutch!" 5/16/69, p. 9.
"With All My Mind," 5/30/69, p. 9.
"He Who Talks Loudest," 5/30/69, p. 9.
"For Once In a Lifetime...," 6/6/69, p. 14.
"A Dutch Postscript," 6/6/69, p. 14.
"Shape of Things to Come?" 6/13/69, p. 9.
"Church Music Revisited," 6/13/69, p. 9.
"Where Have I Been?" 6/27/69, pp. 15, 30.

1970

"Wanted," 1/2/70, pp. 7, 28.
"Three Cheers For God!" 1/2/70, pp. 7, 28.
"The Ecumenical Hurdle," 1/9/70, pp. 13, 21.
"Our Violent Nation," 1/9/70, pp. 13, 21.
"On Losing Our Traditions," 1/16/70, pp. 7, 22.
"The Silent Majority Deserves What it Gets," 1/16/70, pp. 7, 22.
"Church and State," 1/23/70, p. 9.
"The Confessions of a Conservative," 1/23/70, p. 9.
"A Parable," 1/30/70, pp. 9, 23.
"The End of the Age of Reason?" 1/30/70, pp. 9, 23.
"The Real Enemy," 2/6/70, p. 11.
"Priorities," 2/6/70, p. 11.
"Crime Does Not Pay?" 2/13/70, p. 9.
"Full Circle," 2/13/70, p. 9.
"The A.K.V.," 2/20/70, pp. 9, 22.
"A Winter Soliloquy," 2/20/70, pp. 9, 22.
"On Synod Meetings," 2/20/70, pp. 9, 22.
"Who Said It?" 2/27/70, p. 9.
"Unity Whither?" 2/27/70, p. 9.
"Ireland Again," 3/6/70, p. 9.
"St. Madelyn, Pray for Us," 3/6/70, p. 9.
"Why Are They So Angry?" 3/13/70, pp. 9, 22.
"Liturgical Renewal," 3/13/70, pp. 9, 22.
"When Old Traditions Become New Discoveries," 3/20/70, p. 9.
"On Re-reading Old Books, 3/20/70, p. 9.
"Law and Order," 3/27/70, p. 11.
"Who Killed Him?" 3/27/70, p. 11.
"For Whom the Bell Tolls," 4/3/70, pp. 9, 22.
"A White Easter," 5/1/70, pp. 9, 21.
"What Do You Remember?" 5/1/70, pp. 9, 21.
"The Most Expensive Piece of Real Estate in Town," 5/8/70, p. 9.
"Concerning the Salutation," 5/8/70, p. 9.
"The Booby Trap," 5/15/70, pp. 9, 22.
"The New Conservative," 5/15/70, pp. 9, 22.
"Church-going in Europe," 6/19/70, p. 11.
"The Dickens Centennial," 7/17/70, p. 11.
"A Word About Zwingli," 7/17/70, p. 11.
"The Credibility Gap," 7/31/70, p. 9.

"Election Day in Newark," 7/31/70, p. 9.

"The A.K.V. (continued)," 8/14/70, pp. 9, 30.

"How to Grow," 8/14/70, pp. 9, 30.

"Pre-evangelism," 8/28/70, pp. 9, 30.

"The Reformed World," 8/28/70, pp. 9, 30.

"What Makes a Church Member?" 9/11/70, pp. 21, 30.

"The Decline of the English Empire," 9/11/70, pp. 21, 30.

"East vs. West," 9/25/70, pp. 9, 28.

"Pilgrim's Regress," 9/25/70, pp. 9, 28.

"In the Name of Religion," 9/25/70, pp. 9, 28.

"Some Notes on Church Attendance," 10/2/70, pp. 9, 21.

"We Can Sing Together," 10/2/70, pp. 9, 21.

"The Reformed Diaspora (Again)," 10/9/70, p. 9.

"Meditation by a Lake," 10/9/70, p. 9.

"The Downfall of Work," 10/16/70, p. 9.

"How did You Get Your Minister?" 10/16/70, p. 9.

"Confessions of a Middle-Aged Preacher," 10/23/70, pp. 9, 22.

"For Ministers Only (But Laymen May Have a Peep)," 10/23/70, pp. 9, 22.

"Reflections on a Small World," 10/30/70, p. 9.

"But It's the Same Street," 10/30/70, p. 9.

"London Religion," 11/6/70, p. 13.

"On Believing the Worst," 11/6/70, p. 13.

"Lord Paisley of Orange?" 11/13/70, pp. 9, 21.

"No Hiding Place," 11/13/70, pp. 9, 21.

"Who Changes What?" 11/20/70, pp. 9, 21.

"The New Pietism," 11/20/70, pp. 9, 21.

"The Affluent Militant," 11/27/70, pp. 9, 22.

" Just for Fun (Or Is It?)" 11/27/70, pp. 9, 22.

"The Book Corner," 11/27/70, pp. 9, 22.

"Carnalea," 12/4/70, pp. 9, 30.

"Just for Fun," 12/4/70, pp. 9, 30.

"An Unmarked Anniversary," 12/11/70, pp. 9, 21.

"Some Irish Statistics," 12/11/70, pp. 9, 21.

"Let the Bible Speak for Itself," 12/11/70, pp. 9, 21.

"Faith of Our Fathers," 12/18/70, pp. 9, 28.

"The Gastronomy Column," 12/18/70, pp. 9, 28.

"And We Their Children...," 12/18/70, pp. 9, 28.

"A New Year's Resolution," 12/25/70, p. 11.

"Random Notes About Preaching," 12/25/70, p. 11.

1971

"Radicals and Traditionalists," 1/8/71, p. 9.
"On Calling to Worship," 1/8/71, p. 9.
"The Shape of things to Come?" 1/15/71, p. 9.
"Justice—American Style," 1/15/71, p. 9.
"Our Credit Card Economy," 1/22/71, pp. 9, 22.
"A Personal Word," 1/22/71, pp. 9, 22.
"Confessions Old and New," 1/29/71, pp. 9, 21.
"The Post-Christmas Slump," 1/29/71, pp. 9, 21.
"An Elegant Cop-Out," 2/5/71, pp. 11, 22.
"The Unexamined Slogan," 2/5/71, pp. 11, 22.
"In MEMORIAM," 2/19/71, p. 9.
"Run for Your Money," 2/19/71, p. 9.
"What's in a Name?" 2/26/71, p. 9.
"Us Four—No More," 2/26/71, p. 9.
"Lost in Paper," 3/5/71, p. 9.
"Which Side of the Street?" 3/5/71, p. 9.
"Jesus Christ Superstar," 3/12/71, p. 9.
"Extremes Do Meet!" 3/12/71, p. 9.
"The South African Puzzle," 3/19/71, p. 9.
"It Happens in Amsterdam," 3/19/71, p. 9.
"Shoe on the Other Foot," 3/26/71, p. 9.
"Maybe Ignorance is Bliss," 3/26/71, p. 9.
"The Book Corner," 3/26/71, p. 9.
"Money, Money, Who's Got the Money?" 4/2/71, pp. 9, 22.
"A Policeman's Lot Is Not A Happy One," 4/2/71, pp. 9, 22.
"But Will They Still Fire?" 4/9/71, pp. 11, 30.
"A Reminder and a Question," 4/9/71, pp. 11, 30.
"The White Riot," 4/16/71, p. 11.
"Remnant or Core?" 4/16/71, p. 11.
"A New Look at Youth," 4/23/71, p. 9.
"Later Than We Think," 4/23/71, p. 9.
"The Religious Revolution," 4/30/71, pp. 9, 22.
"Episcopar Nolo Aut Volo," 4/30/71, pp. 9, 22.
"The Road to the Purple," 5/7/71, pp. 9, 20.
"Come Unto Me" 5/7/71, pp. 9, 20.
"The Living Hymnal," 5/14/71, p. 11.
"Children and Communism," 5/14/71, p. 11.
"Requiem for COCU," 5/21/71, pp. 9, 22.

1972

"The Basic Need," 11/24/72, p. 19.
"As Others Saw Us," 12/1/72, p. 11.
"But How?" 12/8/72, p. 9.
"Our Plated Culture," 12/8/72, p. 9.
"Case Dismissed," 12/15/72, p. 9.
"How Rome Fell," 12/15/72, p. 9.
"It Might Have Been," 12/22/72, pp. 17, 24.

1973

"Which Way Did It Go?" 1/5/73, p. 9.
"At Least We're Here," 1/5/73, p. 9.
"The Irish Question Again," 1/12/73, pp. 11, 23.
"Opinion vs. Confession," 1/12/73, pp. 11, 23.
"East and West," 1/19/73, pp. 11, 21.
"A New Direction From the Dutch," 1/26/73, pp. 7, 21.
"In Defense of Mysteries," 1/26/73, pp. 7, 21.
"A Dutch Mosque," 2/2/73, pp. 11, 22.
"What Would You Have Done?" 2/2/73, pp.11, 22.
"Mental Seduction," 2/9/73, pp. 7, 23.
"7Q5," 2/9/73, pp. 7, 23.
"Whither Bound," 2/23/73, pp. 9, 23.
"The Little Matter of License," 2/23/73, pp. 9, 23.
"Big News For You!" 3/2/73, pp. 9, 23.
"On the Danger Of Making Up Your Mind," 3/2/73, pp. 9, 23.
"How to Save Money," 3/9/73, p. 7.
"The Other Shore" 3/9/73, p. 7.
"Sink or Swim Time," 3/16/73, pp. 7, 22.
"Between Sex and Sex," 3/16/73, pp. 7, 22.
"What Century Would You Like?" 3/23/73, p. 7.
"X-Rated," 3/30/73, pp. 9, 22.
"Insoluble?" 3/30/73, pp. 9, 22.
"Wishing Won't Make It So!" 4/6/73, pp. 9, 21.
"Prophets of Doom," 4/6/73, pp. 9, 21.
"The Last Puritan," 4/20/73, pp. 9, 24.
"Reverse Success," 4/20/73, pp. 9, 24.
"And He Is We," 4/27/73, pp. 7, 22.
"The Other Side of the Coin," 4/27/73, pp. 7, 22.
"The Secession," 5/4/73, pp. 9, 23.
"The Church Attendance Game," 5/4/73, pp. 9, 23.

1974

"Church Growth," 2/22/74, p. 30.
"Are You a Thief?" 3/8/74, p. 30.
"Have a Look At Alaska," 3/8/74, p. 30.
"The Voice of the Spirit," 3/22/74, p. 30.
"Anything to Sell?" 3/22/74, p. 30.
"The Business of Bibles," 4/5/74, p. 30.
"History or Propaganda?" 4/5/74, p. 30
"Where Have All the Radicals Gone?" 4/19/74, p. 30.
"There's Profit in Redundancy," 4/19/74, p. 30.
"Holy Applause," 5/3/74, p. 30.
"At It Again," 5/3/74, p. 30.
"New Best Seller," 5/17/74, p. 30.
"Urban Safety," 5/17/74, p. 30.
"Sign of the Times?" 5/31/74, p. 34.
"I Don't Believe It," 5/31/74, p. 34.
"New Tongue," 6/14/74, p. 30.
"Some Thoughts on 1976 CRC-RCA," 6/28/74, p. 30.
"Aaron Burr and the RCA," 7/12/74, p. 30.
"What's the Name of the Game? Sky-Way 838," 7/26/74, p. 30.
"Back to the Bible," 8/9/74, p. 30.
"Question 80," 8/9/74, p. 30.
"Church Attendance," 8/23/74, p. 30.
"Church Politics in Rumania," 8/23/74, p. 30.
"Our Battered Colleges," 9/6/74, p. 30.
"What's in a Name?" 9/6/74, p. 30.
"Creeds and Commerce," 9/20/74, p. 30.
"Good News in Color," 10/4/74, p. 30.
"Left-Right," 10/4/74, p. 30.
"Honesty Begins at Home," 10/4/74, p. 30.
"Word About Hymns," 10/18/74, p. 30.
"One Way To Do It," 10/18/74, p. 30.
"Our National Psalm," 11/1/74, p. 30.
"A New Center For Church Music," 11/1/74, p. 30.
"Let's Be Honest," 11/1/74, p. 30.
"Computerized Church," 11/15/74, p. 30.
"A Fixed Easter," 11/15/74, p. 30.
"In Honor of John Wesley," 11/29/74, p. 30.
"Weighty Problem," 11/29/74, p. 30.
"Let's Trade Churches," 11/29/74, p. 30.
"Unfinished Business," 12/13/74, p. 30.

"Happy Loss," 12/27/74, p. 30.
"Word About South Africa," 12/27/74, p. 30.

1975

"Another Church Union," 1/10/75, p. 30.
"The Diaconia Road," 1/10/75, p. 30.
"Signs of the Times?" 1/24/75, p. 30.
"GK," 1/24/75, p. 30.
"Process of Clarification," 2/7/75, p. 30.
"Built to Burn," 2/7/75, p. 30.
"Religion and the Future," 2/21/75, p. 30.
"The Problem of the Aging," 2/21/75, p. 30.
"The Most Bombed Church," 3/7/75, p. 30.
"Seated One Day at the Organ," 3/7/75, p. 30.
"What Shall I Wear?" 3/21/75, p. 30.
"Job Wanted," 3/21/75, p. 30.
"False Alternatives," 4/4/75, p. 30.
"How Grim Was My City," 4/4/75, p. 30.
"Whose Ox is Being Gored?" 4/18/75, p. 30.
"The Hartford Heresies," 4/18/75, p. 30.
"Hemispheric Parochialism," 5/2/75, p. 30.
"Easter Noise," 5/2/75, p. 30.
"Deja Vu," 6/13/75, p. 30.
"News From Indonesia," 6/13/75, p. 30.
"Canadian Jubilees," 7/11/75, pp. 30, 28.
"General Synod Gets Weightier," 7/11/75, pp. 30, 28.
"Independence Day Musings," 7/25/75, p. 30.
"The Fairness of Doctrine," 7/25/75, p. 30.
"The Eastern Establishment," 8/8/75, p. 30.
"The United Reformed Church," 8/8/75, p. 30.
"Whom Do You Believe," 8/22/75, p. 30.
"Give Us Six Months," 8/22/75, p. 30.
"The Fourteenth Colony," 9/5/75, p. 31.
"For the Record," 9/5/75, p. 31.
"Pilgrim Church Comes," 9/19/75, p. 30.
"We're Getting Smaller," 9/19/75, p. 30.
"Church Union in Belgium," 10/3/75, p. 30.
"The Infidelity of Evangelicalism," 10/3/75, p. 30.
"Lost Stanzas," 10/17/75, p. 30.

1976

1977

"Professional Education," 10/6/78, p. 31.
"New Biblical Discovery," 10/6/78, p. 31.
"Pop Goes the Pudding," 10/20/78, p. 30.
"Communist or Russian?" 10/20/78, p. 30.
"Touching the Untouchable," 11/3/78, p. 30.
"A Song of Hope," 11/3/78, p. 30.
"The Reformed Church in Black Africa," 11/17/78, p. 30.
"The Great Divide," 11/17/78, p. 30.
"The Liturgical Bible," 12/1/78, p. 30.
"Truth in Burial," 12/1/78, p. 30.
"Our Most Expensive Election," 12/15/78, p. 30.
"Apartheid and Apathy," 12/15/78, p. 30.
"Mindless Religion," 12/29/78, p. 31.
"Advent Musings," 12/29/78, p. 31.

1979

"The Dutch Reformation was Different," 1/12/79, p. 30.
"Rise Up, O Men of God," 1/12/79, p. 30.
"A Layman's Guide to Inflation," 1/26/79, p. 31.
"The RCA in Politics," 1/26/79, p. 31.
"Our Holy Year," 2/9/79, p. 31.
"Russian Roots," 2/9/79, p. 31.
"Changing Celebrations," 2/23/79, p. 31.
"The Teaching Ministry," 2/23/79, p. 31.
"A Question of Semantics," 3/9/79, p. 30.
"Which Bible do You Read?" 3/9/79, p. 30.
"A Vintage Year," 3/23/79, p. 31.
"Happy Birthday, Brooklyn!" 3/23/79, p. 31.
"Hey, Wyoming!" 4/6/79, p. 31.
"What Would You Like?" 4/6/79, p. 31.
"Our Private Creed," 4/20/79, p. 30.
"What Did We Do Wrong?" 4/20/79 pp. 30, 29.
"Middle City," 5/4/79, p. 30.
"A Place to Stand," 5/4/79, p. 30.
"A Word About South Africa," 5/18/79, p. 30.
"And What Are We?" 5/18/79, p. 30.
"The Shape of the Future," 6/1/79, p. 30.
"Forgotten Bits of Church History," 6/1/79, p. 30.
"Welfare, Anyone?" 6/15/79, p. 30.

1980

"It Still Happens," 4/4/80, p. 31.
"The Psychology of Anonymity," 4/18/80, p. 30.
"An Invitation to Thinking," 4/18/80, p. 30.
"A Canadian Trio," 5/2/80, p. 31.
"Urban Puzzles," 5/2/80, p. 31.
"The Credit Crunch," 5/16/80, p. 30.
"Straws in the Wind," 5/16/80, p. 30.
"A Responsible Press," 6/13/80, p. 31.
"Brooklyn at the Inauguration," 6/13/80, p. 31.
"The Heidelberg Liturgy," 6/27/80, p. 30.
"The Quebec Referendum," 6/27/80, p. 30.
"A Modern Zacchaeus," 7/11/80, p. 30.
"The Lost Art of Psalm Singing," 7/11/80, p. 30.
"On Going Home," 7/25/80, p. 30.
"Shared Facilities," 7/25/80, p. 30.
"Praise the Lord," 8/8/80, p. 30.
"The Glorious Fourth," 8/8/80, p. 30.
"The Story of Isaac Stahl," 8/22/80, p. 23.
"It Was No Mistake," 8/22/80, p. 23.
"The Spirit of the Age," 9/5/80, p. 30.
"Bound in One Bundle," 9/5/80, p. 30.
"The Koran and the Gospel," 9/19/80, p. 30.
"The Christian Year," 9/19/80, p. 30.
"On Clerical Dress," 10/3/80, p. 30.
"Freedom to be Foolish," 10/3/80, p. 30.
"Styles of Church Life," 10/17/80, p. 30.
"Things that Matter," 10/17/80, p. 30.
"Language Persistence," 10/31/80, p. 31.
"God is Doing Better," 10/31/80, p. 31.
"What Makes the Swiss Miss?" 11/14/80, p. 30.
"A Belgian Church," 11/14/80, p. 30.
"Happy Thanksgiving!" 11/28/80, p. 30.
"Reformed County," 11/28/80, p. 30.
"Trouble to the North," 12/12/80, p. 30.
"Selective Generosity," 12/12/80, p. 30.
"Back to Boots and Saddle," 12/26/80, p. 31.
"At Our Worst," 12/26/80, p. 31.

1981

"Get the Facts Straight," 1/9/81, p. 30.

"Cracks in the Ecumenical Wall," 1/9/81, p. 30.
"A Hymnological Reflection," 1/23/81, p. 30.
"A Personal Word," 1/23/81, p. 30.
"The Class of 1881," 2/6/81, p. 30.
"What About De-Inspiration?" 2/6/81, p. 30.
"Are You From the Mideast?" 2/20/81, p. 30.
"The Lecturer," 2/20/81, p. 30.
"The Sick Bear," 3/6/81, p. 30.
"A Nervous Preacher," 3/6/81, p. 30.
"Eroding Infallibility," 4/3/81, p. 30.
"Keeping a Balance," 4/3/81, p. 30.
"Our National Sense of Humor," 4/17/81, p. 31.
"Media Impact," 4/17/81, p. 31.
"Stone Churches," 5/1/81, p. 30.
"The New Idolatry," 5/1/81, p. 30.
"Back to the Beginning," 5/15/81, p. 30.
"How Do We Lose Them?" 5/15/81, p. 30.
"Levitical Clans," 5/29/81, p. 30.
"Back to Canada," 5/29/81, p. 30.
"Preacher, Repent!" 6/12/81, p. 30.
"In the Eye of the Beholder," 6/12/81, p. 30.
"The Schwenkfelders Conquer Washington," 6/26/81, p. 30.
"The Green Card," 6/26/81, p. 30.
"How Great Thou Art!" 7/10/81, p. 30.
"As of Old St. Andrew," 7/10/81, p. 30.
"The Homelander's Revenge," 7/24/81, p. 30.
"The Philadelphia Story," 7/24/81, p. 30.
"The British Agony," 8/7/81, p. 22.
"The Dutch on the Delaware," 8/7/81, p. 22.
"Liturgy Back to Front," 8/21/81, p. 30.
"A Change in Approach," 8/21/81, p. 30.
"The People of the Bulletin," 9/4/81, p. 22.
"What's in a Name?" 9/4/81, p. 22.
"1982," 9/18/81, p. 30.
"The Right End of the Stick," 9/18/81, p. 30.
"The Union Church," 10/2/81, p. 30.
"Cults in Reverse," 10/2/81, p. 30.
"An Ornamental Ministry," 10/30/81, p. 30.
"Our American Glue," 10/30/81, p. 30.
"This is My Father's World," 11/13/81, p. 30.

"True Confession," 11/13/81, p. 30.
"Holy Nicknames," 11/27/81, p. 31.
"Rewriting History," 11/27/81, p. 31.
"The Good Old Hymns," 12/11/81, p. 30.
"Crime Capital #2," 12/11/81, p. 30.
"The Bad Fruits of Prosperity," 12/25/81, p. 34.
"The Age of Intolerance," 12/25/81, p. 34.

1982

"Happy Birthday, Dear Creed," 1/8/82, p. 31.
"Signs of Mortality," 1/8/82, p. 31.
"The Rich Get Richer," 1/22/82, p. 30.
"Our Oldest Name," 1/22/82, p. 30.
"Protecting Shadows," 2/5/82, p. 30.
"Pagan New York," 2/5/82, p. 30.
"The Unchurched American," 2/19/82, p. 30.
"Kitchen Seminaries," 2/19/82, p. 30.
"Winter Vacations," 3/5/82, p. 30.
"Church and Sect," 3/5/82, p. 30.
"A Time of Silence," 4/16/82, p. 31.
"The Jewel in Our Crown," 4/16/82, p. 31.
"The Folly of Belittling," 4/30/82, p. 30.
"James Smart," 4/30/82, p. 30.
"Off Our Backs," 5/14/82, p. 31.
"Signs of Hope," 5/14/82, p. 31.
"A Time for Religion," 5/28/82, p. 31.
"The Paper Business," 5/28/82, p. 31.
"General Synod," 6/11/82, p. 30.
"Old Church Museum," 6/11/82, p. 30.
"Anniversaries," 6/25/82, p. 31.
"A Reversal of Roles," 6/25/82, p. 31.
"Reforming Choirs," 7/23/82, p. 46.
"Rose Rent," 7/23/82, p. 46.
"The Captains and the Queens Depart," 8/20/82, p. 31.
"On Paying Taxes," 8/20/82, p. 31.
"Pennsylvania Dutch and New York Deitsch," 9/3/82, p. 30.
"Watch It!" 9/3/82, p. 30.
"To Market, to Market," 9/17/82, p. 31.
"In Praise of Trains," 9/17/82, p. 31.

1983

"The Place Thereof Shall Know It No More," 9/2/83, p. 31.
"Disappeared or Disappearing," 9/16/83, p. 31.
"Go With the Flow," 9/16/83, p. 31.
"The Best Seller List," 10/7/83, p. 30.
"Lost Causes," 10/7/83, p. 30.
"Words Can Hurt," 10/21/83, p. 30.
"Ursinus Commemoration," 10/21/83, p. 30.
"Appointed to Be Read," 11/4/83, p. 34.
"The Age of the Catalogue," 11/4/83, p. 34.
"Was Calvin a Lutheran?" 11/18/83, p. 34.
"In Praise of the Hudson Valley," 11/18/83, p. 34.
"O Mother Dear, America," 12/2/83, p. 30.
"Angel's Eyes,"12/2/83, p. 30.
"All That Glitters Is Not Gold," 12/16/83, p. 34.
"Secular or Religious?" 12/16/83, p. 34.

1984

"The Urban Scene," 1/6/84, p. 30.
"Compassion," 1/6/84, p. 30.
"Looking At Our Past," 1/20/84, p. 30.
"1984," 1/20/84, p. 30.
"Now It's Our Turn," 2/3/84, p. 31.
"Christmas Hymns," 2/3/84, p. 31.
"My Least Favorite President," 2/17/84, p. 30.
"What's Your Horoscope?" 2/17/84, p. 30.
"How Not to Read the Bible," 3/2/84, p. 38.
"Washington Worshiped Here," 3/2/84, p. 38.
"Our First American Ordination," 3/16/84, p. 30.
"The Aging Mind," 3/16/84, p. 30.
"The Lost Tribe," 4/6/84, p. 31.
"Where the Money Goes," 4/6/84, p. 31.
"Right in Your Own Living Room," 4/20/84, p. 30.
"Winter Soliloquy," 4/20/84, p. 30.
"An Apology," 5/18/84, p. 30.
"A Partial America," 5/18/84, p. 30.
"Religious Reporting," 5/18/84, p. 30.
"Unsolved Puzzles In Our History," 6/1/84, p. 30.
"A Return to Religion," 6/1/84, p. 30.
"When the Market Place Fails," 6/15/84, p. 30.

1985

1986

"No Hiding Place," 4/4/86, p. 31.
"The Class of 1886," 4/18/86, p. 31.
"Confessions of a Hit and Run Preacher," 4/18/86, p. 31.
"Orthodoxy and Orthopraxis," 5/2/86, p. 31.
"Ecumenism in Practice," 5/2/86, p. 31.
"Thoughts After Twenty-Five Years," 5/23/86, p. 31.
"Put Up Your Sword," 6/6/86, p. 34.
"The Bible Alone?" 6/6/86, p. 34.
"Our Pluralistic Church," 6/27/86, p. 30.
"Irish Divorce," 6/27/86, p. 30.
"Adherents," 7/25/86, p. 30.
"O Pioneers!" 7/25/86, p. 30.
"Mr. Liberty," 8/15/86, p. 31.
"Our Mixed Heritage," 8/15/86, p. 31.
"The Country is Shrinking," 9/5/86, p. 31.
"A Postscript," 9/5/86, p. 31.
"Immigrant Faith," 9/19/86, p. 23.
"How the Story Grows," 9/19/86, p. 23.
"Ministerial Dropouts," 10/3/86, p. 30.
"Victims of Success," 10/3/86, p. 30.
"The War On Drugs," 10/17/86, p. 30.
"A Wasted Inheritance," 10/17/86, p. 30.
"Our United Reformed Cousins," 11/7/86, p. 34.
"Where Has the Color Gone," 11/7/86, p. 34.
"Pilgrims and Puritans," 11/21/86, p. 30.
"A Postscript," 11/21/86, p. 30.
"Our Lost Advent," 12/5/86, p. 31.
"Thoughts on the Election," 12/5/86, p. 31.
"Re-thinking Christmas," 12/19/86, p. 31.
"A Christmas Psalm," 12/19/86, p. 31.

1987

"It's Only Perspective," 1/2/87, p. 31.
"Theme With Variations," 1/2/87, p. 31.
"American Classics," 2/6/87, p. 30.
"Not So Benign Neglect," 2/6/87, p. 30.
"Our National Shame," 2/20/87, p. 31.
"A City's Churches," 2/20/87, p. 31.
"Lost Dimensions," 3/6/87, p. 30.

1988

"Member of the Parish," 1/15/88, p. 31.
"The Dutch in 1788," 1/15/88, p. 31.
"The End of the Eighties," 2/5/88, p. 31.
"Trivia," 2/5/88, p. 31.
"Behind the Scenes in Central America," 3/4/88, p. 31.
"Glasnost and Protestants," 3/4/88, p. 31.
"Some Thoughts on Identity," 3/18/88, p. 30.
"On Selecting a Candidate," 3/18/88, p. 30.
"The Christian Passover," 4/1/88, p. 30.
"The Cruelest Month," 4/1/88, p. 30.
"After Twenty-Seven Years," 4/15/88, p. 31.
"The Kirkpatrick Doctrine," 4/15/88, p. 31.
"The Evil Empire," 5/6/88, p. 30.
"Who's in Charge," 5/6/88, p. 30.
"Church Extension by Canal," 5/20/88, p. 31.
"Depending on Where You Are," 5/20/88, p. 31.
"Tired Dragons," 6/3/88, p. 31.
"Political Ghosts," 6/3/88, p. 31.
"Swedish or Dutch?" 6/24/88, p. 31.
"The Newcomers," 6/24/88, p. 31.
"Languages of Zion," 7/22/88, p. 30.
"Second Vocations," 7/22/88, p. 30.
"Conflicting Anniversaries," 8/12/88, p. 31.
"The Resurrection of the Dutch," 8/12/88, p. 31.
"New Goals in Life?" 9/2/88, p. 31.
"Too Popular," 9/2/88, p. 31.
"Changing Landscapes," 9/16/88, p. 31.
"Summer Manners," 9/16/88, p. 31.
"Missionary Territory," 10/7/88, p. 31.
"Seminary Dropouts," 10/7/88, p. 31.
"Fundamentalism, Roman Catholic Style," 10/21/88, p. 31.
"Reformed Architecture," 10/21/88, p. 31.
"Ecclesiastical Terms," 11/4/88, p. 31.
"The Olympics," 11/4/88, p. 31.
"Confessional Embarrassments," 11/18/88, p. 31.
"An Interruption," 11/18/88, p. 31.
"Advent 1988," 12/2/88, p. 30.
"Where Must We Go From Here?" 12/2/88, p. 30.
"Thank You, Zephaniah," 12/16/88, p. 31.
"O Little Town of Bethlehem," 12/16/88, p. 31.

Books, Essays, and Articles
(not published in the *Church Herald*):

1948

Our Reformed Church. New York: Half Moon Press, 1948.

1950

"Liturgical Revival," *Theology Today* 6 (January 1950): 490-505.

1955

"With a Dutch Accent," *National Council Outlook* 5 (June 1955): 5-8.

1957

Review of *Whither South Africa?* by B. B. Keet. *Religion in Life,* 26 no. 3 (Summer 1957): 444-450.

Review of *You Are Wrong Father Huddelston,* by Alexander Steward. *Religion in Life* 26 no. 3 (Summer 1957): 444-450.

Review of *Naught for Your Comfort*, by Trevor Huddleston. *Religion in Life* 26 no. 3: (Summer 1957): 444-450.

1959

The Calvin Strasbourg Service. Philadelphia: Board of Education, United Presbyterian Church in the U.S.A., 1959.

"The Religious Life of New Netherland," *Halve Maen* 34(3) (Spring 1959): 7-8.

"Three Reformed Liturgies," *Theology Today* 15 (January, 1959): 507-520.

1960

"Can Church Music Be Reformed?" *Reformed Review* 14 (December, 1960): 19-28.

1961

We Call This Friday Good. Philadelphia: Muhlenberg Press, 1961.
The Book That Reads You. New York: RCA Board of Education, 1961.
"Religious Boom and Moral Bust," *Christianity Today* 5 (February 13
    1961): 16-18.
"Reformed Worship: Yesterday and Today," *Theology Today* 18 (April
    1961): 30-40.

1962

*Pulpit and Table: Some Chapters in the History of Worship of the
    Reformed Churches.* Richmond: John Knox Press, 1962.
"Liturgy and Mission," *Theology Today* 19 (July 1962): 169-170.
"The Heritage of New Netherland," *Halve Maen* 36 No. 1 (1961): 9-10.

1963

Predestination. Philadelphia: Fortress Press, 1963.
"Coming-of-Age of the Liturgical Movement: Report on Section IV of
    the Montreal Conference," *Studia Liturgica* 2 (December 1963): 256-
    265.
"Liturgical Place," *Princeton Seminary Bulletin* 56 (February 1963): 29-
    39.
"Heidelberg Catechism as a Means of Christian Nurture," *Theology and
    Life* 6 (Autumn 1963): 239-254.
"Tribute to the Heidelberg Catechism," *Reformed and Presbyterian
    World* 27 (Summer 1963): 201-206.
"Guilt, Grace and Gratitude" In *Guilt, Grace and Gratitude: A
    Commentary on the Heidelberg Catechism, Commemorating its 400th
    Anniversary*, edited by Donald J. Bruggink, New York: The Half
    Moon Press, 1963.
"The Catechism in Christian Nurture" In *Essays on the Heidelberg
    Catechism*, edited by Bard Thompson. Philadelphia and Boston:
    United Church Press, 1963.

1965

With Ruth Douglas See. *That the World May Know.* Covenant Life
    Curriculum. Richmond, Va: CLC Press, 1965.

1968

Evenhuis, R. B. *The Founder of the Reformed Church in America*.
  Translated by Howard G. Hageman. *Halve Maen* 43 No. 3 (1968): 7-8.

1969

"Liturgical Development in the Reformed Church of America: 1868-
  1947," *Journal of Presbyterian History* 47 No. 3 (1969): 262-289.
"Colonial New Jersey's First Domine," *Halve Maen* 1969 44 No. 3: 9-10,
  14 and 44 No. 4:17-18.

1972

"Henricus Selyns," In *Cultural Mosaic of New Netherland: Seminar II*.
  Rensselaerville, N.Y.: Institute on Man and Science, 1972.

1973

"The Liturgical Origins of the Reformed Churches," In *The Heritage of
  John Calvin* edited by J. Bratt. Grand Rapids: William B. Eerdmans
  Publishing Company, 1973.

1974

With J.C. Baker. *Easter*. Proclamation: Aids for Interpreting the Lessons
  of the Church Year. Series C. Philadelphia: Fortress Press, 1974.

"Old and New in the Worshipbook," *Theology Today* 31 (October 1974):
  207-213.

1975

Lily Among the Thorns. New York: Reformed Church Press, 1975.
"In No Strange Land," *Princeton Seminary Bulletin* 68 (Autumn 1975):
  48-52.
"Need and Promise of Reformed Preaching," *Reformed Review* 28
  (Winter 1975): 75-84.

"The Law in the Liturgy," In *God and the Good,* edited by C. Orlebeke. Grand Rapids: William B. Eerdmans Publishing Company, 1975.

1976

Review of *Rome and Canterbury through Four Centuries*, by Bernard Parley and Margaret Parley. *Review of Books and Religion* 5 (January 1976): 12.

Review of *Dutch in America, 1609-1974*, by Gerald F. De Jong. *Journal of Presbyterian History* 54 (Summer 1976): 282-284.

Review of *Angels: God's Secret Agents*, by William F. Graham. *Theology Today* 33 (October 1976): 310.

"William Bertholf: Pioneer Domine of New Jersey," *Reformed Review* 29 (Winter 1976): 73-80.

"Response to J. N. Tollendi on Calvin on the Relationship Between Christ's Cross and the Lord's Supper," In *Renaissance, Reformation, Resurgence*, edited by P. De Clark. Grand Rapids: Calvin Theological Seminary, 1976.

1977

"Eucharistic Prayer in the Reformed Church in America," *Reformed Review* 38 (Spring 1977): 166-179.

Review of *Denominationalism*, edited by Russell E. Richey. *New Review of Books and Religion* 1 (May 1977): 8.

Review of *Valley of Discord: Church and Society along the Connecticut River, 1636-1725*, by Paul R. Lucas. *New Review of Books and Religion* 1 (January 1977): 13-14.

"Die Reformierte Kirche in Amerika" In *Die Refomierten Kirchen* edited by K. Halaski. Stuttgart: Evangelisches Verlagserrk, 1977.

1979

"The Reformed Churches: Enlarging Their Witness," *Christian Century* 96 (February 21, 1979): 177-181.

Review of *Saint Nicholas of Myra, Bari and Manhattan: Biography of a Legend*, by Charles W. Jones. *Theology Today* 36 (October 1979): 461-463.

Review of *An Introduction to the Reformed Tradition*, by John H. Leith.

Theological Studies 39 (March 1978): 176-178.
"New York's First Domine," *Reformed Review* 31 (Spring 1978): 119-126.

1980

Review of *Klinkend Geloof*, edited by A. C. Honers. *Hymn,* 31 (January 1980): 72-73.

Review of *Study of Liturgy* by C. P. M. Jones and Geoffrey Wainwright. *Theology Today* 36 (January 1980): 611-612.

"The Reformed Church in America and Nineteenth Century Architects," *New Brunswick Theological Seminary Newsletter,* Vol. 9, No. 3 (March): 3-4, 21-24.

1981

"Katholisch und Reformiert," In *Jahrbuch fur Liturgik und Hymnologie* 25. Kassel: Johannes Stauda Verlag, 1981.

"Preaching is Alive and Well," *Theology Today* 37 (January 1981): 493-497.

"South, Middle, North: Dutch Reformed Leapfrog in New York," *New Brunswick Theological Seminary Newsletter,* Vol. 10, No. 3 (March): 3-6, 10, 23-24.

1982

"A Brief Study of the British Lectionary," *Worship* 56 (July 1982): 356-364.

Review of *The Word in Worship: Preaching in a Liturgical Context,* by William Skudlarek. *Journal of Supervision and Training in Ministry* 5 (1982): 217.

"A Philadelphia Story," *New Brunswick Theological Seminary Newsletter,* Vol. 11, No. 9 (November): 3-6, 15, 20-21.

1983

"A Forgotten Anniversary," *Reformed Journal* 33 No. 1 (January, 1983): 5.

"The Lessons of Mercersburg," *Reformed Journal* 33 No. 9 (September 1983): 4.

"The Golden Age," *New Brunswick Theological Seminary Newsletter*,
Vol. 12, No. 9 (November): 3-7.

1984

Two Centuries Plus: The Story of the New Brunswick Seminary. With
chapter 13 by Benjamin Alicea, Grand Rapids: W. B. Eerdmans
Publishing Co., 1984.
"Changing Understandings of Reformed Corporate Worship," *Reformed
Liturgy and Music* 18 (Fall 1984): 155-158.
"A Heritage Forgotten," *Reformed Journal* 34 No 7 (July 1984): 2-3.
"Some Notes on the Use of the Lectionary in the Reformed Tradition,"
In *The Divine Drama in History and Liturgy*, edited by J. Booty.
1984. Allison Park, Pa: Pickwick Publications, 1984.
"Reformed in Four Languages," *New Brunswick Seminary Newsletter*,
Vol. 14, No. 3 (Spring): 6-9.
"The Synod of Dort and American Beginnings," *Reformed Review* 38
(Winter 1985): 99108.
"The Heritage of the Holland Society," *Halve Maen* 59 No. 2 (1985): 8-9,
20.
Review of *Dutch Calvinism in Modern America: A History of a
Conservative Subculture*, by James D. Bratt. *American Presbyterians*
63 No. 4 (Winter 1985): 404-405.

1986

"In Flanders Fields," *Reformed Journal* 36 No 11 (November 1986): 6-7.
"Reformed Spirituality" In *Protestant Spiritual Traditions* edited by F.
Senn. New York: Paulist Press, 1986.
"The Lasting Significance of Ursinus" In *Controversy and Conciliation*,
edited by D. Visser. Allison Park, Pa.: Pickwick Press, 1986.
"The Story of Rejoice in the Lord," *New Brunswick Theological
Seminary Newsletter*, Vol. 14, No. 12 (Spring): 8-10.

1987

"The First Boston," *Reformed Journal* 3 (March 1987): 6.
"Rioting in Switzerland," *Reformed Journal* 37 (October 1987): 7.
"Holy Week Celebrations," *Reformed Worship* No 2. (Winter 1987): 31-
33.

"Needed: A Liberal Dialogue," *Unitarian Universalist Christian* 42 No 4.
    (1987): 20-22.

1988

"Colonial Outreach," *Reformed Journal* 38: (November 1988): 6-7.
"The Eucharistic Prayer in the Reformed Tradition," *Reformed Liturgy
    and Music* 22 (Fall 1988): 190-193.
Review of *The Funeral: A Service of Witness to the Resurrection,
    Reformed Worship,* prepared by The Office of Worship for the
    Presbyterian Church (U.S.A.), *Reformed Worship* 7 (Spring, 1988):
    44-45.

1989

"Saintly Churches," *Reformed Journal* 39 (August 1989): 8.
"Chalice and Loaf or Cups and Cubes," *Reformed Worship* 13 (Fall
    1989):17-19.

1990

"Songs in the Night," *Reformed Journal* 40 (November 1990): 9.
"A Catholic and Reformed Liturgy" In *Scholarship, Sacraments and
    Service* edited by D. Clendenin. Lewiston: E. Mellon Press, 1990.
"Dominies and Witches," *de Halve Maen,* 63 No. 1 (1990): 4-6.

1992

"Common Prayer, Book of,"; "Geneva Gown,"; "Nevin, John Williamson
    (1803-1886)," In *Encyclopedia of the Reformed Faith*, edited by
    Donald K. McKim. Louisville, Kentucky. 1992.

Unpublished Material (located in the Hageman CollectionGardner Sage Library, New Brunswick Theological SeminaryNew Brunswick, New Jersey):

Workshop for the Consistory, April 23, 1960. A lecture, entitled "The

Office of Elder," delivered at Warwick Estates, Warwick, New York.

Out of the Shackles of Traditionalism. One thirty-minute audiotape of a lecture at the National Ministries Conference, Montreat, North Carolina, August, 1967.

Untitled. 1968. A sermon preached on Good Friday in Newark, New Jersey.

New Days, New Ways. One seventy-five minute audiotape of an address at the National Ministers' Conference, Montreat, North Carolina, August 1968.

Mass Media and American Protestant Liturgy, 1969.

A Twentieth-Century God. Six audiotapes [133 minutes] of six sermons delivered at the Blackstone Conference Center, Blackstone, Virginia, Sept. 29-Oct. 3, 1969.

A Funny Thing Happened on the Way to New Brunswick. 1973.

Questions about Church Growth. Thesis Theological Cassettes No. 8 Spring 1977.

On Being A Real Parson. May 18, 1978.

Editor, with others. *Bibliography of Liturgical Studies, 1981.*

Into the Third Century. January 18, 1985.

A Personal Word. undated.

Lord's Supper I & II. Lectures delivered at Western Theological Seminary, undated.

Untitled and Undated. A ten-page manuscript focused on hymnody and prayer.

Index

224